D0312677

The Life of
GRAHAM

Also by Bob McCabe:

The Pythons Autobiography By The Pythons
Dark Knights and Holy Fools
The Authorised Biography of Ronnie Barker
George Clooney
Sean Connery
The Exorcist: Out of the Shadows

The Life of GRAHAM

The Authorised Biography of Graham Chapman

BOB McCABE

First published in hardback in Great Britain in 2005 by
Orion Books
an imprint of the Orion Publishing Group Ltd
Orion House, 5 Upper St Martin's Lane,
London WC2H 9EA

1 3 5 7 9 10 8 6 4 2

A CIP catalogue record for this book is available from the British Library.

ISBN 0 75285 773 8

Typeset by Deltatype Ltd,
Birkenhead, Merseyside
Printed in Great Britain by Clays Ltd, St Ives plc

www.orionbooks.co.uk

Chapter One

Seeing somebody else's body parts is always a formative experience. But when you see them dismembered, ripped apart – a severed arm here, a booted foot there, a decapitated head that's shot through a nearby shed roof – then it sticks with you for life, especially when you see your father, the local policeman, charged with the task of putting all these pieces back together – the right head with the right torso and so on – and then getting them into body bags. It's bound to be life changing.

It happened one afternoon in Leicestershire in 1944, and the bodies belonged to nine Polish airmen. Their plane had exploded above the town, and their component bits and pieces had rained down on the local inhabitants and their houses. An unopened parachute adorned a tree, pieces of human liver littered the grass. Another head had crashed through the roof of a nearby house.

The three-year-old boy looked on as his father tried to reassemble those parts. And then word came: one of the men had missed the flight – there were only eight bodies to reassemble. Police officer Walter Chapman would have to empty out the bags and start again.

Not many three-year-olds get such a lesson in anatomy. Pondering this experience, it is not all that surprising that the three-year-old would grow up to become a doctor. What is surprising is that he would also become one of Britain's most successful comedy actors and writers.

Graham Chapman was born in the small town of Wigston Fields, south of Leicester, on 8 January 1941 to parents Walter and Edith, preceded by a brother, John, four years earlier.

Walter, who was born in 1911, had once trained as a French polisher before joining the Leicestershire constabulary, and had at times thought of joining the colonial service and seeing something of the world. But these ambitions were replaced by the requirements of a young bride and a young family – and, of course, the Second World War.

Despite the appearance of an occasional Polish airman's lung hanging from a tree above the playground of Long Street Modern School, Walter's second and final son Graham's childhood was a fairly uneventful one. In later life Graham spoke of the great poverty the family lived with, citing such examples as having to put card in the soles of his shoes, colouring it black so people wouldn't notice the holes. John Chapman believes this to be a bit of fanciful embellishment on Graham's part. After all, a policeman's job was a pretty secure one during wartime.

'My parents were actually very generous and did without things themselves so that Graham and I could have things we wanted,' he recalls. 'We weren't well off, so my father used to make toys for us rather than buy them. That was partly because there weren't many toys in the shops in those days, during and just after the Second World War, but we never lacked for shoes anyway; we may have worn them a bit longer than our growing feet would have required normally, but we were never into that level of penury.'

They were a frugal and disciplined family and, naturally enough for a policeman's house, had a strong set of values. Edith

Chapman was known to point out proudly that she had never been to a hairdresser in her life, seeing it as a waste of money. She was obviously a strong woman. One night when her husband was out on patrol, she was left manning the station when a man brandishing an axe he had recently used on someone came in. She managed to talk him down and get the axe away before further damage could be done.

'She was, for the time I knew her, just a housewife and a policeman's wife,' recalls her eldest son. 'At that time in a rural constabulary, the policeman's wife was the telephone answerer and took messages when the policeman was out. She took the messages about air raids during the war and from people complaining about things. If you had a break-in, you'd call and she'd answer, "Well, the policeman isn't here at the moment, but I'll see if I can find him." She had various points throughout the area that he was covering where she could reach him, usually at certain times, so she knew she could get him within the hour at least and let him know, rather than having to jump on her bike and go riding round trying to find him.'

Walter and Edith had married in 1935. They met in Edith's home town of Hinckley, where Walter was stationed. She had previously worked in a local hosiery factory. Her father, also a policeman, had been killed in the First World War.

After the couple met and were married, Constable Chapman and his new bride found themselves living the itinerant life of a local policeman, moving first from Hinckley into Leicester, then shortly after this, when Walter was transferred, to nearby Market Harborough and finally to Wigston. It was here, in late November of 1936, that their first son, John, was born.

The outbreak of war ensured that they remained in Wigston for its duration, the once quiet town having become a much more active place courtesy of the Leicester Regiment's local barracks.

John Chapman was just under three years old when war broke out, and it informs his earliest memories. 'I was aware of there being lots more soldiers around than there were normally. And I know that we were aware of the air-raid warnings, the sirens going off. And we used to watch the searchlights, with aircraft flying overhead. I soon knew how to recognise the sound of some of the German aircraft. I think it was the Dornier bombers coming over, usually on their way to somewhere like Coventry, although Leicester itself was bombed.'

Graham was born one year and four months into the war in January 1941 at the local nursing home, and shortly after his birth, at the insistence of Edith, Walter Chapman was forced to dispose of the family dog, an Alsatian, although the dog was reluctant to go.

'My mother didn't like the idea of having the dog and the baby,' John Chapman recollects. 'He had an Alsatian dog and she felt it was a bit of a threat with a baby around, and my father actually gave the dog away. He wasn't a police dog, because there weren't police dogs in those days, but he used to go out with my father around the village when he was on duty, and when they were around somewhere like the local factory, the Two Steeples, if they went in through the gate, the dog would go round one way and my father would go the other way and they'd meet, and he knew if he met the dog there was nobody on the premises, not even the night watchman, because the dog wouldn't go past anybody. And when the air-raid sirens went, there were lots of temporary firemen who had to be warned – some of them weren't on the telephone – so my father used to go out on his bike. But the dog would be a bit of a nuisance when that happened, so he stayed chained to his kennel outside in the back garden. But on several occasions the dog broke the chain, somehow got out, leapt over the back gate, which was about five feet high, and would run round the village until he found my father, dragging this damn great chain behind him.

'But when Graham was born, my father was told to get rid of the dog, so he gave it to an old farmer friend somewhere near Coalville. Four or five days later my father received a phone call saying that the dog had disappeared; they thought it was living wild in the countryside around. My father got on his bike and went all the way over to Coalville, called the dog and he came straight up to him. It nearly broke his heart to leave it there again, but he did.'

A local girl named Mary Honour soon took a shine to baby Graham and was often to be found helping Edith out with him. As John Chapman recalls, 'There was one girl, Mary, in her early teens at the time, who used to take Graham out for walks in the pram and help my mother. Her father was one of my father's special constables. They had recruited lots of old men and retired policemen to come back into the police force because the young chaps went off to the armed services in the war and her father was one of them. We had a big, black, coach-built pram that he went around in – it was probably the same one that I went around in when I was smaller. I can remember we played with things like train sets out in the front room, clockwork train sets; for a while at least we had one big actual model steam train that we ran round tracks in the front room, spilling burning methylated spirits, little bits of oil and dirty water all over the carpets, which my mother didn't like. To my mind, Graham was often being a bit of a nuisance because he used to walk over and knock things over, as small children do.'

One of Graham's other interests as a very young boy was the police station's dog pound. It was one of his father's duties to maintain the pound attached to the station house, where stray dogs were corralled and kept, and one of Graham's earliest childhood memories was of visiting these animals, but because his father always reminded him that a policeman's lot was to be constantly posted to new locations (and given Edith's uncertainty over dogs and small children), Graham was never allowed a dog of his own, despite there being several at any one time just waiting there in the station's pound to be adopted.

As Graham grew, the war impinged more and more on his life and his imagination. A large house, known locally as The Grange, became a prisoner-of-war camp for Italian soldiers after their surrender. Both the Chapman siblings could recall these interned soldiers leaning over the walls of the grounds, talking to the local children and carving them small toys out of pieces of wood that they would pass to them over the wall.

Then, of course, towards the end of the war, the Americans rolled into town. 'We were aware of enormous convoys of arms and vehicles, particularly when the Americans came over before the D-Day landings,' says John Chapman. 'Enormous numbers of Americans continually going past up the road in their lorries, and kids waving to them, and them giving us chewing gum and chocolate, and stuff which we couldn't get at the time. And I was also aware of us riding around with my father and mother on bikes, when we had the opportunity, in the countryside, and the sight of hundreds and hundreds of little Nissen huts with canvas ends to them storing armaments, shells and grenades and that sort of stuff, all the build-up of material for the invasion of Europe.'

More than anything, of course, Graham later recalled vividly the crash of that Polish-manned Dakota, and the horrific sights it offered up to him.

The family remained strong, if at times stoic, throughout the war, and stayed in Wigston until well after the conclusion of the conflict.

'In 1947 we moved to Braunston, another part of Leicester's suburbs, following my father's promotion to sergeant,' recollects John Chapman. 'Then back to Wigston on his promotion to inspector in 1951, and then to Melton Mowbray for a period of some years. As an officer, you had to live virtually on the job because you had to have a telephone there so that you could be called out and get to any problems in a fairly short time. So we had five different houses before I left home at the age of seventeen, and then my father was eventually promoted to chief inspector and that's the rank at which he retired.'

Throughout their childhoods the two brothers were certainly friendly, but never all that close. 'Graham was not close enough in age to have many of the same interests that I had. When I was doing things like playing with Meccano, he would not be terribly interested or would very quickly lose interest in it. He wasn't someone who I was able to play games with very much. When we were playing together, I was the one who always had to do the pushing around or whatever. He wasn't desperately interested in things like ball games, cricket or anything like that, which I was quite keen on. We certainly did play together, often with other children around, but we pretty well always had a separate group of friends, appropriate to our age groups really, and because we moved around after – 1946 we never stayed in any one place more than about four years – it meant we were continually having to re-establish and make new friends as well, so we tended to make new groups of different friends. We would be aware of each other's friends but very seldom had any great common interests at all.'

At home, however, the brothers Chapman did both enjoy listening to the radio, with adventure shows such as *Journey into Space* and *Dick Barton, Special Agent* being favourites, alongside such comedy staples as *Much Binding in the Marsh* and *ITMA* (Tommy Handley's *It's That Man Again*). Later they would find another mutual wireless bond with their shared love of the Goons.

But their difference in age, the enormous uncertainty of the last few years and the constant motion demanded by their father's career ensured that their bond was always a difficult one to strengthen, something exacerbated by the fact that, throughout their childhoods, they nearly always attended different schools to each other.

'There was always a distance between us,' recalls the elder brother, 'because I don't think, except for very brief periods, we ever went to the same schools because of the way we'd moved around, so we led fairly separate lives, with different bunches of friends and that sort of thing. By the time Graham was going to school first of all, I was off at another school. He was at the primary school, I was at what was called the elementary school at that time. So we went to entirely different schools. When I went to grammar school, we were living on the south-western side of Leicester. When Graham started at grammar school, we were living on the south-eastern side of Leicester, where his catchment area was for Kidworth Grammar School, mine was to Market Bosworth Grammar School. They were both co-educational county grammar schools.'

The brothers didn't, however, find some commonality in the experience of being the new child in class, albeit different classes in different schools. 'It was a bit inhibiting for the first few days,' recalls John Chapman, 'but I don't think either of us found it very difficult to make friends. We were pretty well always known as "the policeman's children". I used to spend an awful lot of time reading at that time and, of course, when I was five, six, seven, eight then nine, Graham wasn't reading. When he got to reading, and he did a lot of reading as well, I was beyond that stuff. He was very much beneath me really in terms of the stuff I was reading.

'We did have one or two common interests from time to time, but when we were playing, it always seemed to end up somehow with me getting into trouble for doing something. One particular thing that stands in my memory is when we were playing cowboys and Indians, which we'd seen on western films, and we'd made bows and arrows. It was arranged that I would be in the drive, and he would poke his cap on a stick round the corner of the house, and I would shoot at it, and the silly devil poked his head round to see if I was ready and I was, and I hit him right in the corner of the eye with an arrow. I got a hell of a belting for that. It usually finished up with me getting into trouble for being either too vigorous or for resenting something that he was allowed to get away with. I suppose it's a fairly normal childhood really. I don't remember him as having any problems or being an unhappy child. He was a very pretty boy – blond curly hair and all that sort of thing.'

Graham later described this time of his life as a 'semi-country-pork-pie-and-stilton-cheese childhood'.

By 1951 Walter Chapman had progressed to the rank of chief inspector and was posted to the town of Melton Mowbray. His sons became even more distant from each other under this new arrangement.

'I'd only got eighteen months of school to do at that stage, so I went to live during the week with relatives close to Market Bosworth, and Graham was then living at home getting involved with the local group, a lot of friends.'

Having shown aptitude in his early schooling, Graham soon started attending the local county grammar school of King Edward VII, and it was here that his interests really began to develop. As well as beginning to find a natural affinity for science subjects, chemistry in particular, the young Graham, already tall for his age, actively participated in athletics and threw himself into rugby with vigour. Away from the playing fields he was also developing extra-curricular activities, in particular in acting.

'He certainly got interested in amateur dramatics in a fairly big way at that time, which was something that I never had a great deal of time for myself,' says John Chapman, who was by now finding his younger sibling a more engaging personality. 'I was always very self-conscious in those small ventures I made on to the stage, usually in Gilbert and Sullivan, in the chorus and that sort of thing. But Graham was really taken by it.'

He appeared in several school plays, including pieces by Gilbert and Sullivan, but also in *Macbeth* and other Shakespearean plays, with one local paper going so far as to single him out in a production of *Julius Caesar*: 'The biggest star, however, was Graham Chapman. As Mark Antony, Caesar's greatest friend and chief lieutenant, Graham showed an aptitude for Shakespeare acting rarely witnessed behind the amateur footlights. He combined fine diction with an impressive appearance and brought to life the great Mark Antony in a performance that will long be remembered by Melton audiences. He completely dominated the stage . . . '

The delighted young Graham continued to perform throughout his school career. Even his big brother was impressed, offering him advice on how to pick the best roles.

'We talked about what he should do and about his interest in the theatre. I remember being particularly impressed with the Gilbert and Sullivan he did and the ability of the people who had the patter songs and the humorous parts, and I thought that it was sensible for him to try and avoid playing the part of what were often wishy-washy heroes, and to try to take the character parts because it would be a) a bit more of a challenge and b) much better received, as it were. That's the sort of beginnings of getting into the line of being humorous and being a bit outrageous, I suppose, in behaviour, and that sort of thing. But I don't think I can claim any responsibility for directing his career in any way at all.'

As well as sharing career advice, the brothers had also discovered their radio favourites the Goons. Based on the anarchic scripts of Spike Milligan, the now classic radio show featured Spike alongside Peter Sellers and Harry Secombe (and Michael Bentine originally) and was not only a breath of fresh air on the radio waves of post-war Britain but was to prove the most influential comedy show of its day, spawning a generation of devotees that would come to shape British comedy in the next two decades, not least of whom was Graham Chapman himself.

'We used to just roll about laughing,' says John. 'I don't remember my parents being particularly enamoured by that. But often, while we were having Saturday lunch, we'd have the radio on. Frankie Howerd would be on, and he was someone that Graham was very fond of. But *The Goon Show* was the really big feature in Graham's appreciation of other people's comedy.'

At school Graham still excelled in rugby on the field, chemistry in the classroom and amateur acting in the school hall. However, this latter activity was clearly just something to do for fun; it was never going to be a career. For that decision he once again turned to his elder sibling.

'I think Graham followed me into medicine. I went into medicine on the advice of my headmaster. He asked me what I wanted to do. There wasn't a lot of career advice in those days, and I had to decide what I would want to do at the very tender age of fourteen. I was thinking of going into the Navy, because we still had some battleships at that time and a few aircraft carriers. Or going to do forestry or something like that. I would have quite liked to do farming, but there was no prospect of me ever being able to afford to buy a farm, so that was counted out. So my headmaster suggested medicine, and I thought, "That sounds interesting, perhaps I'll try that." I think Graham simply followed on after my decision because I was obviously enjoying my undergraduate medical career.'

Throughout his life, many who knew and worked with Graham would never have described him as a driven man. He was obviously talented and clearly made his way to success, but that underlying burning ambition that fuels many, often seemed absent in him. Those who knew him well claim this was not his ability to conceal any such desire; there simply seemed to be less of a strong need for success than in many others. His decision to follow his brother into medicine was not a casual decision – and it was certainly a profession he later felt strongly and passionately about – but it was a decision made in the absence of anything drawing him to another life.

'He was somebody who followed up opportunities rather than was driven by an overriding ambition. That's certainly the impression I got. Things happened for him, and he made an impression, and therefore more offers came along,' offers his brother, also recalling the influence he had had on Graham as a child. 'That was a justified problem for me afterwards. I was quite frequently in trouble for not exactly looking after him but dominating him and trying to bend him to my way of thinking.'

John Chapman had been lined up for an early university entrance. As a result of this he would sit both his O levels and A levels simultaneously, forcing him to drop Latin, a subject essential for admission to both Oxford and Cambridge at the time. Instead he went to St Bartholomew's Hospital in London. He left home in 1954, often returning for holidays and visits, regaling his younger brother with his tales of the life to be had in medical school.

'Being small-town people in the lower middle class, as it were, our horizons were fairly limited in those days, and we didn't realise what we might be capable of, and the ultimate seemed to be to have a profession and make a good honest living out of working hard.'

Graham's school records show him to be particularly strong in biology, physics and especially chemistry. So in 1958, inspired to follow his brother, Graham also applied to Bart's and was accepted. However, in between, something else happened. Graham always claimed later that around this time he had seen some footage of the Cambridge Footlights on television, and at that moment decided he would go to Cambridge. The encouragement of his brother only added to this growing decision.

'Having had the experience of being the first member of the

family ever to go to university, I felt it would have been advantageous to Graham to go to Oxford or Cambridge,' John Chapman says. 'I wished I had been able to go to Cambridge because I saw people coming down to London to do clinical medicine with me who had had a proper university education rather than a medical-school education. All my colleagues were medical students, and we didn't have anybody reading poetry or history or geography. I felt that this was something I'd missed out on.

'By that stage, Graham had got entry into a London medical school – Bart's – and I had suggested to him – as he had done a full series of O levels including Latin – he should then try to get into Oxford or Cambridge, and he went along to discuss it with his headmaster who was, actually, a few days later entertaining the master of Emmanuel College to dinner. In those days the usual way of getting from grammar school to Cambridge was to take an entrance examination but that had all already happened for the year that he had wanted to go by the time he'd decided that it would be a good thing to explore the possibility of getting into Cambridge. His headmaster was certainly a very great help to him there and agreed that it would be a sensible thing to do.'

So Graham was interviewed by the master of Emmanuel at Melton Mowbray and not at Cambridge and, despite the lateness of his application, was offered a place on the basis of his headmaster's recommendation.

'Basically, it was my suggestion,' says Graham's elder sibling, 'that he try to get into Oxford or Cambridge because I don't think my parents really understood that it would make a significant difference to his life, and it made the *whole* difference to his life, obviously with Cambridge Footlights and that sort of thing.'

The experience of attending Cambridge University was to

prove in many ways the defining moment in Graham's life. It introduced him to a variety of people who were to populate much of his later life. But it was also to throw up a dilemma: medicine (his chosen career) or comedy (the life he happily fell into).

Chapter Two

Around 1956, back home in Melton Mowbray, Graham picked up two attributes that would become, in many ways, props for him; one was a drink and one was a pipe. Tall and athletic, he was recruited for the local rugby team. This involved training during the week, matches at the weekend and drinking in the club bar afterwards; the latter he would retain a fondness for throughout the next twenty years.

Graham's future partner, David Sherlock, recalls how Graham would discuss these days, 'Graham was such a dedicated sportsman, he was very good at athletics, he was a very good rugby player and also he was very tall at an early age. So he told me that around the age of fifteen, he was asked to join the local rugby club, which was nothing to do with school. This was for grown-up men for whom it was a Saturday fun thing, and they invited Graham to join because they'd heard that he was damn good, and he was thrilled. After rugby, and they'd all cleaned up and showered, it was a Saturday afternoon, so they piled into the pub, and Graham told me that if you're going to go into a pub as a fifteen-year-old in those days, when your father's a copper, you'd better damn well look older. So that was when he took to smoking a pipe, which gave him much more gravitas than smoking cigarettes, which he never really liked, and he then took to drinking pints of beer, along with the rest of the boys.

That's the earliest link I can find looking back to how Graham started his boozing tradition.'

'He had quite a marked example from both my father and myself who smoked pipes,' recalls his brother, John, 'and we both smoked fairly heavily, so I suppose it was almost inevitable.'

Many years later his writing partner and fellow Python John Cleese also noted the way in which Graham more often than not had this object handy. As nonchalant as he was about it, it was clearly something he depended on, at least socially. 'When you're filming,' recalls Cleese, 'you just hang around for hours, and there are times when I find I'm going almost crazy with boredom because you can't sit anywhere and read because there's nowhere comfortable to sit; you can't do anything, and so you play all sorts of games or do crosswords, or you might tell jokes or whatever. On this particular occasion I saw Graham put his pipe down. It was a very silly thing to do, but because I lacked the insight to understand what I was doing, I took his pipe and I popped it in my pocket, and when he turned round and found his pipe was gone, he became so agitated that I realised after quite a short time that something was going on that I didn't understand. So I told him that I'd taken it for a joke and handed it to him, at which point he stepped towards me and literally kneed me in the groin. Fortunately he did not hit the testicles, he hit the bone, which hurt a bit but not a lot, and afterwards I remember thinking, "What on earth was that about?" And then I began to see that that pipe meant a great deal more to Graham symbolically than just being a pipe. It was a strange incident.'

Shortly before leaving home for university, Graham's father taught him to drive, getting him to drive him to various appointments round the town. He failed his first driving test, however, and did not get behind a wheel again until he hit the age of forty and had sobered up.

The then still-present pipe and sporty attitude, however, certainly suited the environs of Cambridge University when Chapman arrived in 1959 to study medicine at Emmanuel College. In many ways, though, at the time of Chapman's arrival Cambridge was something of a schizophrenic institution. It was, on the one hand, still the bastion of tradition it had been for hundreds of years, but, in recent times, it had begun to produce the people who would come to attack and satirise the very establishment that had produced them. The contradiction must have suited Graham perfectly, the young pipe-smoking man in tweed, slowly nurturing what would prove to be an extremely subversive, anarchic sense of comedy.

Cambridge had originated the idea of the university revue on their campus – often known as a 'smoking concert' or 'smoker' – as far back as the late 1900s, the Cambridge University Footlights Club itself first seeing the light of day in 1883. These early musical comedy shows were typically parochial, humorously topical (in that they dealt with events of the university year) and involved plenty of occasion for drinking – and smoking – and were the exclusive province of the male students of the university. This tradition persisted for many years to come.

But as British post-war humour developed, led in many ways by the rule-breaking insanity of the Goons, people started to become more serious about their comedy. Jonathan Miller, a medical student who arrived at Cambridge in 1953, was seen as a figurehead for this unplanned movement. He was among the first of the Cambridge comic performers to venture beyond the confines of the university's boundaries, largely performing his own monologues in *Out of the Blue*, a Cambridge revue that briefly transferred to the West End in 1954, followed by another London transfer, *Between the Lines*, the following year. These two shows garnered Miller press attention and announced to the world that Cambridge was developing into a breeding ground for a new hard-edged, satirical form of comedy. With his medical background, lugubrious wit and ability to fend off any criticism with absurdity, Miller and Chapman would later become acquaintances.

Standing in the firmament behind Miller was another tall, understated performer, by the name of Peter Cook. As a schoolboy, Cook had written for the humour magazine *Punch* and, like just about all of his contemporaries, he found his life changed by the arrival of *The Goon Show*, later citing instances where he would pretend to be ill at boarding school so he could listen to the show in the infirmary. From this and other influences he developed a unique stage persona, at once aloof and caustic, with a natural affinity for the absurd, demonstrated often in one of his key characters, the bizarre, rain-coated monologist who became known as E. L. Whisty. The influence of Cook and his performing style – as well as his love of the surreal and the inexplicable in humour – would prove to be a dominant influence over the generation that followed him, Chapman and his contemporaries being a prime example.

Cook, in turn, was followed by David Frost, a deadpan performer who was the man who would very shortly harness the new-found excitement of what came to be called 'the satire boom' and bring it to the masses, via television. However, at this time, the shadow of Cook's prodigious talent hung over the Footlights, especially over Frost, which was just the way Cook liked it. As Chapman noted in his *A Liar's Autobiography*, 'Peter Cook . . . had an obsessive disregard for David Frost, and came back to punish him by being funnier and more intelligent at the smoking concerts.'

It was into this milieu that Chapman arrived. Although he never neglected his studies, convinced that his future lay in medicine, the lure of the Footlights was strong. There was only one problem – you couldn't join. In a strange, almost Catch-22-like example of bureaucracy, the long-standing rule of the Footlights committee was that you couldn't be allowed to audition in one of their smokers until they had actually seen you perform. In essence you had to audition to be asked to audition.

Humphrey Barclay, later a highly influential radio and TV producer, who ushered along the careers of many of his contemporaries, went up to Cambridge in 1960 and recalls seeing little of Graham initially. 'He hadn't emerged to attract the attention of the Footlights by then, so that must mean he wasn't doing smokers or anything, otherwise he would have been picked. It's possible that when you get to Cambridge, the Footlights seem a bit grand and a bit high and you could never aspire to it. So a lot of people tended to muck about in college revues, rather than daring to aspire to the Footlights. I only got in because I was doing comedy parts in plays and was spotted. But obviously Graham hadn't put his head above the parapet at that time.'

Graham later spoke both in interviews and during his US-university lecture tours of that pivotal moment he had seen the Footlights on TV, but this may well have been retrospective story-telling on his part. During his first year at Cambridge he never approached the Footlights, concentrating instead on his studies. It may well be that Chapman was deterred by the somewhat laborious nature of the Footlights' auditioning process, but when he returned to Cambridge the next autumn in his second year, likely spurred on by the absurdity of the whole thing, Graham set about staging his own smoking concert at Emmanuel, inviting Footlights secretary Frost, and Footlights president Peter Bellwood to attend. Graham later joked that it was the vast amount of claret he plied them with that secured him an audition spot at the next Footlights smoking concert. He attended and performed two pieces – one in which he impersonated a carrot, and another in which he played a man with iron fingertips being pulled off stage by a large magnet.

Chapman was accepted for a place in the Footlights, as was another young performer, John Cleese, from Downing College, who was auditioning at the same time, although Cleese, who was in his first year, would later underplay their mutual achievement: 'If you wanted to audition in the Footlights, you would approach them, show them your piece as a sort of pre-audition, and then you would actually do it in front of the membership of the club. Then, after you performed, a decision was taken in the next few days as to whether you would be invited to join them. I don't ever remember anyone being turned down, although theoretically I suppose they could have been.'

Both Chapman and Cleese were nervous about the auditioning process, although, as Cleese puts it, 'It was daunting, but sometimes when you're younger you do things without thinking about them much.' Part of the audition process involved both men being forced to sing and dance, something that Chapman later claimed they personally ousted from the Footlights.

On their first meeting Chapman and Cleese, who would form a lengthy writing partnership, went for a drink at the nearby Kenco coffee house. Cleese recalls that his first impression of Chapman was one of dislike, albeit irrational dislike: 'It was an absolute gut feeling that I was not able to identify at all. Just a feeling of really not liking him.'

At Cambridge, as he would throughout most of his life, Graham moved between worlds. His academic work was strong, as were his ties to the medical college and his colleagues, but he also had the Footlights Clubhouse, at 5 Falcon Yard, to hang out in. This was not just a place for like-minded souls, but a place on campus where you could get a drink late at night, something Graham had become increasingly fond of on a social level.

Graham's initial invite to audition for the Footlights ('a piece of cardboard' as Cleese recalls it) had asked him to bring along not only the sketches they had seen him perform at his own smoker but also requested him to 'bring as much material as you can muster'. Alongside his first tentative steps as a performer, Graham was now beginning to write. He had always been well aware as he listened to the Goons that the scripts were written by Spike Milligan; indeed, with all the radio comedy he listened to, Graham always took note of the writer, so for him to begin penning material was a natural development. Throughout his life Graham never seemed to favour one over the other. Although his writing career was, by definition, more prolific, he never really seemed to separate the two. He did not perform to preserve his own material; he simply saw no issue in doing both.

When they reconvened after the summer, Cleese – no longer displaying any worrying feelings of antipathy towards him – started to write with Chapman.

'I don't think I saw Chapman again until the beginning of the next academic year, which was my second and his third. And, for reasons that I cannot remember, we immediately fell into writing together, the sense of dislike just evaporated, and we spent a lot of time that year sitting together, usually in my room, writing stuff, a fair amount of which made it into the Footlights revue of that year.'

Graham recalled the first sketch he and Cleese ever wrote together: 'A policeman came in, beat a bloke up, and then said, "Just a routine enquiry."' It was not so unusual then that later critics would notice a propensity for violence, even sadism in their subsequent work together.

The decision to write as a team was never really discussed between the two; the idea at the time just seemed to take shape naturally, as if it would, in many ways, be easier to pen comedy as a team than as individuals.

'I do remember,' Cleese states, 'sitting down to write was a bit like dating. Your ego was, to some extent, at stake, and you didn't want the other person to turn down too many of your ideas or think they weren't funny. Similarly you were fairly careful and tactful if they came up with something you didn't like. I remember we had no experience, we had no confidence. I think it was more a case that we were unconfident and hiding our lack of confidence more.'

It was not an obvious match as Cleese wrote, by his own confession, far more obsessively, struggling over every word and construction, while Chapman was more prone to throwing out comic ideas, running with them and seeing where they would end up, if indeed anywhere. Although at the time both men never discussed the process, both instinctively seemed to know that this was a combination that not only benefited their disparate styles and abilities but generally added something to the other's work – Cleese gave Chapman structure and was willing to put in the hours to hone the material; Chapman could take a simple idea and elevate it to unexpected absurd levels. It allowed both writers to fall into place and follow the flow of each other's approach.

But then again, none of this was serious; this was just university – Cleese had a career in law lined up, Chapman was on his way to becoming a doctor like his older brother. And by no means were they exclusive. Although they found writing together to be conducive, they were still working alone or, in various combinations, with other members of the Footlights. (At this time in the Footlights' history, the other members were inevitably male, the likes of Tim Brooke-Taylor, Bill Oddie, David Hatch and Humphrey Barclay were all passing through. Women were still not being admitted to the club as members but were occasionally recruited for shows. Miriam Margolyes was the current female on hand, and she later claimed that she and Chapman 'loathed' each other.

Unlike John Cleese's strong initial feelings towards Graham, Humphrey Barclay claims not to have too much of a recollection – Graham was just there. 'I don't know that I have any particular impression of him. He sort of went around with Cleese, and they had some material. He was also fairly close to Tim Brooke-Taylor. This sounds almost pathetic; I'm not covering anything up, just we were all doing the bits we could do. We all fell into things. We'd say, "This is going on, are you going to come along?" There was no feeling of making a professional decision to go and write some material. It was better than going and doing some work – sit around the Footlights Club after a bun and a beer. It was more fun to sit down and write something for the forthcoming smoker than it was to go and do some work.'

The result of much of this collaboration would be the 1962 Footlights revue, *Double Take*. Directed by Trevor Nunn, Chapman appeared alongside Cleese, Humphrey Barclay, Robert Atkins, Tim Brooke-Taylor, Nigel Brown, Alan George, Tony Hendra and Miriam Margolyes.

For the previous two years the spectre of *Beyond the Fringe* had hung over the university revue in general. When Cambridge graduates Peter Cook and Jonathan Miller were teamed with Oxford graduates Alan Bennett and Dudley Moore to bring a revue-style show to the West End of London, it revolutionised not only British theatre, but British society in general. What had previously only been seen within the confines of such relatively elite university establishments was now common tender in London. Where once it had been a secretive notion to mock the government and institutions around you – often knowing full well that those doing so would soon end up the very pillars on which these institutions rested – now it was made available to all. The austere years of post-Second World War Britain were crumbled by something the media chose to brand as 'satire'. The effect was both liberating and dramatic. David Frost quickly jumped into the fray and took satire to television, in the form of *That Was the Week That Was*, a topical comedy show that was not only a hit but began Frost's mighty television legacy.

Double Take found itself hanging in the shadow of all this rapid change – and decided to ignore it. This revue eschewed topicality and satire and moved in a simply more comic direction. In a strange way that itself was now like a breath of fresh air. Here was absurdist, silly humour, featuring the like of Chapman wrestling himself off the stage. Graham wasn't at this time a very politicised animal, so this form of show suited him perfectly.

The show debuted at the Cambridge Arts Theatre to generally good reviews. The *Guardian* singled out Graham for praise: 'Graham Chapman showed a real comic gift which, save for his impersonation of a carrot, he had too few opportunities to display . . . ' Closer to home, the *Cambridge News* was less enthusiastic while still offering some praise: 'Graham Chapman, Tony Hendra and Alan George also add mimicry, energy and wit to the show – the last two particularly . . . '

Audiences responded well to *Double Take*, with the show proving a popular success at the King's Lynn Festival in Oxford before becoming the first Footlights revue to play on the Edinburgh Fringe.

'They gave us this huge house in Edinburgh which somebody had willed or left to Edinburgh University,' recalls Cleese, 'and there was nothing in it except a bathroom with taps that had water coming out of them, and we all slept on inflatable plastic things with dirty sheets and had a great time.'

During the Edinburgh run the show was coupled with a production of Ibsen's *Brand*. Chapman and Cleese both had small roles in the latter and, to get out of the show, they started performing material as a double act in a local coffee house.

The show then transferred to the Oxford Playhouse, where the local *Oxford Mail* provided the two writer-performers with their first negative review. Noting the level of sadism in their pieces, the critic pointed out that Chapman and Cleese were 'responsible for a lot of the poorer material'.

Both Chapman and Cleese refused to be put off by such notions. 'What I discovered,' Cleese recounts, 'was sometimes when Graham and I were writing, a funny "hard" line would come along and I would think, "Well, it's only the Footlights, let's try it," because even if I don't know them all it was friendly, and it would get the biggest laughs. So I would put what I call these harder lines in more and more, and I was rewarded with the biggest laughs. So I learned that it was okay, well, better than okay; I learned that it worked, and that what I would laugh at with Chapman, in fact the audience would laugh at too.'

Nonetheless this appeared to mark the end of Graham's university-revue career. He had graduated from Emmanuel and followed his brother to St Bartholomew's in London to continue his medical studies.

'With hindsight,' Graham once said, 'I realise I always wanted to write and perform, but at the time I thought I wanted to do medicine for the good of humanity.'

John Chapman was now a junior lecturer at Bart's, and even though he saw his younger sibling quite often, the closeness of their relationship remained defined by the four-year age gap between them. That and the fact that John was now married, to Pamela, starting a family and living in the suburbs – a very different world from the central-London lifestyle that Graham now found himself in.

However, Graham did not seem all that keen to leave the extra-curricular side of life at Cambridge behind, and one of the first things he did upon arriving at Bart's was to stage a smoker of his own, bringing in the troops for the occasion.

'Previously at Bart's they'd had Christmas shows, that sort of thing,' remembers John Chapman, 'but Graham organised a smoker and brought quite a lot of people down from Cambridge – Bill Oddie, Anthony Buffery, Humphrey Barclay and people like that. Tim Brooke-Taylor was certainly one of them. John Cleese was there as well. That was the first smoking concert in the Abanethean Room at Bart's, in Charterhouse Square. It then became an annual tradition, and after that it was primarily Bart's people doing it, rather than imported talent from Cambridge.

'There was only room for an audience of around a hundred. It wasn't in a formal theatre or anything; it was just the Abanethean Room, adjacent to the bar, conveniently, and it was a place that also used to run the Saturday-night hops. It had a small stage – a raised dais, which normally had a piano on it, on which the performance was done.'

One of the first people Graham met at Bart's became a close and lifelong friend, Alan Bailey. 'When he came to Bart's from Cambridge he was in my wife's year, and we only became contemporaries because he went around in that world. He came to her attention because they were in Women's Outpatients, Gynaecology, this is in '63, and there was a very strict sister there. All the sisters at Bart's were incredibly well turned out and very strict, and medical students were the shit: they really didn't like medical students. They were badly dressed and they didn't fit in well and they were herded around, and Graham was discovered boiling an egg in one of the sterilisers. When the sister discovered that there was this egg boiling in her steriliser, she just panicked, and nobody had ever seen her panic before, and she screamed and she rushed down. She said, "There's something terrible!" It had boiled for so long all the white had come out and bubbled up and Graham was laughing.

'The other time I remember Graham, one of the first memories, was of him wandering along. He wasn't a terribly extrovert fellow in those days, I don't think, but he came up to one of these big, red London pillar boxes and he looked in it and then started cranking this imaginary handle, like a "what the butler saw" machine. This was this weird fellow who'd come to Bart's. We hadn't seen anything like this. We were all "three-piece suits" in those days with stiff collars, and this amazing loony had come up to Bart's. But underneath the three-piece suit if he got bored he'd start doing loony things. He had no fear internally, but externally . . . I'm not so sure.'

Graham and Bailey bonded significantly when they helped run the students' recently formed Wine Committee and took over the running of the Bart's in-house bar, previously an institution managed by one of the hospital porters, that was open only one or two hours a night. Chapman and Bailey soon put a stop to all that.

'It used to open from about six o'clock to eight o'clock in the evenings, that's all, and it was not terribly convenient as far as times were concerned,' recalled John Chapman, 'and it was run by one of the college porters. And while Graham was there, the Wine Committee was formed, which took over the running of the bar, and they organised a rota of their own people and opened it for much longer. Consequently it started to make money, and they were able to plough some of that money into various activities – promoting social functions and things like that. They were a bright bunch of people. We had a junior warden at the time, and it was his job to make sure the bar closed promptly at 10 p.m. Time was called and everybody got out, and then, of course, he went up to his room and went to bed, and then the bar could open again, often until two o'clock in the morning!

'This was social drinking. At that time the ethic among medical students was to work only after the bar had closed. We all tried to acquire our knowledge by stealth and display it only under the maximum provocation, as it were. The majority of people were drinking, usually beer, and it was really an extension of the rugby-playing group. We had a thriving rugby club running five teams every week, and everybody finished up down at the bar in the evenings. It was always a very boozy affair really – you came off the field and the first thing was these enormous jugs with about a gallon of shandy in it, just to quench the thirst.'

Prior to this new regime a Bart's student's quest for booze could lead to some unusual places. 'By the time Graham had joined, we'd got Whitbread, who provided us with the beer, to build a bigger bar and an extension in the residence in College Hall,' Alan Bailey remembers. 'And, of course, Graham, who liked to drink, went on to the Wine Committee straight away. I was the treasurer by that stage. We didn't want to upset the people that we'd been going to – the pubs around – so we'd open it for a bit for a drink before dinner, and then we'd have our supper, and then we'd go to the pub we wanted to go to, and then we'd open our bar when the other pubs closed. So it was pretty illegal, but it didn't really matter, because if you wanted a late-night drink in Smithfield in the sixties, you went down to the police station opposite the hospital, and they'd give you a drink. So the only night we were raided, the Snow Hill police, who were city police in Charterhouse Square, came at our invitation and had drinks there. Then we were raided by the Clerkenwell police, and they all knew the Snow Hill police, so we had a really good drunken evening that night.'

Although not as frequent a prop at the college bar, Graham's elder brother also took advantage of the hospitality of a somewhat lax police view on drunken behaviour – as did most of their contemporaries. 'You got to know the City of London policemen,' says John Chapman, 'because quite a lot of medical students did silly things from time to time, and their silly things were better tolerated by the City of London Police than by the Metropolitan Police. I remember getting stopped in a friend's car; there were five of us going at some speed down the City Road with the old bells clanging behind, and the City of London Police were getting out and coming and talking to us, and they're saying, "Well, okay chaps, you're not far from home, you'd better carry on now but just remember in future that had you by any means been drinking and had you also been caught speeding home and been caught drinking, we would have had to throw the book at you. Fortunately you weren't caught on this occasion."'

'The rule at our bar,' says Bailey, 'was that when the last drunk had fallen over, then we would close the bar, and Graham and I often ran that late and we'd have to get a cab home. There was one chap who used to go to sleep a lot when he was drunk but hardly ever fell over, so we'd push him when everybody else had gone home, and then he'd fall off and we'd say, "Well, the last one's gone."'

Graham's decision to join the Wine Committee and essentially instigate a coup of the bar was fuelled by his own predilection for alcohol, something that had been formed back in those post-rugby-match days in Melton Mowbray.

'From the time I knew him he was as heavy a drinker as I was, and I was one of the heaviest drinkers at Bart's,' states Alan Bailey. 'I don't think he had any fear, particularly when we'd had a few drinks, and he was much more fearless than I was. People would do mad things at Bart's. There was one chap who got on a bus and drove it into a butcher's shop. He didn't know how to drive a bus. People would light fireworks and put them up dogs' arses; Graham never did that. It was very horrid, but we were funny people in those days. We did the most terrible things. You'd be locked up for them these days.

'Graham was chairman of the students' union in '65, and I was chairman of the students' union in '66. I followed him the year later and Bart's were playing the London Hospital in the finals of the rugby cup, and they were our biggest rivals. It was at the Richmond Athletic Ground. In previous days it was such a little amateur ground that no medical student ever paid – they just jumped over the wall or whatever – so they built this bloody great turnstile, and the bus with all the Bart's supporters arrived, and the driver got out to say, "What's all this?" and the chap on the turnstile said, "Well, how many people have you got in there? This is a forty-seater bus, I want forty times a pound." Somebody got in the driver's seat and just drove the bus into the turnstile and knocked it down. This brand-new turnstile at the Richmond Athletic Ground which they were so proud about! Then the Dean got a bill for £600 to rebuild this thing. Being chairman of the students' union, I get called in and the Dean says, "Apparently one of our buses knocked down the turnstile," and I said, "No, no, that wasn't us, that was the London Hospital supporters," and he said, "Good, good!" and sent the bill to the London Hospital. And I imagine that bill's still going backwards and forwards. That was the atmosphere that we were brought up in. And Graham somehow made it more loony and made us think we could get away with even more things. He had a huge foresight. He wasn't worried about anything in those days, particularly when he'd had a drink. Nor was I.

'He didn't instigate in an extrovert way. He encouraged. So if somebody said something like, "Let's go and steal the mascot from Guy's," he wouldn't suggest it, but he'd be the first out there, ordering cabs and getting us all over to Guy's and talking strategy. He'd have his pipe in his mouth, saying how we ought to go in and do it. And then the next day he'd say, "That was terribly childish, we'd better go and do some work this morning," and he'd go off and sit in the library for three hours. He was that sort of fellow. You either loved him or hated him. A lot of people couldn't take that, and there were a lot of people there who thought we were making a lot of noise in the bar or coming in late at night and still roaring around.

'We were completely isolated from the rest of the university. That was one of the great criticisms about medical education after the war: that it was all done in units that had no other discipline to them. And that is now not government policy.

You've got to be educated with arts and sciences and all sorts of other things, because we turned out to be a really narrow-minded race.'

As ever, despite such social interludes, Graham remained very adept at his studies; if anything those around him seemed to feel that medicine came almost too easily to him, even his brother, John, who was several years ahead of Graham in his studies. 'He was always bloody bright. He was a lot brighter than me.'

'He didn't have to work very hard at medicine,' concurs Graham's sister-in-law, Pam Chapman. 'That was always the impression we got. He was extremely bright, but he wasn't a slogger. He didn't have to swot for exams. He was just one of those annoying people,' she laughs.

Although they only had a limited degree of social interaction at Bart's, John Chapman was keenly aware of his younger brother's study patterns. 'He made lots and lots of meticulous notes, he obviously attended lectures and took notes fairly religiously. He did not neglect his studies, certainly at that stage, but he was able to take that in his stride and do much more. Whereas I was more interested in playing cricket and rugby, he developed other things.'

This period was proving to be a pivotal time not only for Graham but for the majority of his Cambridge Footlights contemporaries. The year after he left Cambridge, the Footlights' end-of-year revue ran under the somewhat difficult title of *A Clump of Plinths* (believed to be the result of the meeting of the Cleese and Brooke-Taylor minds). The show was directed by Humphrey Barclay, himself a performer (and a very decent cartoonist) from the previous year's *Double Take*.

'I decided I shouldn't be in the revue for my third year,' says Barclay, 'because I ought to succeed in some exams, and Tim

Brooke-Taylor came and asked me if I would direct it. I said, "Why?" and he basically said, "Because there's nobody else." It was a surprising choice, but I had kind of sidled up to Trevor Nunn the year before and worked very closely with him, and we sat up all night writing silly lyrics. Nowadays I think of him writing silly lyrics for *Cats* and earning millions!

'We didn't have a good title. I was only trying to be sensible and *You Can't Call A Show Cornflakes* was one of the titles that was considered. For a show like *A Clump of Plinths* you'd remember good sketches from the smokers that year and who did them and who were the good performers, so it just wasn't very difficult to collect what you'd got and then see what you hadn't got. There wasn't any feeling of "if I do a good sketch here I might get into the revue". It sounds incredibly haphazard, but it was in those days. There were certain people who everybody knew would be in the revue, then there might be a question of who "the girl" would be, and there might be a question of how many people you actually wanted in the end. The Footlights' membership was sixty or seventy, but most of them were not good enough or interested enough to be in a show. It was pretty much a sort of self-forming A-list.'

For Barclay – and his contemporaries – a future in performing or working behind the scenes in television was a distant prospect. But it was one they would soon learn could be achieved.

'When I was acting,' Barclays recalls, 'a girl said to me once as I came off stage, "Oh, you are good. You are going to do it professionally, aren't you?" and obviously it was in her mind, but it had never crossed mine. Frost was evidently set on it from the word go. People from Granada and the BBC came to recruit at Cambridge. There was a BBC production-trainee post that you could compete for, so a career in broadcasting wasn't a million miles away from some people's minds, but a career as a performer would never have occurred to any of us. Of course, the one person who had turned professional from our background was Peter Cook in that he had had material accepted by West End revues, where it was performed by Kenneth Williams. But it never crossed our minds that it would happen to us.'

Alongside Tim Brooke-Taylor and John Cleese, *A Clump of Plinths* featured Bill Oddie, Chris Stuart-Clark, David Hatch, Anthony Buffery and Jo Kendall. The show played the Cambridge Arts Theatre and headed on to Edinburgh and may well have then been finished with. Instead, West End impresario Michael White caught one of its performances and decided to take it to London.

By now John Cleese, having graduated, had passed on his career in law to take up an offer to work as a writer for the BBC. Having renewed his relationship with Graham, he would often find himself staying at Bart's.

'I was usually able to find a bed in Bart's,' recollects Cleese. 'One guy would be out for the week, so I'd stay in his room, and he'd come back and someone else would go.'

Soon he and Graham, along with Tim Brooke-Taylor and a colleague of Graham's, Benny Chi Ping Lee, were rooming together in Manchester Square, but, as Cleese recalls, 'I don't remember spending very much time with Graham. He would go off, to medical school, earlier in the morning than I did. I'd go into the BBC, usually walked in and did a full day's work and if I saw him, I saw him in the evening.'

Although they saw little of each other, when Cleese and Chapman were together they did make time to argue. 'He seemed to me to have very extreme views on selfishness. He had an idea of a kind of perfect unselfishness, and I remember when I praised the Buddhists or certain aspects of Buddhism to him, he was very dismissive of them and thought they were very selfish, presumably because they took time to themselves and meditated and did things like that, which he saw as very selfish. I also noticed that he got much more aggressive when he was drinking, whereas when he wasn't drinking he was very eloquent. Almost too weak. That was something that I became much more aware of later too. It was as though his aggression could only come out when he'd been drinking. He found it very hard to assert himself. It ties up psychologically – some kind of over-idealised view of selfishness with an inability to assert himself.'

During his time in London, Graham had not forsaken his fondness for performing. Working in a double act with Tony Hendra (who had once considered taking orders as a Benedictine monk and later helped found *National Lampoon* magazine), they would occasionally play such noted clubs as Peter Cook's The Establishment. But it was really little more than a hobby. His flatmate Cleese meanwhile was working at the BBC during the day and gearing up for a run in the West End at night, in *A Clump of Plinths*, recently retitled *Cambridge Circus*. 'A slightly boring title,' concedes Barclay, 'and a confused bunch of people expected animals.'

Cambridge Circus debuted at the New Arts Theatre on 10 July 1963. Picking up the slack from the recently departed long run of *Beyond the Fringe*, the show proved an immediate hit with audiences and, to a lesser degree, with most critics; the *Observer* catching the prevailing tone: 'You cannot expect every Cambridge Footlights review to start a new wave or spew up a vast amount of talent. But of course you do, and of course they don't. *Cambridge Circus* . . . does the expected rather well . . . ' Bernard Levin meanwhile in the *Daily Mail* opined, 'Have they got a new Jonathan Miller among them? I may as well get the answer over right away. No.' The show, however, was immensely successful, and its three-week run was extended to five, before transferring to the Lyric Theatre, on 14 August 1963, for another hundred-plus performances.

Just prior to this transfer, however, one of its original performers decided to forsake the stage and return to academia. 'Tony Buffery left when we got to the West End,' Barclay recalls, 'and it was a general agreement that Graham was available to be added to the cast, thank goodness. It didn't take much thinking about.'

Bart's proved to be amenable, and now Graham found himself doing ward rounds by day and treading the West End stage by night.

Chapter Three

'St Bartholomew's Hospital – bless it!' Graham once told the writer Roger Wilmut. 'A marvellous place – has always been one of the few medical institutions that favours the loony, the oddball character – which has often had very good results medically; there's a rather impressive list of innovative characters associated with the place – as far as activities outside medicine were concerned, they rather encouraged them, provided Bart's were mentioned in the programme notes. Of course, appearing every night for three or four months, it was rather difficult getting up at eight in the morning to rush in for a ward round.'

Despite the pressure, Graham was clearly relishing the sheer activity of appearing in *Cambridge Circus* and the fact that he was being offered another chance at this more glamorous side of life. As with so many things in his career, Graham did not actively pursue or crave them, but when they fortuitously landed in his lap, he knew how to make the most of them. In the last month of *Cambridge Circus*'s London run Chris Stuart-Clark also left to return to academia and Humphrey Barclay took over his roles. Despite leading this double life – Graham moving between worlds as always – the theatre was still an indulgence, almost a guilty pleasure for the burgeoning doctor.

'After all, Graham was going to be a doctor, so the show was just a fun extra,' Barclay confirms. 'But there was a kind of loopy physicality about him which was very valuable. I remember him most in *Cambridge Circus* for his performance as Arnold Fitch in the big court sketch which ended the show, because he was wonderfully panicked and nervous in that performance, he was acting somebody terrified out of his mind by the bullying of John Cleese's character.

'I think he presented himself as a very ordinary bloke, and yet underneath it, in his private life – and because of his maverick spirit which kind of gave rise to his comedy performance – there was a rebellious streak. There was a "let's break the rules" kind of lunacy that was provocative. He liked to provoke people, and yet he wasn't the sort of person who would go around, as it would be now, with spiky hair and pierced body parts to provoke people that way. He just liked to surprise people with what was under the surface.'

Among those who saw Graham in the London run of *Cambridge Circus* was Oxford contemporary, and later collaborator, Terry Jones, who found himself particularly impressed with Graham's performance. 'I remember thinking John was wonderful,' Jones recollects, 'but being even more intrigued by Graham. You could see exactly where John was coming from when he walked on the stage . . . but Graham came on the stage and you had no idea what he was doing there. Graham was like a mystery. A wonderful mystery. Why was he funny? Was he funny? What on earth was he doing on a stage? With Graham one always thought, "How on earth?" '

The show was later performed in Edinburgh with a different cast, which included another Cambridge graduate and future collaborator, Eric Idle.

In between the West End and what would later prove to be a globe-trotting tour of the show, Barclay could always rely on his Footlights contemporaries to drop everything and come and put on a show on a more personal basis – case in point, their appearance at his sister's birthday party.

'The Footlights boys very kindly used to come down whenever I needed a cabaret and they came and performed at my sister's twenty-first. I remember being in the kitchen of our house in Shere in Surrey, and everybody was wonderful, pitching in to do the washing-up and the kitchen seemed extraordinarily full and busy, and then Graham suddenly said, "I hope you all notice how busy I'm looking," and all he was doing was walking up and down at the end of the room, looking busy. He wasn't doing anything at all.'

The show transferred to radio in a one-off collection of sketches, also going by the name of *Cambridge Circus*, broadcast on 30 December 1963. The success of this show led, the following spring, to the creation of the cult radio comedy sketch show *I'm Sorry I'll Read That Again*. Having appeared in the first broadcast, Chapman was absent from the cast for the next three, due in part to hospital commitments but also in part due to producer Barclay.

'I remember taking a decision, which feels quite harsh now, that for the radio series, we should substitute Graeme Garden for Graham Chapman. And that was my decision, and it was because of Graeme Garden's versatility voice-wise, his great ability to mimic and all that. I just thought he would be more useful. I don't know whether Graham was upset by it, or whether he was too busy being a doctor. I don't think I ever did know.'

While the likes of Cleese and Brooke-Taylor had now forsaken the idea of their respective careers in law in favour of work at the BBC – and Humphrey Barclay had been offered a job in radio production – Graham seemed to be the only remaining member of the cast who was still actively considering his original career. Medicine for him was still what he was going to do with his life. He was eventually persuaded to change that opinion by royal appointment.

Following the success of *Cambridge Circus*'s run in London, an offer was made for the cast to bring the show to New Zealand, in a deal arranged by producer Michael White. For most of those involved this would potentially be a life-changing commitment. Humphrey Barclay needed to be released temporarily from his recent BBC contract, as would Cleese (the Beeb were amenable in both cases). As for Chapman it meant taking a sabbatical from his medical studies, something that his parents were reluctant to agree to.

However, in his position as secretary of the students' union at Bart's in 1964, Graham was obliged on one occasion to take tea with the Queen Mother when she came to open a new biochemistry building. In conversation he mentioned that he had just been offered the chance to travel to New Zealand and tour in a show he had previously played in London. The Queen Mother thought it was a splendid idea.

'They'd put a lot into his education and they were a bit against him being over-adventurous in the show-business world,' recollects John Chapman. 'So Graham was at the table with the Queen Mother and was just making conversation with her, and he was asked by the Queen Mother what his interests were and things like that. When he mentioned that they'd been offered the chance of taking *Cambridge Circus* over to New Zealand, the Queen Mother called over the Dean of the medical school and said, "You must let him go." She put in a good word. It was in his last year of clinical studies.'

The New Zealand run of *Cambridge Circus* was up and running. Humphrey Barclay once again produced and directed the show, with another Cambridge student, Jonathan Lynn, joining the already well-established cast.

'He went off and did a six-week tour of New Zealand,' says John Chapman. 'I don't know what my parents felt about it at that stage. I think they were by then beginning to think, "Well, maybe there is something to this, maybe it's an opportunity that shouldn't be missed. He's got so far with his medical career now, it's not going to be completely lost if he goes over at this stage; it can be retrieved later on. Why not take the chance and take the opportunity?" I myself felt that it was an opportunity that shouldn't be passed over and had to be taken.'

John's wife, Pam, recalls the general impression that this was still a temporary thing for Graham. 'There was the feeling at the time that it was something that was great fun and everything, and it probably wouldn't last. I suppose we almost had a parental attitude, because we were young newly-weds with a new young son and everything, so I can remember having fun with Gray. But I never thought his comedy career would last.'

'He'd got a real job that he could come back to,' concurred John.

Before heading to New Zealand, Humphrey Barclay reconvened the cast for a brief period of rehearsal and performance in Yorkshire. One of the additions to the show was a sketch by Terry Jones, a graduate of the Oxford revue scene and admirer of Chapman. Jones had written the 'Custard Pie' skit (performed here under the title 'Humour Without Tears'), in which slapstick comedy was performed, commentated on and effectively deconstructed, which proved to be a sizeable hit in the show, in effect creating the first significant link between the Oxford and Cambridge teams that would later form Monty Python's Flying Circus.

★

Following in the wake of a recent tour by the Beatles, the cast of *Cambridge Circus* headed Down Under in May 1964. Along the way Graham, who was meticulously noting all his expenditure in a notebook, bought himself a camera for the first time. Upon arrival he sent his parents a necessarily brief telegram. It simply read, 'Arrived safely. Graham.'

It's impossible to underestimate the life-changing impact this tour of New Zealand had on many of the performers present. Where before performing on stage had been an extension of the japeries of university life, now here they were travelling halfway around the world to bring their own brand of humour to a whole other audience. They were comedy ambassadors on one hand but, much more importantly, professional stage performers on another. Then, on a purely practical level, there was the nature of the travel itself. In 1964 travel of this magnitude was not generally experienced by what was essentially a group of provincial graduates. It was something their own generation and the generations before them had not had the opportunity to explore. The lengthy flight alone was daunting, the sense of isolation once you got there even more so. Yet they embraced it – a trip to a new world seemed to indicate the path forward to a new life.

'At the beginning of the summer of that year, suddenly somebody started saying, "Well, hey, guys, what about coming to New Zealand and probably going on to Broadway,"' Cleese remembers, 'and, of course, at that age I don't think anyone was married or thinking about getting married, so you kind of think, "Why not? It sounds a lot of fun". So we all met up again and rehearsed for a couple of months, got on a plane and flew thirty-six hours to New Zealand and arrived in this strange time-warp place that felt like England 1923, south coast, it had that sort of feeling about it, and we had an hilarious six weeks with a great deal of laughter, a lot of it at the expense of the New Zealanders.'

For Graham New Zealand was the moment when he realised, even if he were loath to admit it, that there might be a career in this. Medicine was still his calling, but it was becoming a more and more distant voice.

'It did seem a very remarkably long journey that we took because it was sort of thirty hours or something getting there, and yes, there were various adventures en route. I think John got locked in a lavatory,' Barclay recalls.

Upon their arrival in Christchurch the troupe found themselves billed as 'Masters of Mirth' and housed in a wooden temperance hotel, devoid of heat as much as it was of alcohol. 'We stayed in this terrible hotel in Christchurch, which was run by this dreadful woman,' Barclay continues. 'It was rather old-fashioned and there was no heating, and I think Graham said he was reduced to running hot water in his basin and saying embarrassing things to himself to make himself blush to keep warm. I think that was how he dealt with it. Somebody else went to complain to the lady running the hotel and she said, "Well, if you're cold, dear, run up and down the corridor." It was a very bizarre hotel. We weren't allowed to sit next to each other at breakfast because each room was supposed to sit at a certain table: that was the rule. And the menu said cereal or porridge and we said, "What's the cereal?" and she said "Porridge." And then fruit or prunes. We asked what the fruit was and she said, "Prunes." It was really very bizarre. It was in that hotel that John asked for a three-egg omelette and he got an omelette with three fried eggs on top of it.'

Graham later wrote that upon sight of said omelette, 'Even people three tables away threw up.' The troupe promptly left the temperance hotel and checked into another, this one, much to Graham's relief, with a liquor licence.

The show's opening night in Christchurch set the tone for the rest of the tour: 'On Monday night, playing to a packed house for its NZ premiere, *Cambridge Circus* provided Christchurch with more laughs to the aching inch than any previous show of its kind,' wrote their first reviewer, B. J. Southam. 'Notable for an absence of the aggressive social-political satire that has been prominent in England recently, it seemed to be based on a "humour for humour's sake" approach.' The ball was rolling . . .

At this time Graham's homosexuality was hidden from his fellow cast members. While he later claimed to have had homosexual experiences during his time at Cambridge, it was also true that he was dating women and at the very least experimenting as he came to terms with himself. When on later tours with Cleese, in the Python days, Graham would almost always absent himself from the social aspect of touring. In New Zealand, however, the troupe clung together, strangers in a strange land, with some of them determined to see as much of this new world as time – and the perennial lack of money – allowed them. When they decamped to South Island, Chapman, Cleese and Brooke-Taylor hired a single prop, four-seater Cessna to explore the mountains, landing on a glacier, at which point – according to Chapman – an air-sick Cleese promptly threw up.

In between sightseeing *Cambridge Circus* took time to impress the antipodeans. Beginning in Christchurch, the show moved to the town of Dunedin and then to the even smaller town of Timaru, where it was recorded for television by the New Zealand Broadcasting Company. In addition to this and their stage performances the *Cambridge Circus* troupe also found time in Wellington in New Zealand to transfer their material to radio in the form of four shows, each of which ran under a different title.

'It was just a case of what rubbish can we do?' Barclay remembers. 'What can we do that will work all right in sound? And we gave those radio shows some rather silly names – *The Cardinal Richelieu Show* was one and *The Peter Titheridge Show* – Peter being our great mentor at the BBC – and then there was *The Mrs Muir Show*. Mrs Muir was the landlady at the place that we were sent to in Wellington – a little Scottish lady who was confused as to who these people were, but she knew that the movie *Zulu* was opening in town, so she opened the door to us and received us very kindly and said, "Are you the Zulus?" And we tried to persuade her that we weren't, but she'd got this idea into her head and she said, "I've got a brother in Africa, do you know him?" and we decided to call one of the shows *The Mrs Muir Show*, just so she could say to her friends, "These Zulus turned up and named a radio show after me!"'

The shows on stage meanwhile didn't always run smoothly – Barclay recalls one night when Graham skipped half a monologue (possibly due to the effects of alcohol) and had everyone backstage frantically scrabbling around to get ready for the impending next sketch. 'It was a total panic because nobody had their costume on for the next number,' says Barclay.

Nonetheless the show – which moved on to the capital, Wellington, before completing its run in Auckland – proved to be a big success. The reviews were generally ecstatic: 'Nobody with weak abdominal muscles should be allowed to see this show. It is too remorselessly achingly funny,' with Graham often being singled out for praise: 'I must make mention of Graham Chapman's hilarious wrestling match with himself . . . ', ' . . . the Tati-like Chapman . . . '

The *Timaru Herald* even picked up on Graham's royal

appointment story: 'The royal remark was fortunate as Chapman is a wonderful comedian . . . Becoming an inanimate object, a carrot, he is drawn across and off the stage by a magnetic force attracting his fingertips. He mimes a wrestler who has no opponent but, not wishing to disappoint his audience, wrestles with himself . . . The combined result is that *Cambridge Circus* has a character all of its own. It is very refreshing, unlike anything seen on the professional stage here before.' And to think, given the title, some people still showed up expecting to see lions and trapeze acts!

'It was a mixed experience, New Zealand,' Barclay concludes, 'but we were incredibly lucky to be there. It was good fun.'

Before their arrival in New Zealand there had been some talk of a run in New York. Already legendary TV mogul and presenter Ed Sullivan had bought the US rights to the show when it was still running in London, before selling them on to theatrical impresario Sol Hurok.

While travelling between Christchurch and Auckland, word came through – they were indeed headed for Broadway. It was an amazing turn of events, and one that led Graham to question his future career even further, although some part of him still held fast to the notion of medicine. If Broadway was in the offing, it was surely as far as he could go. He would enjoy the experience and then get back to the life he had planned out for himself; a respectable life that his parents approved of and his brother had forged for him in many ways.

Graham went through a large part of his life following the path that was mapped out for him by others. He was not always driven by his choices, although he was extremely capable at whatever he lent his hand to, be it in medicine or comedy writing or acting. These were all things that seemed to come easily to him, and while he was seldom overtly passionate about either or any of them, he was extremely adroit at all when required to be. Medicine had always been there – ever since his brother had led the way. Graham simply followed.

'He wasn't ever driven to go into medicine in the first place. It wasn't his life's ambition, it was probably something he followed me into in the absence of a great ambition to do anything else particularly.'

Similarly, Graham's subsequent career as a writer was predicated on his relationships with writing partners. Cleese was the first to commandeer him, but later working relationships with Barry Cryer and Bernard McKenna were also based on Graham's dependency on having somebody else in the room to bounce his ideas off.

John Cleese recalls writing with Graham during this period. 'First of all he was always a little bit in a world of his own, and secondly he was lazy. His main way of earning money was to go from one writing group to another to another. So he'd leave me and go to work in a group with Barry Cryer and then go and work with someone else. Thus, without making a major contribution in any group, he would be getting one third or one half of the fees for three different shows.'

McKenna recalls though, 'I think it's an important point to say the least work can be balanced by the best lines.' Cleese concurs, 'He was worth it for two reasons. He was the greatest sounding board that I've ever had. He was extraordinary in the sense that if Graham thought something was funny, then it almost certainly was funny, and you cannot believe how invaluable that is, and I think that's why we tended to write in pairs, because I think it would have been too scary writing on our own to know whether we were doing something funny or not. Whereas I discovered that if Chapman thought something was funny, it almost always was. I knew it from very early on.

And at the beginning, while he was still more in the swing of being at Cambridge and training as a doctor, he was more focused than he was later on and made a bigger contribution.'

Although Graham later told his partner, David Sherlock, that his first homosexual experiences pre-dated their time in Ibiza years later, in his own book *A Liar's Autobiography* he recalls his nascent feelings for a local New Zealander he called Mike Cormack. As he said himself, ' "What a bloody fucking waste of time," I thought three years later when I was hugging David in a tent feeling more liberated and happy than ever before in my life. I realised then that I didn't have to have women all the time, and that guilt is the weapon used by a muddled society to stop people having a good time.'

Though for all the wonder of hindsight, Graham still felt obliged to at least attempt to indulge his heterosexual feelings when the lengthy flight home from New Zealand allowed the troupe to stop off in Hong Kong, where Chapman, Cleese and Brooke-Taylor decided to take some time to visit the family of their old friend Benny Chi Ping Lee.

While they were met with perfect hospitality by the family, Chapman and Brooke-Taylor – on their last day in town – decided to explore some of the country's more personal environs. They went to a massage parlour, surely an untold delight for two boys from Cambridge University in the mid-1960s. According to Graham's record of their visit, they both politely declined to be 'assisted' in the shower and both deeply regretted it afterwards, Graham blaming it on his accursed Englishness, something he embraced fully but never seemed to be comfortable in accepting. 'We had to rush back to meet Mrs Lee, but quite frankly I could have fucked a letterbox,' he later wrote. 'As opposed to fiction, I wanked three times within an hour of the plane leaving Hong Kong.'

With only a brief sojourn back in England, during which Graham arranged to extend his sabbatical from the medical profession, the "*Cambridge Circus*" troupe were on yet another long-haul flight, this time to New York. If New Zealand had been something of a culture shock for this group, then the notion of opening a show on Broadway itself, while being fêted in New York, was an alien way of life. Most of the group seemed to take it in their stride, admitting to a certain degree of shock as to where their larking around at university had taken them.

The show opened on Broadway at the Plymouth Theatre on 6 October 1964. 'That was rather bizarre,' recalls Barclay. 'I remember just standing outside the theatre staring up at the marquee saying "*Cambridge Circus*" and trying to pinch myself and trying to imagine that it was real. It was very strange and very, very frightening because we opened cold; we didn't tour anywhere. I went a little ahead and then the others came on, and I think the whole thing was on within a week of our arrival or something bizarre. We did some run-throughs of the material for the backers, who were sitting in a darkened auditorium, and we did the whole show, which by then was pretty good; it was in very good shape. We were very proud of the show and we knew it worked, and I went down into the auditorium to see the backers, and I said, "Well, that's our little show," and they said, "Yes, well, do you have a different opener? We don't like that opener."

'"Um, no, and what else?"

'"Well, the first half, that's no good at all, and the number that opens the second half, no, I'm afraid not."

'That was our Oscar Wilde parody, which was supposed to be really terrific, and they said, "That won't mean anything here," and they just went through and they took out half the show, so we had panic sessions in a hotel in the middle of the night saying, "What do we do? Do we just go home or do we try?" and so we racked our brains and all sorts of odd things came in, and I think it was probably at that stage that Graham started to do Tony Hendra's old Mark Antony piece: "Friends, Romans, countrymen," where he was carrying the body of Julius Caesar which got too heavy for him. We were pinching material from everywhere because we were desperate: we were opening in two or three days on Broadway and the backers had ruled out half the show.'

Despite such last-minute anxiety – an Eric Idle-penned Beatles parody (early shades of The Rutles) was also included, with Graham and Co. rushing out to buy Beatles wigs on Broadway – the show opened and was generally received quite well.

Time magazine said of the show, 'It thinks small and carries a big slapstick . . . ' citing Idle's Beatles pastiche, 'I Wanna Hold Your Handel', as a highlight; *Journal America* described it as 'another intimate British revue with a cast of kids (six boys, one girl) and a stealthy approach to humour which I found magnificent', while industry bible *Daily Variety* gushed, 'Probably not in a generation has a Broadway audience laughed as hard as at *Cambridge Circus*, tonight's opening at Plymouth Theatre . . . the normally self-contained first-nighters were helpless with mirth . . . '

All in all not too shabby as notices go. But there was one holdout – the all-powerful *New York Times*. When its review proved to be tepid, the show's backers seemed to lose faith in their product, despite the other glowing notices, causing a degree of concern and depression among its eager young cast.

'We opened and got very, very good notices from a fellow on the *Post*,' recalls co-star Cleese. 'We played for three weeks, and we couldn't understand why they didn't publicise it.'

After those three weeks the show closed, with several members of the cast making noises that they felt the whole thing had been staged as a tax write-off for the US producers, although the *Variety* review of 15 October seems to suggest a more practical reasoning behind its initial failure (*New York Times* review aside): 'The import arrived on Broadway without advance build-up, despite a run in London and was presumably aimed largely for the concert-type tour of short stands Sol Hurok frequently sponsors. With the favourable New York reviews as promotional ammunition, such a tour should do well. The show has the markings of a sleeper hit on the basis of the hilarious reaction of the first-night audience. The absence of preliminary ballyhoo and the lack of advance sales impose a severe handicap on a potential Broadway run, however, particularly since the public appetite for British productions is apparently dwindling.'

The show closed on 24 October, a Saturday night. As the cast sat licking their wounds, they were only half consoled by an article that appeared in an early edition of Sunday's *New York Herald Tribune* singing their praises. Barclay later said that the reaction from all was not a casual one: 'We were very soppy that night.'

Nonetheless this early relative failure was to turn into something of a success. The troupe were invited to transfer the show to the smaller, but altogether hipper, locale of the Square East Café Theatre in Greenwich Village, where it ran for more than three months. (Among those who saw it there was Terry

Gilliam, then the assistant editor of national humour magazine *Help!*, who co-opted Cleese to do some work for his magazine – a chance meeting, the impact of which would be felt just a few short years later.)

'I loved it there,' Cleese says, 'because it's rather lazy really. There were only about two hundred people in the audience. It was a nice room and you didn't have to knock yourself out getting your voice to the back of these big theatres, you could play at a much more naturalistic level, which suited me better. I was happier. And we did it there for some months, and then we put together a second revue, and it was during the time that we were doing the second revue that one or two people left. Graham left because he felt he should get on with his medicine.'

Before he left, Graham had taken some time to do some American publicity for the show, as Barclay fondly recalls, 'I remember Graham having to give an answer to a newspaper journalist on "What's the difference between American and British humour?" And Graham said, "They're spelt differently," which was a very good reply.'

When the show's run came to an end, Cleese opted to stay in the States, landing himself both a role in the Tommy Steele Broadway smash *Half a Sixpence* and a stint as a journalist for *Newsweek* magazine. His erstwhile partner returned to London, once again resuming his career in medicine.

Humphrey Barclay also headed home. 'I stayed with the show until Christmas. I enjoyed it much less when it was playing in Square East in the cabaret place, because there wasn't much for a director to do, and then I returned because my job at the BBC had been kept open if I returned by the end of the year. So I left them to it and came back to England and started to try to reconstitute a radio revue show.'

This involved bringing his contemporaries – slowly making

their way back from the States – back to BBC radio for what turned out to be a long-running show *I'm Sorry I'll Read That Again*, with the majority of his *Cambridge Circus* cast still in tow. Cleese was absent for the first series, due to his remaining in America, and as a result Chapman was not part of the show, replaced once again by former Footlight Graeme Garden, who like Chapman was also concurrently embroiled in medical studies.

Chapman's sexuality was something that those around him never questioned at this time. His public image was that of a tall, athletic type, a rugby player for the hospital, fond of a pint and a drag on his pipe. Socially he dated numerous women from the hospital, eventually developing what appeared to be quite a serious relationship with Lesley Davies-Dawson, who would go on to become the first female dean of Bart's. If there were any sexual indiscretions or experimentations – and Graham was to indicate to his later partner David Sherlock that there were – they were handled carefully and kept hidden away.

His friend and colleague Alan Bailey later came to understand Graham's approach to his sexual life during these years. 'Deep down I think Graham probably had a mind which said, "I'm going in this direction," every now and then. He had some heterosexual relationships at Bart's which didn't work out in the end, so I can imagine Graham being analytical and saying, "Well, this isn't very good, let me do something else," and finding out that homosexuality was different.

'I only knew Graham was involved with a couple of women. He might drunkenly have fondled a few people and woken up the next morning and wondered what the hell he'd done, but I doubt there was anything more than a bit of late-night drunkenness.'

In 1976 Graham candidly told American broadcaster and friend Ken Levy of some of the experiences of his heterosexual lifestyle at this time. 'I had a girlfriend at the hospital at this same time. She'd been treated rather badly to the extent of him putting her head through the railings, and he just got violent, which wasn't too nice, and then this unfortunate girl got me, and then I decided to tell her after about a year that I thought I was probably gay, and she's had a very bad time out of me. A very bad time out of everybody, actually.'

For a man making his way in the medical field in the mid-1960s, any hint of homosexuality could easily mean the end of his career. 'When I met Graham he had the greatest cover story going,' recounts Cleese. 'What I mean is, the cover story is the way he behaved. He was a medical student who wore rather hairy tweed jackets and woolly ties and smoked a pipe and wore big brogue shoes and who played rugby and drank a lot of beer and went mountaineering. He was as un-camp as you can possibly get. And I knew that he was not exactly extrovert in female company because he once asked [*Cambridge Circus* co-star] Jo Kendall to a ball and he'd done so the previous year, and Jo told me she'd said to him, "Shall I bring a book this time?" In other words Graham tended to sit back and suck his pipe and not say much, even in male company, and I think he was even more like that in female company.'

Chapter Four

While Graham was continuing his studies, his writing partner, Cleese, was traversing America, eventually ending up in a touring company performing a show based on material from Peter Cook's London satirical nightclub, The Establishment. It was at this point that Cleese received two offers of work back in England. The first was an invitation to rejoin many of his *Cambridge Circus* colleagues in the second radio series of *I'm Sorry I'll Read That Again*. The second, more significant, offer was to become one of David Frost's repertory company of performers (alongside Ronnie Barker and Ronnie Corbett) in a new television show he was making for the BBC. It was titled *The Frost Report* and drew on a huge range of comedy writers, many of whom had passed through the Cambridge–Oxford milieu. The team comprised, among others, Dennis Norden and Frank Muir, Barry Took and Marty Feldman, Anthony Jay, Keith Waterhouse, Michael Palin and Terry Jones, Eric Idle, Barry Cryer, David Nobbs, Peter Tinniswood and more. As a performer on the show Cleese suddenly found his profile considerably raised; but as a writer he once again found himself in need of a sounding board. Had Cleese not recruited Chapman to be his writing partner on *The Frost Report* there's a possibility that Graham would have indeed stuck with his original plan and stayed in medicine. But once again fate intervened and Chapman fell in step, partly putting his medical life on hold, as he joined what was at that point the most prestigious comedy-writing team ever assembled for a British TV show.

Chapman's presence on the show was minimal – ('I was at Cambridge with John Cleese, and Eric Idle was there, and Michael Palin and Terry Jones were at Oxford, and we met up really quite by accident because we were all writing for the awful David Frost,' Chapman later recalled) – he was, after all, in his last eighteen months at medical school and needed to find some time to take his training seriously. But, then again, demands on his time for Frost were not overwhelming. Writers would attend one major meeting per week during which ideas were pitched for that week's topic (each weekly show was themed around one central idea, such as 'Authority', 'Class' and so forth). Then the rest of the week would be spent away from the studio writing their material, which would eventually be pared down by Frost, Anthony Jay, head writer Marty Feldman and others. (Eric Idle once joked that the BBC would send a taxi to pick up his writing, but he had to make his own way to the network via the London Underground.) Although there was no guarantee that your material would be used in any given week, Chapman's partnership with Cleese – one of the key performers on the show – ensured that more often than not their sketches would get on and Graham, as a writer, would get paid. In addition Graham was providing a certain amount of material – again via Cleese, although Graham never seemed to resent this – for the radio show *I'm Sorry I'll Read That Again*. Cleese was also writing a fair amount of material on his own, and on occasion in tandem with Bill Oddie. But Graham was so supportive of the radio show that he would regularly drag along a bunch of medical friends for its weekly recording at the Playhouse Theatre in London.

'Graham would take a party of us along,' regular, Alan Bailey, recalls. 'He always had half a dozen tickets, and we'd sit in the front row and laugh a lot. And Graham appeared in it once or twice when somebody was ill. The others were post-university, but Graham was still a student in those days, and we used to talk about what we were all going to do, who we were going to marry and all those sorts of things, and those were very good evenings. Cleese was awfully bad about coming into the pub afterwards and having a drink, and we'd say, "Come on, John! You've got to have a drink," and he'd drink something, maybe a little half of beer, and Tim was quite bad about having a drink. Then Graham and I would go back to Bart's. But it was Sunday night: we used to have a little rule not to keep the bar open too late Sunday so we started Monday fairly fresh in the morning.'

By now, however, Graham had already toured two other continents, appeared on both television and radio and was currently ensconced at the BBC. His medical studies – while still prevalent – were taking a backseat more and more. *The Frost Report* was proving to be a huge success and ran for two seasons on the BBC. More than anything else it allowed David Frost to fully establish his empire in television. Each of his lead performers would be given series of their own, all of which were produced and marshalled by Frost's Paradine Productions. He was also expanding into movies and passed that particular baton to the partnership of Chapman and Cleese. The first attempt at a screenplay was titled *Rentasleuth* – at various points it had Ealing veteran Charles Crichton (later the co-director, with Cleese, of *A Fish Called Wanda*) attached as director. The project was quickly shelved and emerged six years later in 1972 as the lamentable *Rentadick*, a movie that both Chapman and Cleese attempted to have their names removed from, replacing their own monikers with pseudonyms – 'additional material by Jim Viles and Kurt Loggerhead'. Not deterred, however – and funded once again by Frost – they began writing a vehicle for Peter Cook, Frost's old Cambridge contemporary, who, despite great success on television with Dudley Moore in the series *Not Only . . . But Also*, had largely failed to reach the heights that his Footlights compatriots had predicted for him.

The result of this Frost-inspired screenwriting notion was *The Rise and Rise of Michael Rimmer*, a satirical tale of an efficiency expert overloaded with power, on his way to becoming Britain's prime minister. 'When we started on *Rimmer*, we sat down with the director, Kevin Billington, and after the first session, when we walked into a restaurant in Hampstead, I remember Kevin saying to me, "Is Graham usually this quiet?" And it hadn't even struck me that he'd been particularly quiet. In other words his contributions were very sparse, but what he was so good at was throwing in a completely new angle, and my weakness is that I get so interested in the logic that I can disappear into a logical vortex trying to get everything to fit in a mathematical way, and Graham was great at suddenly taking the sketch off in an unexpected direction, which would give it great new energy.'

Although Graham was close to completing his medical training, when the idea of decamping to Ibiza for three months of writing in the sun was suggested, it was just too much of an opportunity to pass up. Even if, as Cleese recalls, the workload remained unequal: 'I would sit inside in the shade at a table writing, and Graham would be on the balcony sunning himself. We would talk through the door.'

This idyll, however, was briefly spoilt for Cleese because of that year's World Cup. 'We went off in '66 to Ibiza because Frost had given us some huge sum of money, like £500, to go and write and write and write. And I came back for two weeks in the middle of that period to watch the World Cup and, having seen our performance against Uruguay, I gave my Cup final ticket away, can you believe? to Bill Oddie, because I knew we'd never get past the semi-finals. [England played – and beat – Germany in the final, for anyone who doesn't remember.] I came back to Ibiza and watched the final in a café in Ibiza surrounded by Germans.'

When not watching the football, Chapman and Cleese rented a villa; at various points over the summer they would be joined by Marty Feldman and his wife, Loretta, Tim Brooke-Taylor and Frost himself, who made one appearance to see how the work was going. The reality was it wasn't going too well, with all concerned treating the event as something of an extended holiday; Cleese even taking the time to finally learn how to ride a bicycle. When Frost joined them briefly later in the summer, they had only around ten completed pages to show him; nonetheless he seemed pleased with the progress. Buoyed by this endorsement, Chapman, Cleese and their various guests retired to the beach again shortly after Frost's departure.

Graham meanwhile was enjoying the island lifestyle. Ibiza at the time was a very liberal, relaxed place. Artists of various natures were attracted there by the freedom and spirit of the place. It was an opportunity for exploration, and Graham felt free to explore. It was during this time that he met the man who would become his first serious male lover and his long-time companion, David Sherlock, who was returning to the island, having spent a large part of the previous summer there. Appropriately enough they met on the evening of Bastille Day.

'I was in Ibiza to meet somebody else,' Sherlock recalls. 'It didn't work out, as holiday romances from the year before often don't. I was determined to go back to Ibiza anyway, as it was an extremely beautiful and quiet place to be, except that the cheapest and easiest place to stay was San Antonio, which was the least quiet part of the island. It was the only place I'd ever been where people didn't seem to bother as to whether you were gay or not.

'Ibiza has always been a home for alternatives and left-wing agitators or whatever. For hundreds of years people have always fled to those areas to be themselves. It had had a very chequered and coloured history and of course in the thirties the Nazis made it their holiday home for many years, so there's the German connection with Ibiza too. By the sixties they were still opening houses which had been sealed for thirty years and had belonged to quite important people who had since been seen off after the Nuremberg Trials. So it had a very different atmosphere, but it was definitely becoming a big tourist attraction by then.'

One evening, slightly the worse for drink, Sherlock was approached by Chapman. 'I had noticed Graham in the street: he was fairly striking. The evening I met Graham I'd actually had dinner with a couple of guys who I'd met on the beach, and they turned out to be hardened Mediterranean travellers, and they were a couple of gays. One of them was a designer for the BBC. By the end of the meal I had got through at least a jug of sangria myself, these two were going back home and so I was making my way back to the campsite which had a little bridge over to it. I stopped and there were loads of people, it being the fourteenth of July, Bastille Day. There were lots of French people staying at the campsite and they were streaming out to San Antonio to go partying. As these people were making their way out of the campsite, being slightly tanked up, I looked them up and down and said goodnight in whatever language I thought might be theirs. Suddenly behind me I could hear this very English voice saying, "Good evening," which turned out to be Graham, and I said, "Good evening," and I thought, "This is extraordinary," in that I wasn't unaware of the fact that this could be a pick-up. At the same time here was a man who always looked so straight, with a sort of gravitas that you do not expect from your average pooftah, in those days anyway. That of course is what I always found attractive about him: he behaved just like any ordinary straight man. He had his pipe and he said, "Do you want to go and have a drink at the bar?" So, on top of a jug of sangria, we suddenly found ourselves at the bar surrounded by lots of French people who were jumping in the pool dressed in banana leaves they'd managed to make into fancy dress for their fabulous Bastille Day celebrations. I've always joked that the fact Graham and I got together on a day like the anniversary of the fall of the Bastille has a certain ring to it. So we had several drinks at the bar and that was when I found out that he was a writer, that he was living hardly a block away, as the crow flies across the field. Then Graham casually said, "Are you camping here? Can I come and see your tent?" So I said, "Yeah, all right." And then we were into a clinch, and I thought, "Oh, that is what he's up to." At that point I really didn't know, because his manner was just so correct and so straight, and then he decided he would like to spend the night. Of course that night, as it went on, it was virtually impossible to sleep until about four in the morning, being a tiny tent which was really meant for one. Graham's feet stuck out of the end. It was such a tiny area, you couldn't for the life of you get up to very much at all, other than hold your partner. The French were falling across the tent, tripping on every guy-rope, and it was all "Oh, merde!" and suddenly we would find that we were being crushed by falling French people. Which really was the *pièce de resistance*.

'My favourite moment was in the morning, very early –

Graham had to creep back home, and nobody was stirring in the campsite, but the campsite's large Alsatian guard dog sniffed Graham, realised he was not a member of the campsite and he was chased down the road with this dog snapping at his heels! So it was quite a meeting really.'

Graham's family and close friends at this point had no inkling of his sexual preferences, although during these early days with Sherlock, Graham confessed that this was not his first homosexual experience.

'He knew exactly that something was up with his emotional life,' confirms Sherlock. 'After all, he was damn near engaged to be married at this point to the lovely Lesley Davies-Dawson.'

Graham's brother, John, was unaware of any earlier examples of Graham's homosexuality and believes the relationship with Davies-Dawson was as serious as Graham could ever be with a woman. 'I'm not sure Graham was aware of his sexuality until he went off to Ibiza. Then when he met up with David, the relationship started and that was when Graham realised or became homosexual. Prior to that there had certainly been quite a lot of heterosexual relationships.'

Sister-in-law Pam Chapman elaborates, 'While he was at Bart's, at that year's May Ball, he actually asked Lesley to marry him, and she turned him down because she knew that things weren't quite right.'

As he later became more open about his homosexuality, in interview Graham often referred to Ibiza as the turning point. 'I was quite straight until I was twenty-four. I had my fair share of girls. I still do. It wasn't something that happened quickly. Then I was writing a film in Ibiza . . . Life seemed great and far from the conventions of English life. I suddenly felt free to take the sexual decision, to give it a whirl. And I did. I was greatly relieved. I enjoyed the experience very much indeed. I felt fulfilled. It was definitely an important moment in my life. I felt better for having admitted to myself what I already knew.

'I have known so-called "normality" as a student,' he would elaborate. 'I went around with a few girls and enjoyed it very much. But there came a point when I realised it was a real chore to sleep with them. I had to acclimatise myself to being gay because of my background. Melton Mowbray, grammar school, then Cambridge. I didn't realise what was going on at Cambridge at the time. There's a gay bar in every town in the country and a gay club in most. I had a lot of mind-blowing to do before I could be open about it – but I knew that I would really prefer to live with a man for the rest of my life. Subconsciously I probably always knew that, but there are tremendous pressures from society to settle down, marry and produce children. I nearly married once – in my last year of college – but fortunately I didn't. It would have been disastrous.'

The rest of Graham's time in Ibiza was divided between writing with Cleese, socialising with whoever happened to drop by from London and secret assignations with David Sherlock. Cleese and the other guests were unaware of David's existence during this time, and this was a situation that Graham wanted to maintain upon his return to London. Sherlock soon joined him, as he was starting at drama school in London that autumn. Chapman had already determined to keep the relationship going and maintain its clandestine nature.

'It was the autumn of '66 when I came to London as a student,' Sherlock recalls, 'having left Graham on the station at Euston, gone home to Cheshire for about six weeks only and then come straight down to London and started my course at the Central School of Speech and Drama in Swiss Cottage. We were both in the same boat to an extent. The Central School at that time was terrified of overloading their school with gays, so they were extremely anti-gay, which was very funny considering there were an awful lot of unmarried ladies who seemed to be shacking up together. But about eighteen months before, the story goes, some of the students had been openly having affairs with some members of staff and this caused a huge ruction in the school. So there was a certain amount of paranoia at my college, to say the least. I was living in South-East London, in a Methodist hostel almost directly opposite where the Kray brothers were removing toes and fingers from people, and I was an extremely nervous country lad who was not used to this sort of thing.'

Still pursuing his medical career, although increasingly distracted by his work as a writer, Graham knew the importance of keeping his homosexuality hidden from his peers. 'Me being hidden away for a year was essential from Graham's point of view, because Graham had not yet made a decision as to whether he was going to be a writer or not. And it was still the case in medicine that if you are not married, it takes you twice as long to get anywhere.'

'Doctors have a special horror,' Graham would explain, 'or rather they're the object of special horror if they're homosexual. Why this should be, I can't say – no one gets uptight about the possibility of straight doctors feeling up little girls.'

On his return to London Graham found his career in comedy was beginning to eclipse that of his being a practising doctor. This was in part brought on by a demand from the Inland Revenue for back-tax earned on his writing, something that Graham was unable to pay unless he kept writing.

Away from the shadow of Cleese he took on extra work writing for Roy Hudd's radio show, *The News Huddlines*, which for the first time proved to Graham that he could write on his own when required.

While Graham often worked in tandem with another writer, David Sherlock remembers that he was still eager to remain independent. 'There was still this old belief that a battered typewriter, a bottle of Scotch and packet of Gitanes beside him is what makes you be a good writer. That was certainly the case. A lot of those writers always said that their agents really didn't find them work. One often thinks that that's an agent's job, but this particular crowd always seemed to get their own work somehow or other by being in the right place at the right time. There was an awful lot of time when Graham was working on his own, particularly in the early days when he was working for Roy Hudd and the BBC asked him to write the links for Petula Clark and whatever. Some of those jobs, I think, came from hanging round the BBC bar.'

This new-found independence, however, did not keep him away from Cleese, courtesy of *The Frost Report* and their on-going film projects, and now Frost was opting to spin off his three key co-performers (Barker, Cleese and Corbett) in shows of their own. Significantly Graham joined the cast of what Frost had conceived as Cleese's spin-off project *At Last The 1948 Show*.

On his brief trip to Ibiza, Frost had mooted the idea of a show to highlight the undoubted talents of Cleese and Tim Brooke-Taylor; Cleese was quick to add Graham as a performer. This was undoubtedly a huge leap forward for Graham, who was previously seen as Cleese's attached writer but in terms of British TV or radio had no strong form of his own at this time. Yet both Cleese and Brooke-Taylor knew of Graham's abilities from their work together on stage and were eager to make use of them on what they both rightly saw as their break-out showcase. In addition both of them opted for Frost's head writer, Marty

Feldman, to join them. Having enjoyed a varied career in radio – penning such classics as *Educating Archie* and *Round the Horne* – Feldman was an accomplished writer and had some performing experience as part of a music-hall act. But his rather particular looks, finished off with his very noticeably protuberant eyes, had not made him a natural for television appearances. Certainly Frost thought so, but at the others' insistence, Feldman was cast as the fourth member of the team and a star was born. (Feldman went on to even greater success with his own show, *Marty*, which offered yet another opportunity for Chapman and Cleese to provide material as writers and later received international acclaim through his association with Mel Brooks in such movies as *Young Frankenstein* and *Silent Movie*.)

Although John and Graham still wrote together as a team, *At Last The 1948 Show* offered the opportunity to experiment with all of its principal cast – Brooke-Taylor and Feldman included – and for the four of them to write in various combinations. The scripts were generally assembled by the four together in what was inevitably a late-night session, with some of this material later going on to be recycled and reperformed, especially in live shows that involved the Pythons – for example *The 1948 Show* saw the television debut of Graham's wrestling himself sketch, as well as the debut of 'the Four Yorkshiremen', a much-beloved piece that would become a staple of later live shows.

Even though *At Last The 1948 Show* was Graham's first significant job as a performer, he was still reluctant to sever ties with Bart's and his background. 'Cleese has no perception of the fact that Graham, for many years, wanted to keep open the ability to return to medicine,' says Sherlock, 'and that meant keeping a damn good check on the people who still worked there and could give him a houseman's job, because he would only ever have started again as a houseman and gone back into having to work his way up, because of course he'd never done his houseman's training. He was constantly deeply unsure as to whether he would always be a writer, even though he'd made that decision. It wasn't clear cut at all.

'He did actually ask me what I thought he should do,' recalls Sherlock, 'and being the young drama student at the time, I said, "Heck, go for the big time!"'

Because of this concern, during the two-season run of the *1948 Show* Graham did come to complete his medical training, earning himself the right to call himself 'Doctor Graham Chapman' even if – strictly speaking – he wasn't qualified to practise.

'He was provisionally registered,' Alan Bailey explains. 'He passed all the exams, then you have to do a year under supervision, and he did two weeks in a locum, where the chap was away on holiday, and it was for the ENT [ear, nose and throat] consultant, and the ENT consultant was a really peculiar man. I know him quite well now, but Graham didn't like it at all. This was his first two weeks in real medicine, even though it was under supervision at Bart's. Graham was very funny because he did this two-week locum after he qualified, but he didn't like that two weeks; it was all a bit of a let-down. And then the world just took him over.

'But they'd just computerised the medical directory, and when you were provisionally registered – in other words you were allowed to practise only under supervision in a hospital before you were really qualified – you had an asterisk by your name, and for some reason the next year the directory came out, the asterisk had gone from against Graham's name, so he was therefore allowed to prescribe and all sorts of things as a result of the asterisk having gone from his name. And it was a technical fault: he never did that year, but for some reasons he was in the register as a fully registered doctor. You qualified, then you registered. He was fully registered by mistake, and he always used to laugh about that.'

'He was still very deeply emotionally attached to Bart's Hospital,' Sherlock concurs. 'He had his pals there, and he continued to return there on a regular basis, even when we were living together. He'd say, "Just got to drop in to the bar at the hospital," and in those days it was one of the few places where after banking hours, he could change a cheque, and he was often off to change cheques at Bart's Hospital and of course drop in to the student bar to join the lads. And he continued to edit some of the ward shows and all of that.'

Graham's fondness for cashing cheques late at night at Bart's became almost the stuff of legend among his closest friends and partner. Early on, during the *1948 Show*, it was in many ways his excuse to leave a writing session that had simply gone on too long for his liking. With the benefit of hindsight those who knew him well saw it as a three-tiered series of possibilities. First and foremost it was his opportunity to both get a drink – something that was becoming more and more of a concern for him as he enjoyed the good life that television offered him away from the relatively staid confines of life on the ward. Secondly some saw it – David Sherlock in particular – as a means of simply keeping his hand in with the Bart's crowd, and of his obvious reluctance to sever those ties, despite what should have been the reassurance of his new-found celebrity status. Thirdly many of the Pythons, and his other writing partners, later saw it as his means of going off to meet up with Sherlock, something that was hidden from all his contemporaries for over a year after Ibiza. (Of course, he may have just needed to cash a cheque.)

By now Graham had moved out of medical-school accommodation and was looking for a place to stay. Humphrey Barclay came to the rescue, offering him a room at his place on Prince of Wales Terrace in Kensington.

'There was nothing close between us in any way,' Barclay recollects. 'What happened was my father had rented a flat for my sister and me to have in Prince of Wales Terrace – this would have been 1967. We paid him £13 a week for the rent. Then she had gone off to get married, so I had a spare room and I needed people to help with the rent. So Graham moved in.'

Like all his contemporaries Graham kept Barclay in the dark vis-à-vis his relationship with David Sherlock. 'He knew David at that time but he never brought him to Kensington. Certainly they didn't sleep there or anything like that, as far as I understand.'

At Last The 1948 Show was a breath of fresh air for all those concerned. Freed from the formulaic resistrictions and intended topicality of Frost's shows, Cleese, Chapman and Co. could follow their own wildest fantasies, their own flights of comic fancy. They conceived of the show as a series of unrelated sketches linked by a dancing girl who generally gave the impression she might be in charge, if anyone that vacuous could ever be in charge. Cleese and Brooke-Taylor scoured London nightclubs to find just such a woman (Chapman was undoubtedly off cashing a cheque at Bart's at the time), while the others settled on/discovered the delightful Aimi Macdonald in the process.

Meanwhile, on the writing front, all four of the show's stars had decided that this was their first real opportunity to cut loose. Where previously Frost's producer, Jimmy Gilbert, had excised certain sketches on the grounds that they 'wouldn't play in Bradford', now Chapman, Cleese and Co. decided that Bradford be damned. The result was an instant success and British television's most surreal and ambitious comedy series to date, as close to a precursor of Python as there ever was.

More than anything it established all four performers – who, with the exception of Cleese, were best known as behind-the-scenes writers – as recognised televisual faces. Graham had finally made it in front of the camera as well as behind, and this presented him with a dilemma. Here he was, a man who was covertly conducting a serious homosexual relationship with a partner, who was now finding his name and face regularly adorning the pages of the *Radio Times* and the national press, at a time when homosexuality among consenting adults of twenty-one or over was only just beginning to be recognised as something other than a criminal act. His own sense of logic dictated that he now had to address this issue, and the fact that he did showed, more than anything else, that Graham had realised that his future lay in entertainment, more so than in medicine, something that he finally knew he didn't have to be dependent on. Having left his temporary lodging with Humphrey Barclay, Graham had taken the first step of moving David Sherlock into his new abode. His success on television had allowed him to afford an admittedly tiny, but decent flat on Gayton Crescent in Hampstead, which Graham rented from his old medical colleague Benny Chi Ping Lee.

Although they were still not that close, over the next year John Chapman and his wife, Pam, did start to sense a change in Graham's lifestyle. As John recalls, 'I saw him from time to time. He was now living in Hampstead. He'd got a flat, a small flat, and we used to go and visit him there. It was an occasional thing; we met up once a month or once every six weeks or something – that would be about it at that particular time. I was working. I was often on duty at weekends and living out in the suburbs, in Harrow. Graham would come out to us sometimes and have a meal when he'd got a bit of spare time to be able to do that. But I didn't see him frequently. We didn't become any closer at that time because our paths were diverging, and our spare time was taken up by things related to our careers. After the relationship was established, Graham would come on his own to visit, not with David, but then when we were going down to visit Graham, David would be there in the house. So it was something we became aware of before it was openly spoken of. It wasn't anything that was hidden but it wasn't flaunted, as it were. It was certainly initially hidden from my parents because I think my brother was worried about what my father might think about it. In fact I think my father realised that it was going on and he was worried what my mother might think about it when she learned about it.'

Living for a year with David Sherlock as his surreptitious lover had a profound impact on Graham. This together with the fact that, as well as writing for Roy Hudd, he was now in demand writing links for the likes of Petula Clark and Cilla Black for their prime-time TV variety series gave Graham a new-found level of confidence. Coupled with his success as a performer on *At Last The 1948 Show*, and the considerable rise in profile this gave him, Graham was riding the crest of a wave. He could have simply coasted; instead he chose what many could have seen as a drastic gesture. He was in love with David Sherlock, they shared a life together, and Graham clearly wanted others to be aware of that. Never one to do things by halves, Graham conceived of an elaborate party in which he unveiled David to the world. But, before such an event could take place, there were a handful of people he felt a responsibility to tell first. After all, he was always one for the grand gesture but rarely at the expense of other people's feelings. One of these was his writing partner, John Cleese.

'In my absence in Ibiza, when I went back for the World Cup game, Graham had met David and his life had changed, but he didn't tell us for a further twelve months.'

During that time Graham and David had led an active social life, just one that excluded his professional partners. 'We socialised together at the local pub in Hampstead – the William the Fourth, which was notorious as a gay pub,' David recalls. 'We would go out to eat in Chelsea, sometimes up to three times a week to the same place. Apart from that I was at the Central School in Swiss Cottage, so a lot of my friends either came out to eat in the evening or would be around. Graham would often write at home – and there would be many evenings when I'd be at home and he'd be off to Bart's and on the other evenings we'd go out together.'

Cleese recalls the moment Graham came clean to him on his twelve months of clandestine activity. 'I always remember going on summer holiday with my girlfriend, Pippa, and we came back and went to a party, and I think I went off to watch the football on television, and when I got back Pippa said to me, "Graham has been talking to me and he wants me to tell you that he has decided that he's gay and he has a boyfriend," and I remember saying to her, "What are you talking about? What is this about? Is this some joke? He's set you up!" And it took Pippa a very long time to convince me that she wasn't fooling. I remember that the same evening she said to me, "Graham wants you to tell Marty," so I rang Marty up, whom I hadn't seen for some time during the summer, and I said, "Marty, Graham's got a boyfriend," and he got quite ratty with me and he said, "What do you want? Why did you call me?" and I said, "No, look . . ." and this conversation went on just like the one I'd had with

Pippa two hours before. And then Graham had a sort of coming-out party when he was living at Gayton Crescent, and we met David.'

According to David Sherlock, it was Graham himself who broke the news to the Feldmans, again shortly before his announced party. 'He was so scared of telling anybody that it took an enormous amount of courage at the time, and he had no idea what the reaction was going to be, so he decided to tell the person he thought would be most relaxed about it and that was Marty Feldman's wife, Loretta, who howled with laughter and then said she would tell Marty. They were in bed at the time, and he apparently fell out of bed laughing so much, because both of them had a much broader view of the world and they had an extraordinary mix of friends. In fact I would say the Feldmans at that time almost ran a salon in that you could meet people from the jazz world, from light entertainment, all sorts. They were for me anyway, my role models in some way, because the people they knew and introduced us to were unlike any I'd met before, and I thought they were part of a much wider world than just light-entertainment BBC. So, that over, then Graham had his party where everyone was invited.'

Alan Bailey was another person that Graham informed early on, although their fondness for drink may well have precipitated that conversation. 'At that time we'd both got very pissed together, and I expect we drank about the same amount, and I think when the pressure came on Graham, he doubled and trebled his drinking. He'd got tremendous tolerance to it, and I stayed fairly regular.

'I was one of the first people at Bart's that he told about his homosexuality, in the back of a taxi. I lived in Highgate and he lived with Dave in Hampstead, and so we'd get a taxi together up to Highgate, and then I'd get out and walk down Highgate

West hill and he'd go on, and that night he said, "Look, I've got to tell you something which I've never told anybody before at Bart's, but I'm living with a boy and I'm gay." Although he wouldn't have used the word "gay"; I think it was "queer". This was two or three in the morning, and we were both absolutely rat-arsed, so I said, "Are you really, old man? I'd better come and see your boyfriend," and so I stayed in the taxi and went back to see Dave. That's when I first met him.

'Nineteen sixy-six, which was the year we qualified,' Bailey continues, 'that was just before homosexuality was legalised, and Bart's would have been horrified. Homosexuality was still thought of as a disease in America. They did nasty things to you if you were homosexual and they showed you pictures of men doing things, pornographic pictures of men, and gave you electric shocks and then showed you pictures of women fucking, and men and women fucking and gave you sweets, and it was that sort of treatment. And that's what Graham was really worried about, so we had to keep it deathly secret. Mind you, another friend of ours married a black girl. And we had to keep that away from his father and mother.'

Graham later discussed his own antipathy towards what he was increasingly seeing as the hypocrisy of the medical profession with American interviewer Ken Levy. 'Certainly I've got a great deal of anger about doctors because they pose. They pose to be something which they are not. They claim to have knowledge of ailments which they don't have. It's happened for years. It's just like witchcraft. If they pose successfully, you will get better because you're galled by it . . . it's a con business; they don't know how to make you better, no hope. There are certain illnesses . . . You can have a broken leg and hopefully you can do something about that. You can have syphilis and that can be cured, right, okay? But they don't know how, they don't know why. They're not really scientists. Science is an exact art, medicine isn't . . . there are two reasons. One is that I couldn't stand when I went into the final stages of the medical curriculum in England to do locums for other people and to go to other hospitals and act as a locum for another doctor, and the people that I met there were so bloody boring. They were either extremely interested in medicine and nothing else, or they were extremely interested in earning money and nothing else. Whereas they should be interested in people. I've met some good doctors; there are some good ones, but it's incredible the way that most people, I suppose, go into medicine because they think it's a way to help people, but you get disillusioned by that very quickly when you realise why everyone else had gone into medicine.

'It's largely, I suppose, that the general practitioner has replaced in the minds of the public the vicar of years ago. That they've given up religion so they think science has got an answer, which it often hasn't. It certainly has no moral answers, although I don't believe in morals at all, so that doesn't really matter, as far as I'm concerned. But another reason why I couldn't be a doctor as well, in that it was something that stopped me going ahead with medicine, was that I'm a homosexual largely, not totally – I'm heterosexual as well – but on balance I'm homosexual and I perhaps mistakenly thought, "Good heavens, I can't carry on like this because I might finish up molesting someone. I mustn't do that if I'm a doctor." So I just go around molesting people now, which is much nicer.

'I don't have to worry about getting struck off, right. You know, an amazing story in my own hospital. I don't think I should tell it . . . I've forgotten the name, but the Professor of Medicine was found washing this young boy's hair. Now that is not a thing that a professor of medicine should do – it's not part of his duties: you'd let a nurse do it – and the family complained, because the boy told, little rat, and it was all hushed up, fortunately, that was fine. But these things happen, they happen in everyday life.'

Graham's brother, John, was already aware of the developments in Graham's personal life, albeit in a fairly unspoken way. 'Obviously the propensity must have been there. What makes people homosexual? Is it an innate thing, or is it an acquired thing? I've no idea. I don't think anybody else knows why it occurs. I was first aware of it when they went off to Ibiza to do some writing. John was there, Marty Feldman was there. I was certainly aware of his heterosexual behaviour prior to that, but I've no idea how the changeover came, or when it came.'

'I always thought of him as very heterosexual,' adds Pam Chapman. 'He was an attractive chap and I'd flirt with him, my husband's brother, as one does. But you were never quite sure of him, never quite certain how he was going to react. There was a certain uneasiness there. He had lots of girlfriends, lots of them. Lesley Davies-Dawson had a chat with us and said he'd had almost every girl in Bart's at one time.'

'It may have been there for a long, long while without anybody being aware of it,' continues John on his brother's burgeoning sexuality. 'I don't think it was Cambridge. I perceived it as a change, and it was associated with going into the show-business world. It was much more acceptable in the show-business world than it would have been in medicine, for instance. I'm aware of quite a few people in medicine who have had long-lasting homosexual relationships, but I think at that particular time in the 1960s it was not something that was looked upon favourably. But one accepted his being something one couldn't influence in any way at all, and unless you wanted to alienate him, you accepted it really. I didn't understand it and

I may be fairly honest that I still don't understand it to this day as to how it comes about, but it is sufficiently obvious that it is so common that it's not something that one should be taking a particular exception to. The fact you don't understand it doesn't mean to say you can't accept it, but whether it's innate, whether it's hormonally determined, whether it's behaviour at any particular time of life . . . I suspect, like many other things, there's a multiplicity of factors involved and not a single one, and nature and nurture will probably both play their part in it. Opportunism also plays a part in it. Acceptability among the peer group is another factor which must play a very large part, and why it is so acceptable in what I call the show-business world and the artistic world – art, music, acting, literature generally. I'm thinking of the Noel Cowards and Somerset Maughams. I think it must have multiple causations and no single factor in anyone's life determines what happens.'

Despite his acceptance of his brother's nature, Chapman admits to finding himself disappointed in some ways. 'I suppose in a way one was, in that it was obvious that there was going to be no nephews and nieces from that direction at all for my family to establish relationships with. So, yes, there would be some element of disappointment about it. But not anything that one felt should lead to any alienation, as it were.'

Graham also took the time to discuss his sexuality with his father, although he was reluctant to speak to his mother on the subject. 'He told my father,' John Chapman explains, 'because he thought my father would be a little bit more understanding than my mother. Because my father had obviously been involved in prosecuting quite a lot of homosexuals during his police lifetime, it was difficult for him. My mother was always aware of it and unhappy with it and feeling "Where did I go wrong? It must be my fault somehow." And I'm not sure that she ever properly came to terms with it.'

'I think she blamed other people for leading Graham astray,' adds Pam Chapman. 'That was her interpretation.'

'I don't think she ever felt that she understood it,' continues Graham's elder brother. 'I don't ever think I ever understood it, but then I think it's very difficult for somebody who is entirely heterosexual to understand quite how it comes about really, to accept it.'

Yet it was acceptance that Graham wanted, and that more than anything fuelled his coming-out party, the notion that he wanted his secretive life to be secret no more from the people around him that he cared about the most.

Graham's coming-out party was certainly a major event for him and David. It was not only a declaration of love but of a life decision that had now firmly been made, rather than secretly prevaricated over. It was also something of a liberation for Graham. For years he had cultivated the image of the traditional Englishman, prone to the occasional moment of unexpected wild excess and hilarity; now the stereotypes were being left behind. Graham was presenting himself to those closest to him – both friends and colleagues – as a man you couldn't pre-judge. It was a moment first and foremost of self-liberation, and it occurred at a time when Graham obviously felt confident enough in himself not to worry too much if it left anyone else behind.

'Lots of people were deeply surprised,' says David Sherlock, 'and some people were even shocked. But it didn't last long, and when they realised that Graham wasn't going to change his lifestyle, I think they settled down. But I get the feeling that John Cleese was certainly more than a little shocked and surprised, and it took John a long time to get used to it.'

Cleese freely admits that it was something that on some level unexpectedly threw him. 'We were doing the *1948 Show* together, and Graham in the middle of a script meeting in the evening would suddenly look at his watch about a quarter past ten and say, "Oh, um, I'd better go up to Bart's and cash a cheque." We thought he'd got some girlfriend or something, it didn't bother us. And then, all of a sudden, it came out that he'd been with David for a year, and we all got to meet him.'

Cleese wasn't the only one shocked by Graham's revelation. His erstwhile girlfriend, Lesley Davies-Dawson, was also in attendance and didn't really know what she had let herself in for; a rare example of Graham not realising the potential cruelty of his own self-concerned actions, something he admitted seeing in hindsight. 'I threw a coming-out party and invited everyone. The big mistake was inviting my ex-girlfriend. She burst into tears. I felt I'd hurt her unnecessarily.

'None of the Python boys were hostile though. John Cleese had most difficultly accepting it because he knew me better than the rest and he didn't expect or suspect it. I mean, when you're a rugby-playing, pipe-smoking mountain climber, people tend not to think of you in that light.'

'Graham's girlfriend at the time was an extremely intelligent, beautiful woman,' recalls Sherlock, 'and Graham, like many of his contemporaries at that time, grew up in a pretty masculine environment. He didn't have a sister, and I think an awful lot of his generation were actually rather frightened of women; they weren't easy in their company. I think he loved being with his girlfriend when they were together, but he was always off doing other things. She certainly had a career in mind and had an extremely good one, but I think she was genuinely taken aback when Graham had his coming-out party in the summer of '67. He invited her along with some friends from Bart's, who were kind enough to take her home when she realised that she'd had enough . . . I think she would have liked to have been engaged. Graham told me that she had previously suffered in another relationship, and I think she was doubly hurt by two rejections, Graham's being the second, once he had discovered who he was and, from then on, what direction he was going in. I would like to think that he did not string her along, but the fact remains that she was at that party, and I don't think she was even aware that this was his coming-out party, and then she left.'

Fellow Frost writer Eric Idle was also made aware of Graham's change of lifestyle, although Graham chose to make him the butt of a joke, insisting that Eric never really understood what he meant in openly declaring his homosexuality. It was something that remained an issue between them for the rest of Graham's life, and something that, according to David Sherlock, both men later regretted. 'There is this silly story which Graham used to trot out that he had to explain to Eric Idle what it was all about, and I actually think that Graham regretted having made that comment because Eric can be quite sensitive, and in fact that became an issue in the weeks before Graham died. I think this was trotted out again in an interview or something, and Eric wrote a rather angry letter to Graham, and Graham asked me if he should reply to it, and I said, "No, I think you've got far too much on your mind at the moment." So it was left, and I think afterwards that it was something and nothing, it was really irrelevant, but it's one of those little things that niggles at people.'

Idle concurs that this joke of Graham's was something that in some ways haunted and annoyed him for years to come (although at the time of his complaint to Graham, he had no idea of the seriousness of his illness).

John Cleese, who at the time knew Graham better than most,

concurs with Idle's interpretation of Graham's feelings. 'What happened from that time on was that Graham started leading socially a rather different kind of life to the one he'd been leading before. And I don't think he was very happy with it for a long time. I saw a very funny play recently at the Donmar Warehouse in London, it's called *Take Me Out*. It's about baseball, and it's American, and there's a line in it that got a big laugh, about gays always feeling that there are two types of men in the world: the gays and the people who are still in denial. And that was Graham. Graham, at that point, decided that everyone was gay; it was just a question of the extent to which they were gay. Gay until proven innocent. And I don't think he was very comfortable about this, because I think he needed to see that everyone else was gay. He didn't want to be gay on his own, and what was complicated about Graham is he thought of himself, or his image of himself, as very virile, which ties in with the rugby and the mountaineering and all that sort of stuff. And what he couldn't stand was "camp gay", he hated the equating of gayness with being effeminate, and that made him very angry, and he didn't like gays who were effeminate. So I don't think he was ever very comfortable with it really, and that manifested itself as a slightly aggressive promotion of it. Not that he was particularly trying to persuade us, but his advocacy of it was rather aggressive and confrontational rather than being just "that's the way it is". And I have to say, he said I was very shocked, but I don't think he's right. I was surprised, because after years of hairy jackets and brogues and beer and pipes and football he had successfully hoodwinked me and himself, I'm sure, and I was astonished, as was Marty Feldman, because it was the last thing we expected from him. But once we knew it, it didn't bother us at all, and I think Graham thought it did.

'I think an awful lot of Graham's reactions to everything were projections of his own stuff. He thought Marty was very shocked. Now Marty was a lot more worldly than either Graham or me and had spent an awful lot of time in show business and a lot of time around gays. Marty was not bothered by gays, but Graham thought he was. So I think there was an enormous amount of projection going on at that time. I wasn't bothered by it at all once I'd got over the sheer surprise of it. I've never been very interested in people's private lives. I don't care what they do sexually or who they're with, and I always find it quite bizarre that people are so obsessively interested in it, in newspapers or on film sets everybody is watching to see if X is flirting with Y; I don't give a fuck. I think it's rather uninteresting unless you're involved.'

Fellow Frost writer Michael Palin was not close enough to Graham at the time to be invited to the party, but in mid-1970, when he and Graham were firmly working together as part of the Monty Python team, his diary recalls a further discussion about that eventful night. 'A lot of time spent with Graham Chapman, High Priest of Hedonism. Terry Gilliam recently gave what seemed a good clue to Graham's attitude. Terry suggested that Graham, having once made the big decision, it must have been greater than the decisions most people are called on to make, to profess himself a homosexual, [and] is no longer concerned with making important decisions, he is now concerned with his homosexual relationships and perpetuating an atmosphere of well-being which good food and drink bring and on which the relationships thrive. He doesn't want to think too much about himself now, above all he doesn't want to have to struggle. He seems to feel that having stated his position he deserves the good life.'

Despite the odd controversy it threw up, David Sherlock was still pleased finally to be acknowledged – and accepted – as part of Graham's world. 'Things settled down in one way, but also Graham suddenly had an entrée into a whole different society which I knew better than he did, although I was younger. He knew that he was gay but we had no role models in those days. In some ways the Feldmans and their friends became the sort of people one could talk to about anything, and I instantly felt very comfortable with them. So it was fun.'

Still, with Graham's public acknowledgement of a new life, it was time for a new home, and, in 1968, he and Sherlock moved into a much bigger place on Ornan Road, Belsize Park, just down the road from their previous Hampstead flat. They were to remain there for four years.

'Within a very short time though he'd made his mark in the *1948 Show*,' says Sherlock, 'he still thought of himself very much as a writer, but it seemed meteoric to me because within one year we'd moved from a tiny flat in Hampstead to a large mansion-block-type flat.'

Graham, however successful his writing career appeared to be, never felt financially secure, and soon his and David's new home was being shared by a lodger. 'Within a year we were sharing that flat with John Newton Clarke, the designer of the *1948 Show* and then *How to Irritate People*,' recalls Sherlock. 'He was extremely difficult to live with: he would sometimes use Dettol in face-washing water, and you'd end up with what Graham called a phenol rash. He was gay but he didn't know what to do about it. I think he thought that, because we had decided to live together at that point, we probably knew more about the subject and that he could live vicariously through us, and he was awfully nice when he was in a good mood, but when he was maudlin or drunk he was a pain in the arse to be around. Graham would say, "It's unkind to kick him out, he needs somewhere to live," and I said, "Yes, but he's putting such a strain on our relationship, I think it's time to move on." Eventually we had to do alterations to the flat including the room which he was using as his bedroom and study, just to move him on. We felt bad about it, but it had to be done.'

While Ibiza had proved to be a success in terms of his personal life, work-wise, it was less so. The film *The Rise and Rise of Michael Rimmer* was not filmed until 1969 and not released until 1970, at which point both Cook and director Billington shared co-authorship billing with Chapman and Cleese. (Cook having intentionally rewritten his role to parody producer David Frost, who soon caught on to what he was up to.)

Nonetheless back home Chapman's career in general was going from strength to strength. In addition to the ongoing success of *At Last The 1948 Show*, providing links to various variety shows and sketches for Frost, Graham was now working alongside Barry Cryer and Eric Idle on Ronnie Corbett's spin-off sitcom, *No, That's Me Over Here!*, further establishing himself as a writer – or certainly as a writing partner – away from Cleese.

In his private life Graham was revelling in his new lifestyle. While his workload was heavy, he and David were discovering the London gay scene, something that this pipe-chomping tweed-wearer had previously kept at a firm distance. This new approach to life, unfettered by the post-war trappings inbred into him by his upbringing, coupled with increased financial security and the heady mixture of a certain degree of fame, meant that Graham was experiencing life as never before.

'We used to go to a club called the Sombrero, which friends of ours told us about,' Sherlock says, 'and we decided we liked it so much that we became regulars. It had a very young clientele and an awful lot of kids who were students from the Philippines, and they were quite, quite fun, extremely camp and boisterous but great fun, and for Graham, it was the first time really he'd been aware that such places existed. That's not to say that he didn't know they existed, but he'd never been, so it was all new. I often think that Gray had such a serious upbringing that he made up for an awful lot of lost time.'

Despite his increasingly heavy workload – or possibly in spite of it – Graham was quietly becoming more and more dependent on alcohol. For the most part his habits were still, publicly at least, seen as those of the social drinker; a young man who could handle more than a few and then get up early the next day and carry on. His new-found status also gave him a sense of the aesthetic drunk, the image he cultivated of a man for whom a gin and tonic was as much an accessory as a necessity.

But it was clearly becoming more of a necessity. Cleese recalls writing with him at this time. While Graham was never the most forward of the two when they wrote together, preferring to quietly suck on his pipe before often throwing in the key element that elevated their work to new heights (a classic example shortly after this time being the Monty Python 'Pet Shop' sketch in which Graham's primary contribution was the phrase 'How about a parrot?'), Cleese remembers how the mornings were often a means of simply waiting for lunchtime, with Graham eager to head off to the local pub, often the Angel in Highgate, while Cleese preferred to stay behind and carry on the work. 'And often in the afternoon he wouldn't remember the work he'd done in the morning,' Cleese recalls.

'I think Cleese is definitely W. H. Gilbert, who was an absolute stickler for the words being said correctly,' offers Sherlock, casting Graham as Sullivan. 'Cleese is incredibly punctilious and drove Graham barmy by insisting for a day and a half that a comma or a word was in the wrong place, and if it was in the wrong place, he would work and worry and whittle away at the script until it was right. And Graham was a great believer in a broad sweep and then thinking about how it could be shaped. If Graham was with people he knew and with whom he could be relaxed, then he would drop his reserve, but if there was always a huge amount of reserve, then his shyness, rather like his father and rather like his brother, was manifested in very little wasted speech.

'He was conscientious and hardworking in his attitude, but the pub was also part of it,' Sherlock continues, 'and other co-writers were very happy to go to the pub at lunchtime and some crazy ideas came out of those lunchtimes, but of course when Graham was writing with Cleese he would occasionally join Graham at the pub, but I remember him very often saying, "No, I'll have some lunch here," or "I'll stay in, and you go to the pub, and we'll work when you get back." I do think that probably John remembers more of those times than the balancing thing of the fact that they actually got an awful lot of very good stuff done.'

'The going out of Bart's, out of the community that we had and going into television and going round the world and all of that business – that was part of the pressure,' says Alan Bailey, explaining Graham's initial predilection for drink. 'The other part was hoping he wouldn't be sacked from Bart's when they found out he was gay. From the time I knew him he was as heavy a drinker as I was, and I was one of the heaviest drinkers at Bart's. We used it as medical students because we had young healthy livers. Now I expect I'm dependent on it. I hardly ever not have a drink, and Graham got up to a few bottles a day. It's been said three and a half bottles of gin, but in fact he liked gin in the morning and whisky in the evening. And beer in the middle if he was feeling a bit dehydrated!

'I suppose a little bit of it was an issue for me. We used to discuss it together, how we were drinking too much and how much of it had got out of control. It was the change in Graham's life, the success. The success at writing mainly and then suddenly in the performing – I think a lot of that would have fuelled his alcoholic tendencies. He drank because he was really introverted but he had to be extroverted and he had to pretend to be that.'

The pressure of Graham's success was reflected in the amount of work to be done. In addition to writing the Ronnie Corbett sitcom alongside Barry Cryer and Eric Idle, he and Cleese were also corralled by nascent TV producer Humphrey Barclay into adapting Richard Gordon's popular series of 'Doctor' novels to the small screen. The books, following the often amorous adventures of a young intern and his friends, had already proved hugely successful as a series of films, which made a star out of Dirk Bogarde, beginning with 1954's *Doctor in the House*. Barclay wanted to adapt them to a weekly sitcom, and, with his medical background, Chapman seemed a perfect choice. He and Cleese wrote the pilot.

'Frank Muir asked me to join London Weekend, which was starting a licence,' Barclay recalls, 'and after some time there, when I worked with Michael and Terry and people like that, Frank came to me and said, "We're doing *Doctor in the House*, I think you should be in charge of it, and we've got this rather good script from John and Graham." So I did it and John and Graham were not available to write at that time any more than the first episode. I remember John coming to the recording of the first episode where we had a simply magnificent set in the studio, and he said to me afterwards, "If I'd have known London Weekend could do things in this style, maybe we'd have brought Python here," which wouldn't have been a good idea, because it needed to be at the BBC,'

With Cleese unavailable or unwilling, Chapman wrote the rest of this first series with Barry Cryer. Chapman shortly after appeared in the series' last big-screen outing, 1970's *Doctor in Trouble*, a sub-*Carry On* film if ever there was one – and if that's not an oxymoron.

In 1968 Chapman had co-written and appeared alongside Cleese and Brooke-Taylor in a one-off television special, *How to Irritate People*, produced, once again, by Frost's production company. This was largely conceived as one of Frost's many attempts to break into the American TV market. It's an interesting amalgam of theme-related sketches, many written by the team of Chapman/Cleese, but also marks their first real on-screen work with Michael Palin, brought in as a performer here, rather than as a writer.

'*How to Irritate People* was the show which John asked me to do with him in '68,' says Palin, 'and that was quite important because that was the first time I'd ever worked with John and Graham, as an actor, and that was very much like a mini-Python, except that I wasn't writing with Terry. I was an actor with their material, but we changed it a little bit in rehearsal and we'd really enjoyed doing that, even though the end result had not been very successful, largely due to problems with recording. But that was David Frost getting myself, John and Graham, Marty and Tim Brooke-Taylor and Connie [Booth] together in one go, so David had made moves to get a programme which involved certainly myself, John and Graham together.'

The proto-Python amalgam also contained the germ of a sketch that would become a classic Python moment. Originally suggested by Palin, a sketch involving distinctly unscrupulous used-car salesman (played also by Palin) bore more than a passing resemblance to the famed 'Parrot' sketch, before Graham had chimed in with the idea of a Norwegian Blue as opposed to a car.

'I'd married Connie [Booth] at the beginning of '68,' recalls Cleese, 'and we came back to England and arranged to do a special for the Frost organisation. And Graham and I wrote most of it, and Michael Palin was in it, and Connie was in it, and there's a sketch in it that was based on a man called Mr Gibbins, which is Helen [Palin's] unmarried name. And Mr Gibbins ran a garage somewhere in Michael's area, and Michael started to tell me about taking his car in to Mr Gibbins if there was something wrong with it, and he would ring Mr Gibbins and say, "I'm having trouble with the clutch," and Mr Gibbins would say, "Lovely car, lovely car." And Michael said, "Well, yes, Mr Gibbins, it is a lovely car, but I'm having trouble with the clutch." "Lovely car, lovely car, can't beat it." "No, but we're having trouble with it." "Well, look," he says, "if you ever have any trouble with it, bring it in." Michael would say, "Well, I am having trouble with it and I have brought it in," and he'd say, "Good, lovely car, lovely car, if you have trouble bring it in," and Michael would say, "No, no, no, the clutch is sticking," and he would say, "Sign of a quality car, if you had a sticky clutch first two thousand miles, it's the sign of good quality," and he was one of those people you could never get to take a complaint seriously. And Michael and I chatted about this, and I then went off and wrote a sketch with Graham about a man returning a second-hand car, and I know we had to find a car that was no longer being made, and I think the Frost organisation found a Jowett Javelin. When we started to write for Python eighteen months later, I don't know why we looked at the sketch again, but I remember saying, "This has got something funny in it," but Graham and I agreed the car was much too hackneyed. And within a moment we were in a pet shop and we said, "Which is funnier, could it be a dog or a parrot?" and we argued the toss, well, not argued, chewed that around a bit, and decided it was the parrot. But it definitely came from the sketch about the second-hand car.'

However, it would be a few months yet before Chapman, Cleese and the others had even conceived of a beast named Monty Python. In the meantime Chapman and Cleese had also been offered another stab at film-writing. Terry Southern's novel *The Magic Christian* was being developed as a project for Peter Sellers. The opportunity to put words in the mouth of one of their *Goon Show* idols was too good to pass up for Chapman and Cleese. (Even if the final result – released in 1970 – was something of a mismanaged disappointment, once again, proving to be another failed experiment in cinema, even though both writers landed small roles in the finished film.)

'*The Magic Christian* was a huge move into big movie-time for them,' says David Sherlock. 'It was the first time they met Ringo Starr, and Ringo was such a good comic actor, according to Graham particularly. There was one sequence that had the entire crew falling about to the point where they could hardly technically do the film. The rushes the next day were seen by Sellers, and he was so bothered by the fact that the scene was stolen from him at this point that he called the director and had the whole scene re-shot from a different angle so the camera was on him, so a wonderful piece of comedy was just ditched on the cutting-room floor. Graham played a tiny role in that, as Cleese did.'

Humphrey Barclay meanwhile had recently defected from BBC radio in favour of independent television, in particular the franchise Rediffusion. It was for them that he was charged with helping create and shepherd a TV comedy show, ostensibly designed for children, but, given the nature of the times, one that could certainly have the appeal to cross over. Given that the likes of Chapman, Cleese, Brooke-Taylor and Feldman were already firmly rooted in the David Frost Paradine camp, he turned to a handful of other Oxbridge graduates who had also served their time with Frost. Oxford men Michael Palin and Terry Jones had been making a name for themselves, firstly with the filmed segments on Frost and subsequently on such other programmes as *The Late Show* and *A Series of Birds*. Both were eager to perform as well as write, as was Cambridge graduate and Frost scribe Eric Idle; Idle had appeared in Jonathan Miller's televised adaptation of *Alice in Wonderland*, and he, Palin and Jones had all appeared together on top of a hearse in Ken Russell's TV film *Isadora*. Barclay decided they were a perfect match for his new children's show, and soon teamed them with actors David Jason and Denise Coffey. Knowing they were like-minded souls, Idle, Palin and Jones quickly insisted on taking over the writing – and thus essentially the artistic control of the show, turning *Do Not Adjust Your Set* into a series for children. With its anarchic humour, similar in tone to the *1948 Show*, it soon attracted a strong adult audience, including Chapman and Cleese. 'Graham and I used to watch *Do Not Adjust Your Set*. It was our treat on a Thursday afternoon. We would finish early and watch that because it was the funniest thing on television.'

Idle, who had worked with Graham as a writer on Ronnie Corbett's *No, That's Me Over Here!*, was a key player in the writing and performing of *Do Not Adjust Your Set*, and by its second series it also boasted the talent of wandering American illustrator Terry Gilliam, whose way on to British television was courtesy of John Cleese – when he arrived in London, dodging the Vietnam draft and escaping the carnage of the Watts Riots in

Graham as a baby in 1941, with his brother John, who was four years older than him.

DR JOHN CHAPMAN

A family beach holiday with parents Walter and Edith.

DR JOHN CHAPMAN

Walter's pipe-smoking habit was to become one of Graham's trademarks.

Graham, second right, got the acting bug early.

DR JOHN CHAPMAN

Athletics and rugby were Graham's (Back row, centre) favourite sports at school.

King Graham.

Graham at the christening of his
iece and goddaughter, Fiona.

DR JOHN CHAPMAN

Graham as brother John's best man at his wedding to Pamela.

Graham enjoys the fun of the Footlights.

Cambridge students hard at work: Graham is the human wheelbarro

Bill Oddie takes the mike, with Graham and John Cleese looking on during their 1964 *Cambridge Circus* tour to New Zealand. A quiet word from the Queen Mother helped persuade Graham to leave his studies to make the tri

HUMPHREY BARCLAY

Above Graham, Tim Brooke-Taylor and John Cleese in *I'm Sorry I'll Read That Again*, a cult radio sketch show that first aired in 1964. *Below* The cast of *At Last the 1948 Show*, Marty Feldman, Aimi Macdonald, Graham, Tim Brooke-Taylor and John Cleese, which ran for thirteen episodes in 1967.

JIM YOAKUM

MICHAEL PALIN

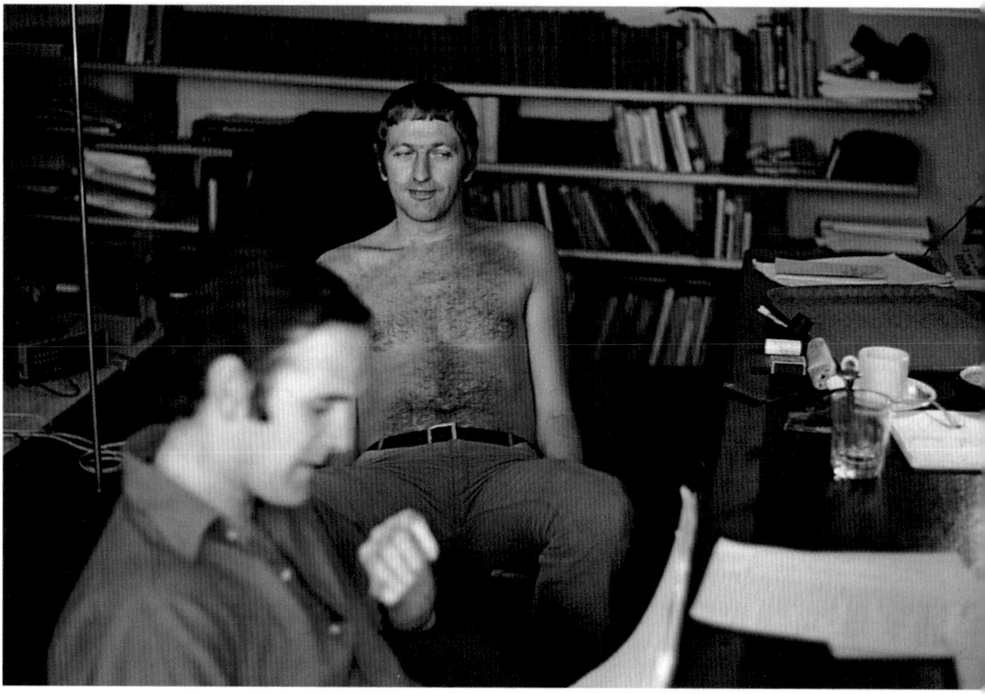

Graham and Cleese make their way through another Python writing session.

The Python team (l to r): Terry Jones, Graham, John Cleese, Eric Idle, Terry Gilliam and Michael Palin.

MICHAEL PALIN

PYTHON (MONTY) PICTURES

Graham had 'this wonderful saintly long-suffering look' as Arthur in *Monty Python and the Holy Grail.*

Resting on the hillside during the shooting of *Holy Grail*, Graham had considered staying sober while filming, but soon abandoned the idea. PYTHON (MONTY) PICTURES

The combination of Harry Nilsson, Graham and Ringo Starr worked together on a project called *Son of Dracula*.

The Python books were another lucrative spin-off. Here Graham and Jilly Cooper celebrate being Authors o the Year.

Los Angeles, he got in touch with Cleese and subsequently met Chapman and the others.

'I really don't remember the moment that Graham and I collided,' Gilliam semi-recalls. 'That was the great thing about Graham, there was a sort of fluidity: he just floated in, he floated out, so you could have met him anywhere, any time. Maybe I never met him! Maybe that's what happened. I never really felt I'd met Graham.'

However, Cleese did have the good sense to put Gilliam in touch with fellow cartoonist Humphrey Barclay, and soon the errant American was doing sketches on the TV show *We Have Ways of Making You Laugh*. This introduced him to Idle, a writer and performer on the show, and Barclay in turn suggested that Gilliam – who had recently tried his hand at some primitive animation – might have something unique to offer the *Do Not Adjust Your Set* team.

'I remember definitely saying to Graham Chapman, "These people are very funny, should we do something with them?" ' recalls Cleese. When he then received an offer to do a series for the BBC, from former Frost writer (by now BBC television's comedy guru) Barry Took, he remembered that conversation with Graham. All the elements were now in place for what was to very quickly become the most influential comedy series in British television history. It almost didn't happen though, because Cleese was still under contract to Frost.

'John Cleese was under contract to his company, and he [David Frost] said, "Oh, wouldn't it be nice if I fronted the show for you," ' Graham later recalled to Ken Levy, in the spring of 1976. 'The BBC wanted to do it with the five of us. And we said, "No, it wouldn't really work, David, thank you very much, we'd like to do our own thing," and so John had to go through a whole court case, practically being sued, but he won, and we went ahead with the programme. The ultimate thing was that we said, "All right, the four of us will do it without John, and John will act just as a writer, and you can't get him there because you've only got him contractually as a performer."

'What happened next was that David rang up Michael Palin and Terry Jones and said, "I hear you don't want to work for Paradine any more?" which is his enterprise, his company. Michael rang me, I was in a restaurant at the time, I went out to a phone box and rang up David and said, "It's quite right, none of us want to work for you any more, so go away," and he was saying, "I heard you don't want to work for Paradine any more, why's this?" So I was very vicious. It's strange though. I mean I quite like the guy. He's just mistaken, that's all.

'But I still go and chat to David occasionally and see him, but he can't understand. I went around about three months ago to see David, and he could spare a few moments. So I went in and waited for about five minutes and then said to the secretary, "Now look, is he coming out or not? Because if he's not, I'll piss off." She said, "He's in a meeting at the moment." I said, "I've heard that one before. Come on, get him down here now," and we had a chat and he couldn't understand that I just wanted to chat to him. He said, "Well, what did you want to talk about?" I said, "Nothing, just have a nice quiet chat, David," because actually I do like the man, but he just can't understand that he doesn't have to be running round earning money all the time. He's completely dim in that way. I hope this gets on to paper and people will read it and realise that, because Cleese has been trying to get through to him for years and can't, but then Cleese is fairly similar.

'I pissed out of his window the other week and didn't clean up the mess,' Chapman continued. 'You won't believe this, but an agent called Sonny Zahl, the agent for Ronnie Corbett – *was* the agent for Ronnie Corbett – was trying to clinch a deal with one of David's aides and actually jumped out of the window in front of him, and this is near Claridges, which is quite a famous place in London, leapt out of the window and fell to his death because, he said, "I couldn't stand it anymore." The police weren't entirely sure whether he'd been pushed or not, because he was quite a wide man and they're not quite sure how he could have got out of that window, but that's the very window that I pissed out of.'

Chapter Five

By the time Graham came to be one sixth of Monty Python's Flying Circus, his drinking had begun to escalate. His new-found freedom at having essentially walked away from medicine and into a new life as a relatively famous TV personality, a highly in-demand writer and an openly gay man, who for the most part had avoided any resentment to his sexual status, had led to a lifestyle of both experimentation and hedonism. David Sherlock was introducing him to a new life in London. As a young drama student, Sherlock was straddling two worlds: hanging out with a group of successfully established writer-performers within the industry and showing Graham the other side of London he had never experienced for himself – the bars and clubs that made up the gay scene of the day, still clandestine enough to be undercover, still on the brink of a far greater liberty. For Graham it was the voyage of discovery he felt he had been waiting for for most of his adult life. Despite their love and closeness, he and Sherlock were quick to establish their relationship as an open one, which afforded Graham the best of both worlds – someone he loved, and others he could simply indulge himself with.

A fair deal of this new-found bravado was fuelled in part by his escalating dependency on alcohol. 'I thought it was brave and perhaps at times foolhardy,' John Chapman says of his brother's increased openness. 'He was becoming quite aggressive about it on occasions in his conversation. But I thought also that part of this was the internal stresses that must have created the onset of his alcoholism, that he was using that to hide from the stresses of his aggressive support of homosexuality and the stress of performing also, because undoubtedly both of those things played some part in his resort to alcohol.'

Away from the nightlife, though not always away from the bottle, Graham found himself joining the Circus. The BBC had more or less given John Cleese a standing offer to do a series with them any time he wanted. Cleese at this time, however, was still very much a team player and enjoyed working in combination with others rather than as a solo performer or writer. He and Graham were now firmly established as a team, but Cleese's ever-present eagerness to move on had attracted him to Michael Palin. They knew each other first from Frost, then from working together as performers in *How to Irritate People*. Palin came with his own other half in the form of Terry Jones. Fresh off *Do Not Adjust Your Set*, they were keen to keep Eric Idle and Terry Gilliam in the mix. And so it was that when feelers were first sent out from the Cleese camp to the Palin camp, these were the camp mates who would eventually go for a curry.

Palin and Jones had recently written and starred in a historical pastiche show for ITV called *The Complete and Utter History of Britain*. The show had met with mixed notices and was not likely to be renewed for a second season. Cleese saw this as an opportune moment to make contact, phoning Palin in light of *Britain* and saying, 'You won't be doing any more of those, then,' and proposing a joint collaboration.

However, Cleese was unaware at the time that Palin, Jones and Idle were concurrently being pursued by Thames Television to make a series of their own. When that was delayed, it was Idle who suggested they should throw their lot in with Cleese and Chapman.

'They were kings of the castle – Cleese and Chapman, as writers,' Palin remembers, 'and we rather liked Graham as a performer, and John was just the best around really, so we were quite excited that John wanted to pitch in with all the rest of us in this kind of experimental form of show. That's what seemed interesting – that we managed to persuade John and Graham, who probably had many more offers, I should think, than we had, to do something that was quite off the wall.'

(Indeed Palin and Jones were very impressed with Graham as a performer and at around this same time had been penning a one-off Comedy Playhouse-style half-hour to star Graham as a small-time zoo keeper, desperately trying to stave off a big takeover – a notion that years later Cleese would use as inspiration for his film *Fierce Creatures*.)

That first curry took place at the Light of Kashmir restaurant in Fleet Road, London, in mid-1969, before adjourning to Cleese's flat in nearby Basil Street. Very quickly the team came together – although it was never really a team. Despite Cleese's desire to work away from Graham and try things with others, the group still split into its old lines – he would work almost exclusively with Chapman, while Jones and Palin remained a double, Idle was content to work on his own, and Gilliam, by nature of his work, had to work alone.

What did unite all six men, however, was a desire to break away from the constraints they had worked within before. All agreed that it was a perfect opportunity for them to try new things in terms of their material – bringing on board surreal flourishes and structural changes, such as the lack of dependency on the traditional punchline, something Graham later elaborated on in interview: 'Our biggest thing really was getting rid of the punchline. For years people had been doing a punchline, and we had to do it too as writers. The producer would look quite blank if there wasn't a punchline, because how can he end it if he can't cue the audience to applaud? You've got to have something there. Well, we don't worry about the audience particularly, let them get on with it.'

It was Gilliam's material that gave them the unifying factor that would define the show. This came via Terry Jones, who was very enamoured of a free-form animation Gilliam had done for *Do Not Adjust Your Set* titled 'Elephants'. His notion was to apply this free-flow of ideas to a whole half-hour show.

'Jonesey saw how animation could give the show something very special,' recollects Cleese, 'and I don't think Chapman and I were that interested in that. We liked the idea of it, but we were excited by just doing completely different types of sketches and not obeying the formats that everyone had developed and seemed to think were necessary.'

After only two meetings the group were so convinced by the direction they wanted to take – and their like-minded pursuit of it – that they found themselves in Barry Took's office at the BBC, pitching him an idea they could hardly put into words. As Cleese enthused about the material and Jones got overexcited about the conceptual aspects of this new show-to-be, Graham quietly sat by, fondling his pipe.

'It was felt that this was the sort of thing we should be doing,' Cleese says. 'We were never great theorisers. We discovered what we were going to do mainly by sitting down and seeing what came out on the sheets of paper at the end of the day, quite literally. And another stage was when we all got together in the same room and were faced not with just writing three minutes of funny material, but how we put the different three minutes of funny material together. That was exhilarating. We had an early script meeting at the BBC, we almost never met at the BBC, they gave us some little underground room, and I just remember coming out of it and thinking, "This was real fun." There was a tremendous liberation, this energising feeling when you break through stuff you felt constricted by, and you suddenly sense that you're opening this gate into the new field, suddenly seeing all the possibilities around.

'There was a real sense of discovery because let's say you want to be a painter; however the paints haven't arrived. There's not much you can do, then suddenly one day the paints turn up, and you start dabbing around, and you're excited by all the possibilities. And when we joined *The Frost Report*, it was very much we were the young ones, we didn't know anything, we had no track record, of course we should shut up and listen to the more experienced people, that was fine. You start doing it that way, then a bit of you says, "Oh, what a shame they wouldn't let me do this." And then next week, "What a shame they wouldn't let us do that," and then as you get more confident that maybe you could make something different work, then the frustration builds up in you. We'd been labouring under these restricted conditions for years, and we were liberated astonishingly quickly. We had a sense of liberation and realised that there was a better and more interesting way of doing it.'

Their enthusiasm for expanding the bounds of television comedy – even if they weren't always able to explain how – was rewarded by the BBC with a commission for a thirteen-show series. On that, for most, writing began in earnest. As soon as the group was formed, it split off into its component parts, except that Cleese went off to write alone initially, as Graham was already out of the door and on his way to a holiday in Ibiza with David, as Michael Palin's diary entry for the day – 23 May 1969 – recalls, 'Graham Chapman disappeared for a week in Ibiza, and the remainder of us began talking about the show. It was a very useful and inspiring discussion, some good material had been written on all sides, and what was more important the Jones/Gilliam/Palin idea of a sort of stream-of-consciousness way of putting the material together was accepted enthusiastically, by John at any rate. So at six we left the BBC feeling a lot better.'

After another week of sex, sangria and liberation with his partner, Graham returned to the fold, very pleased to see the work that had been done in his absence, and resumed his writing role alongside Cleese. Palin noted on 3 June, ' . . . drove up to Graham Chapman's via a bookshop in Hampstead. Graham, very brown from a week in Ibiza, treated us to his usual generous portions of Scotch and was very appreciative of the writing we'd done during the week he was away. He was particularly enthusiastic about the continuity of the show.'

As material began to amass, the group would get together on a weekly basis, more often at Jones's house in Camberwell, South London, or Cleese's flat in Knightsbridge. Here they would present their material before stockpiling it and then attempting to form it into a run of individual shows.

These initial meetings were usually convivial affairs. (Jones later said, his tongue only slightly in his cheek, 'I thought we were all being equal and fair, now I realise everyone was plotting behind my back.') First would come the read-through, in which each would present their own material. Graham never felt comfortable reading out his and John's work, so Cleese would always take that role, as Palin would for himself and Jones. Idle would read his own, and Gilliam would try to explain his extreme ideas in a manner that generally left the others bewildered but confident enough to let him get on with it.

'I think Terry used to really worry about the Cambridge lot being devious, slippery politicians,' Gilliam has stated, 'and he always used to be obsessed about this when he did something, but at the same time I had to agree with him. I thought they were putting things in at particular moments for political reasons because it was going to work that way. You felt with John that he was always jockeying for position, which then Terry was the antithesis of.'

Despite there being some obvious underlying level of competition, laughter was free-flowing when the material deserved it, and all were pleased that this was certainly true of the majority of the work they were doing. What was also true was how well the different sensibilities of the six were gelling together almost from the outset.

'We felt that what had been the problem with shows we'd all been involved in before,' Palin notes, 'is that responsibility had been spread and participation had been spread between a number of people, and sometimes it was just very, very difficult to explain to someone why something was funny. The Python six, the six of us, had a gut feeling about what was funny and you didn't have to explain that really, you didn't have to go into it in great detail, though sometimes we did have debates about what was funny but then they usually ended up in laughter of some kind or another, but the basic thing was we all felt that we had to keep it tight because it was something you couldn't really say quite why it worked, but it did. And we knew that once we spread it out it would lose something, a little bit of the intensity would go. It was extraordinary enough to get six people who have that kind of harmony, and that's what I think we wanted to preserve.'

Nonetheless, despite this apparent harmony, the group meetings would sometimes result in fierce arguments, more often than not led by Jones and Cleese, as the latter recollects, 'There were sometimes tremendous fights about material but the strange thing was it was always about material: it was never about who was going to act what material. We always instinctively knew as actors who was going to make anything work best and that's the way it was. And if you had a light week, you thought, "Well, that's fine, did a light week this week." There was a great sense of we were all in it together, and if the shows were funny we all benefited and if they weren't we didn't, and it didn't matter particularly who got the laughs, it really didn't. But there were catfights about the material. I remember once we decided that one of the sketches should be lit by this sort of candelabra that would be in the view of the camera and we got into a terrible fight about whether it should be a goat or a sheep. What we knew is that it was going to be a light bulb screwed into each of the four feet, and there was this almost vitriolic fight, three against three, I think. Insulting each other, "Fucking sheep!", "What do you mean a sheep?" and I remember halfway through thinking, "This is absolutely insane". There were a lot of those kind of arguments about whether material should go in the show, whether it was good enough, whether it was not good enough. And there was a high degree of energy expended on that. I think Jones and I expended more energy than the others. Michael was probably the natural peacemaker. Graham was happy to put a word in but not ever having the energy. Graham was never quite there. He would come in, say something marvellous and then drift off in his own mind, so he wouldn't have a point most of the time.'

Palin agrees with this point of view – up to a point: 'That's certainly my impression, that Graham would say nothing for a long period and suddenly come out with "Norwegian Blue" or whatever, which was the key thing of an idea. He's such a good performer, Graham, in a style in which none of the rest of us had at all. John had a big authority figure who could bark orders and go completely spare, Graham had this rather sort of decent, British contemplative quality, amusing. He could be slightly mad or angry, but we could complement each other quite well.'

(Terry Jones once wisely said that when Graham performed, you couldn't see where he came from and likewise, his contribution to Python was immense and immeasurable – not only shifting from a dog to a parrot, but coming up with such classics as the famed 'Ministry for Silly Walks', an idea sparked off when he saw an elderly man struggling to walk up Southwood Lane near his home in London. Both him and Cleese being too busy to write the idea themselves, he phoned up Palin and Jones and insisted they write something based on his original observation.)

For a group that was so united, there were clearly divisions within it. Palin still saw some of this as a reflection of the attitudes their respective colleges had brought out in them, an Oxford–Cambridge divide that was particularly reflected in the anger that could be seen not only in both Graham and John, but in what was often viewed as the harsh, almost sadistic nature of some of the material the two of them were writing.

'There seemed to be an edge to the Cambridge people of having to prove themselves. Much more competitive, much more driven and I don't know why it was and maybe it was something in that university background, something like that. We turned out much more easy-going on the whole, and I wondered whether it had gone back to Cambridge days and the fact that the Footlights was a competitive institution in which people dressed up and wore proper evening dress to perform, you were competing with others around you, and whether that was still there and created a dissatisfaction with your own performance and a determination to make sure that you behaved in a certain way – an impatience with anything that seemed like failure of any kind at all. And it was true also in the way the material was written for Python: Terry and myself wrote more than anybody else, that was unquestioningly true, and we also wrote more bad material than anybody else. But we didn't particularly mind. Some things we would just float, which were quite silly. We'd have a go at it, and if it got kicked out, well, it was worth a try, someone else might pick it up. John and Graham were less good at that, they didn't like reading out. John hated reading out material that didn't work; he just really didn't like that. I think he felt that it was somehow a reflection on them, and they should have got it right, and it should have been better and all that. So there's a driven sense I felt to John and Graham in a way, John particularly, which we didn't share in quite the same way, and it gets down to all sorts of things about the difference between us and John's very severe way of dealing with himself and the material and whatever he took on. It wasn't just something you did as a little lark here and there; you had to get this absolutely right, and I think John feels that about the world today; you've got to find out what is the meaning of life.'

In an interview with *Time Out* magazine, Graham concurred on the creative differences within the group. 'John's bigger than the rest of us. I can be fairly fierce, but I don't think there is any friction in that way. I find I tend to align with John as far as choice of material is concerned; we have a much more aligned sense of humour, and Mike and Terry tend to go along the same way, and Eric, poor thing, is on his own.'

Palin, however, saw that a similar sort of anger to Cleese's could often be present in Graham, albeit from a different source. 'Because of his homosexuality, there was a lot of feeling that there were a lot of hypocrites out there in the world really, and

I'm not absolutely certain, but I think that Graham really felt that we were certainly all at the very least bisexual and most people were homosexual, if they'd just admit it and come round the back for a quick snog. That was it.

'All these comments and thoughts about gay, gays and non-gays seem so run-of-the-mill now, but then it was still quite unusual for someone to declare themselves openly to be homosexual. I think the word "gay" had just about come in at that time . . . I think Gray felt that people were hypocritical and they were judging him. Especially when he'd had a drink or two, he really could get very, very angry about people and he would attack people and he'd attack within the group. He'd attack John sometimes. He'd attack any of us if he felt in a certain mood. It wasn't really Graham at all. It certainly wasn't the Graham that I knew later on, but fuelled by drink, and, I think, by a sort of anger at his own life and the way it was, that brought out some very intense feelings.'

Nonetheless, within the group, any such tensions were superseded and kept in check by the overall satisfaction of all involved with the work they were doing and the opportunity they had been afforded. After much discussion the show was finally christened *Monty Python's Flying Circus*, and by the late summer of 1969 it had begun to consume their lives. When they weren't writing, they were filming for an imminent October broadcast date, and in between they were rehearsing in a BBC-hired working men's club in Acton, West London. While this provided a useful space to work in, it also offered the opportunity of a bar next door, meaning that rehearsals nearly always stopped for lunch.

'We would rehearse,' Palin recalls, 'and at twelve o'clock Graham would say, "Oh, time for a drinkee, twelve o'clock, bar's open," which it would be at this working men's club, and he'd go and get a pint, as would [director/producer] Ian MacNaughton, and that would be, as far as I thought, the start of Graham's drinking day. If somebody liked a couple of pints at lunchtime, it wasn't heavy drinking, we did that as well. Terry and I went and had a pint, John and Eric, but we all drank quite a bit then – wine and such.'

Terry Jones recalls the recording of the first few shows in a similar vein. 'When you were doing those early shows, it was really just whether you could remember your words. Then, of course, we hadn't learned the trick in those days of not to drink beforehand. I'm sure we used to have a couple of pints of beer or something before the show. I know Graham did, but I hadn't realised there was a correlation between a lack of mental agility and alcohol intake.'

Just before the recording of the first episode of *Monty Python's Flying Circus*, John Cleese turned to Michael Palin and said, 'Do you realise this could be the first comedy show to go out with absolutely no laughs at all?'

They needn't have worried. The show debuted on 5 October 1969, and despite some initial late-night and regionally non-specific scheduling by the BBC (i.e. if you lived in certain parts of the country you couldn't receive it, it would occasionally be pre-empted in favour of the likes of the International Horse of the Year Show and so on) it quickly became a critics' favourite and a country-wide cult. Within weeks Graham took great delight in the fact that the bar at Bart's would be jam-packed on a Saturday night with medical students crowding round a single television set to watch the show.

As it progressed and its popularity grew, word came down that the Beatles themselves were fans – Paul McCartney was said to curtail recording sessions so he could watch it, while George

Harrison was apparently known to fly back from wherever he was in the world in time to catch each new episode.

'We'd performed at university and that sort of thing,' Graham later recounted for Ken Levy, 'but we earned our first professional money writing or working for other people. Gradually we found that they didn't want to do things that were as stupid as the things that we wanted to do, and so we were the only people around who would be prepared to take that risk and look as stupid as we did. We were not given very much money for each programme by the BBC, who didn't like us, so we only had an hour and a half each week to record each show on tape in front of an audience, which meant that we had to know what we were going to do beforehand, otherwise we wouldn't have had the cameras in the right place and the right costumes or anything . . . I suppose we do seem to get associated with various members of the Beatles in that I've done a bit of work with Ringo and Eric's done a bit with George Harrison.'

In short *Monty Python's Flying Circus* became the kind of show that not only found immense popularity but also came to be something of a cultural event within its time. All heady stuff for a group of six men who wanted to abandon punchlines and simply be allowed the room to do what they felt were the best, and funniest, things they could do.

With such success came celebration, and in Graham's case that meant another large one. Although Graham had clearly achieved a high level of success, he never felt relaxed about it particularly and rarely said no to offers of work. Subsequently, while the others were devoting the majority of their time to honing Python, he also felt he needed to be working on other projects, continuing to write on the 'Doctor' series among others.

'He was really burning the candle at both ends,' David Sherlock notes, 'the pressures of doing the show, doing a whole load of other things, trying to learn lines at the last minute in a cab on the way to Shepherd's Bush to rehearsals, for which he was invariably late, having had a night out the night before. Once he'd got the ability to earn extremely good money, then he wanted to enjoy it and he certainly did. He loved good food, he was an excellent cook, although a very slow one, so sometimes at a dinner party you'd perhaps start a meal at about 11.30 at night, but it would be excellent. He was never a morning person and of course to rehearse at the BBC one has to be, whether you like it or not. Plus of course he drank to give himself confidence and to allow himself to be the sort of social animal he would like to be and that was very difficult for him because of his shyness; however, lots of people never knew he was shy because he was always slightly inebriated.'

Of course, when all this success arrived, the Pythons themselves had little time to enjoy it, still being in the process of either filming the rest of their first series or writing and editing material for their second. Most of them seemed to thrive on it, enjoying the fact that their approach to comedy was now being seen not only as legitimate but dominant. Frost may have nurtured them, but they had now left him far behind.

Graham meanwhile was keenly aware of the opportunities the programme had offered the team. 'I think in fact we got better. In the first series it was really just a revue show, a series of sketches fairly loosely linked together, but later on, when we'd got to know each other and we'd been working together, I think each programme became much more of an entity; even a series became much more of an entity. We would have, say, someone like the Bishop, who wasn't due to appear until five programmes later, appearing five programmes earlier just saying, "I'm not supposed to be in this programme." So it became much more of an entity in that way.'

While Graham clearly enjoyed this notion as much as any of them, he was dealing with it in a different way. 'I used to take Graham into rehearsals,' says Palin. 'It was my penance because I lived nearby. I would go and give him a lift. No one could afford cars then, you weren't picked up and collected like you might be now, and Graham was living in Ornan Road in Hampstead in this tall block of flats, and I'd arrive there at nine. I'd ring Graham and say, "I'm leaving now," "OK give us a toot," I'd get there, park my little Triumph Herald, press the horn and wait and very often, for five minutes, nothing would happen at all, and then a window would go up and a boy's head would appear. It wasn't Graham, it was someone from the Far East, and he'd say, "Hello, he's just coming." I didn't know how to take that and I would wait and then sometimes within ten minutes Graham would appear, sometimes as long as fifteen minutes. I'd just wait out there and I loved dear old Gray, but it was just very, very frustrating and irritating because we'd get into rehearsals, and I was keen on being punctual, I liked order in my life, and so people would think, "Oh dear, here we go again," and Graham would just say, "Oh, traffic," and scratch his head. But the point of this story is that Graham would come down, and he always had this rather strange smell, a real kind of odd toothpaste he'd use. It was a toothpasty smell, but it was a bitter, minty smell, and I never thought anything more about it at all, idiot that I am, for years. Fortunately, as Python got a bit more money, Graham was able to get a car of his own, which was whoopee time for me – just a terrific deliverance from this awful job. But Graham later told me that he'd had to have a couple of quick large vodkas before he could even come out and that was the smell: it was just toothpaste trying to cover up the vodka, and I just had no idea of that at all.'

The show, however, was going from strength to strength,

winning a second series from the BBC, a more regular (i.e. not messed around with) time slot, a chance to represent the Corporation at the prestigious Montreux TV Festival and an expansion into both records and books, something that became the team's first real chance to start earning what Graham considered to be a decent amount of money.

'For all the success it still didn't deliver much in terms of great creature comforts,' states Palin, 'and one has to remember, looking back, we didn't know what was going to happen: Was there going to be a third series? So all these ancillary activities suddenly seemed to be quite important.'

While Python was now becoming a year-round job for most, Graham still had a life of his own, working on other shows with other writers, to financially facilitate his lifestyle. 'Chapman was a one-off,' says Cleese. 'You would never expect to spend much time in the evening with Chapman because he'd be off!'

Part of what fame afforded Graham was the opportunity to speak out about his lifestyle in public. While he insisted he was never a party politician in terms of speaking out for any cause, when asked, he knew how to speak his mind on a simple humanitarian level and knew that if he chose to do so his voice would be heard, if only by virtue of the fact that he was winning awards on television (courtesy of Montreux).

His success in this medium coincided with the rise of the gay movement in Britain, in particular the rise of the Gay Liberation Front. Graham supported the group – he would often attend weekly meetings at All Saints' Church Hall, Notting Hill – but rather than become a public advocate for the group, he instead bought them a tea urn to handle demand when attendance at the meetings swelled to over four hundred a session. However, in a number of interviews at the time and shortly after, Graham made clear where he stood on a number of issues with regard to his position as one of the most high-profile openly out homosexuals in the country.

'If it [the Gay Liberation Front] means that people are prepared to stand up and say, "I'm gay," and someone hearing about it in, say, Oldham will be able to think, "Thank God, I'm not so abnormal after all," it gives a lot of comfort, and it means that the predominantly homosexual man or woman will be able to lead his or her own life instead of making a disastrous heterosexual marriage just in order to have children. We're more sophisticated, I hope, than animals – we don't necessarily have to reproduce ourselves. In fact today with the population exploding in every direction, it's just as well there are homosexuals about to even things up a bit!'

At the time Graham was speaking, 1971, he was acutely aware that while he may well have been able to walk hand in hand with his partner, David, in the street, by kissing him in public he could still be charged with 'public indecency' under the 1967 Sexual Offences Act. A medical man by training, he was equally appalled by the fact that aversion therapy was still being used in the treatment of some homosexually related cases.

'It's treated like a disease. Something to be cured. What's the point? Showing a homo pictures of men and giving him a shock each time may take away his desire for men, but it doesn't make him want women. All he won't want is any more shocks.

'There are two kinds of homosexual love,' Graham espoused. 'The kind where two people enjoy walking the street, doing things together, sharing everything. The other kind goes on in public lavatories and behind bushes and after a chance meeting in a pub – but that happens in heterosexual sex as well.

'People don't know what it's like to be a homosexual. Take for instance the jokes – there are Jewish jokes and black people jokes and hurtful words like "pansy", "fairy", "queen". They don't bother me because I'm a writer and a performer and I don't care what people call me. But the older homosexuals are afraid – they really do mince and talk in funny high voices and flap their wrists – but it is their way of getting over the fact that they are homosexual without admitting it and having to suffer the consequences. They think the GLF will ruin it for them. Any liberating force is important. But when the slaves were liberated in America, they didn't particularly like the idea. There were these liberally minded people who came along and freed them, and suddenly they had money, freedom and no idea of what to do next. It wasn't until a few years later that they started to develop from that point on. That is what's happening to GLF.'

Despite the assured nature of his outspokenness, Graham made it clear that the feelings of his family and, in many ways, the pressures he had put upon them were not a closed book for him. 'Of course I care about the reactions of my parents and my brother . . . they lead such different lives . . . My mother was horrified . . . But as far as I am concerned, I'm not worried. I think people will understand – they always understand more than they are given credit for. And perhaps when they hear a girl say, "I've got to hurry home, my girlfriend is waiting for me" – or the other way around of course – they will accept that for some people that is absolutely right and natural.'

When Graham did choose to discuss his sexuality in public, he was always honest, sometimes more than he needed to be. 'I wouldn't describe myself as totally homosexual. Hardly anyone is entirely one thing or the other. Part of my attitude to myself was clarified when I read the Kinsey Report. He scaled people from nought to six, and most people fall in the middle – tending towards the heterosexual. I am perhaps just on the other side.

But I was surprised at the high number who admitted to homosexual experiences of some kind.'

Having come from what he always saw as a provincial upbringing, Graham was more than aware that being a celebrity in the heart of the nation's capital meant that his own views – which he chose to air – were not going to be universally accepted. 'Public attitude is improving, certainly, especially in London. But it's still terrible outside. I met a girl at a Gay Lib meeting who had been sacked for being a lesbian. The excuse was that they were afraid she would touch up all the girls in the office. Now, by that token, shouldn't they sack all the men?

'There should be no laws on sexual offences of any kind. Just a common law of assault. Nor should there be a particular age of consent, like sixteen for heteros, twenty-one for homos. The age bar has been banished in Sweden, and I don't think the crime rate has increased. I think children in school should be told about both hetero and homosexual behaviour, then they might grow up with a more mature attitude. It's not fair on teachers. A lot of them suffer. It would be odd to think that there were no gay people in the teaching profession. It is one to which they naturally tend to gravitate. But very few, as it were, molest.'

However, at times it is clear that his own views were either a little too idealistic, a little naïve or too deliberately provocative for his own good. 'What I would ask about those rare cases is – what harm do they actually do? I believe that the shame and the guilt are caused much more by what are known as the "due processes of the law". In an incident involving, say, a vicar and a choirboy, it's the interviews and publicity which cause the traumas. George Melly once said that he decided that he felt sorry for pederasts because he remembered being an awful little flirt himself. Now that is an outrageous statement, but it does point out something that is never mentioned. I like saying and doing outrageous things myself sometimes. If they are far enough over the top, I find that people have a stunned reaction, not a shocked one. Perhaps they think I am just being funny. Or perhaps they repeat it and argue and see there is some truth in it. And start to think for themselves and become more compassionate.

'I believe that the only people who should live together are those mature enough to make the decision that they are mutually compatible to live together for a number of years because of a thing I would call love.'

Graham also took time – when talking to interviewer Ken Levy – to discuss his feelings on transsexualism. 'I once went to a meeting at the Royal College of Physicians that was about transsexualism and about people being surgically changed from men to women. And it's the most appalling experience of my life. To see people literally having their penises cut off. A very bloody operation to say the least, and then them trying to make an artificial vagina, which they'd do reasonably. Of course you've got no testicles by then. It's illegal in England anyway, so they'd have to go off to North Africa or Ireland. But these people finish up being nothing. They haven't got their testicles. They haven't got ovaries. They're not "intersex" and they cannot, because of that, there is no way they can have an orgasm. They need to think very hard about what they will lose, and that struck me as the most worrying idea of my life at the Royal Society of Medicine. And I spoke to the man and said, "This is wrong, surely? Why isn't it reasonable, if they feel like this, why shouldn't they just be normal homosexuals?" and the bloke who was giving the lecture and earns lots of money from doing these operations said, "Oh, we always expect some kind of agitator at this kind of meeting: it's an emotive subject." Of course it's emotive. But then for him to advise people to have their genitals cut off, which is what it amounts to, to me it's the most angry-making thing in the world. I wrote an article about it for a magazine which I helped start in England called *Gay News*. I wrote an article about this, and they refused to print it because they thought it would hurt their readers. It's only the fucking truth, that's all. And I mean fucking truth. I met a few. A lot of them finish up as suicide cases, they really do. This man was claiming nineteen out of forty-eight that he had treated, that means made them into women, so he thought, that only nineteen had committed suicide, and that was a good record – it was better than anywhere else in the world. Now, fuck, that's not medicine, it certainly isn't . . . the slides that were shown of his successful patients, not out of the nineteen that committed suicide but the slides that he showed of the others, it just looked like an area of piles; it was appalling. It wasn't at all pretty. Anyway, better move off this subject, as I get rather emotional about it as everybody would. It was one of the nastiest things I've ever seen . . . I guess I'm a troublemaker. A troublemaker that's turning his trouble to his advantage. That's about it.'

Graham was clearly enjoying the freedom he had placed in motion four years before at his coming-out party. Now he was known for what he was – both personally and professionally – and could, when it suited him, be an articulate exponent of both. He would even bring the two together, light-heartedly discussing the difference between his fears of being outed as a medical student at Bart's and the reality of it having occurred during his tenure at the BBC.

'One BBC executive said he couldn't imagine what men could do together and didn't really believe it. What they really draw the line at is words like "piss" and "wee-wee" and anything to do with the Queen' – before going on to discuss his views on the modern homosexual about town – 'There's a great decline in raving screamers these days – who needs them any more? The lisp and limp wrist are on the way out' – as well as his own form of political action – 'When we were filming in Scotland we went into this really dreary rural pub, and to cheer things up I went round and kissed every man in the bar. I was chucked out and the pub closed early, which is quite something in that part of the world. Well, next night I went back, and the feller who'd been most against me was sitting there and made some remark. So I went and sat right next to him and said, "You are a boring man who can only talk about motor cars and the number of women you've screwed." There was a woman sitting with him, and she suddenly exclaimed, "Christ, you're right!" So I enjoy that kind of thing – going up to some rugged character and saying, "I'm a poof . . . " I haven't really done any campaigning in an organised way – it's a more individual method that I use, and it's directed at the most important thing, which is changing people's attitudes.

'After all, there are loads of friendships between men which have a hidden sexual dimension, you know, a guy just likes the look of his friend, but it never comes out in the open. If only people worried less.'

Graham clearly practised what he preached and, as his embracing of the London gay scene moved ahead at full steam, he often worried less.

By the early 1970s Bernard McKenna was as constant a workmate and companion as Cleese had been originally. Having first tried his hand as an actor in his native country, the burly Scotsman was by now a successful television comedy writer, beginning his career supplying sketch material for Ronnie Barker for *Hark at Barker* and the highly regarded one-off half-hour 'The Odd Job' for the series *Six Dates with Barker* (a story Graham would later re-examine in the 1977 movie of the same name). With Cleese eager to pursue other avenues (and increasingly keen to work alone: 'Cleese I don't think at that stage wanted to continue writing with Graham every day, twelve days a week,' remembers McKenna. 'He was happy to do Python, which was just starting . . . but Graham never said no to work so he said, "OK, we'll write the 'Doctor' series"') and having seen out the first series in partnership with Barry Cryer, Humphrey Barclay had the good sense to team Graham with McKenna for a large part of the *Doctor at Large* series and its subsequent follow-ups, although he takes no credit for it, choosing to name serendipity in his place. 'I didn't make any marriages. They just sort of formed themselves really and volunteered their services. I know that sounds extraordinary but I think that's how it was really. They formed themselves. It was wonderfully informal, and I look back on it now that it seems so incredibly exhausting and wearying to get a television show going, in those days it did seem to be easier. Definitely easier! [. . .] But I remember occasionally going to talk through a script with him and Bernard, and I have images of Bernard telling me about how many pints of lager Graham had to have before he could start the day.'

McKenna became a crucial part of the support system that came to surround Graham, although feeling the neophyte on his initial entry, he was quick to realise he was being tested. 'Humphrey put me with Graham before the first Python show. I saw the first Python go out in his flat in Ornan Road with suitably wild, drunken people. Nobody knew what to expect. I was a big fan of Milligan and *The Goon Show* – it was a generational thing that we all were big fans of that. The one thing I'd been told by (in those days) the very, very mini-skirted secretaries who would run up to you and tell you things was one day Graham wore a red leather jacket to a meeting, and one of them said to me, "Do you know he's gay?" or it was "homosexual" or "poof". The word "gay" hadn't quite entered into the vocabulary. So I didn't know anything about him. I knew more about Cleese because of Ronnie Barker and Cleese being on *Frost*. So Humphrey just suggested it, and I went to see the first Python transmission at Graham's place, and it was full of outrageous people. And I wasn't worried – being a drama student I'd known plenty of gay people, but it didn't worry me or frighten me. For years Graham would say, "What are you frightened of?" He was always testing you. "Have you ever tried it?" "No, I haven't, I don't really need to." I knew he could wind me up a bit. When I used to go to his flat, which had on the door the name "Colonel Muriel Volestrangler" – which was one of Cleese's – I used to go there and David Sherlock, Graham's lifelong partner, would come to the door in a purple robe with a fur collar and say, "Yes?" I'd say, "I've come to work with Graham." He'd say, "Oh, all right, then."

'I lived within walking distance of him – I was in Swiss Cottage – and I would get to Graham's at ten, and Graham often wouldn't appear until eleven or half eleven. And there wasn't much I could do about that – he just couldn't be bothered to get up.'

Barclay first tried the pair out by getting them to write links for an ITV Christmas show that contained short seasonal sketches based around the most popular shows of the day. The two gelled and soon the 'Doctor' series seemed the best way to go.

'Graham had the medical knowledge,' recalls McKenna. 'He was very good about saying, "We ought to do one about this," and he would also say, "Oh, I know, this weird thing happened once . . . " and we would try and get that in. I would do the shaping. Graham would very often come from off the wall – you'd never know – with the odd line. Those scripts then were very raucous – all the doctors were lads, and nurses were there to be groped and authority was to be mooted.'

Many of the people who came to write with Graham sensed if not a casual attitude to his work, then one of sporadic interest, within which he could indeed redefine the way a particular sketch or plot could turn. But McKenna was privy to a more competitive side, one that harked back to his medical training and indeed his standing in the British comedy community of the day.

Graeme Garden was a fellow Cambridge graduate and also a medical man, Bill Oddie was an old colleague from *Cambridge Circus* days. Along with another old colleague, Tim Brooke-Taylor, they were giving Python a run for their money at the BBC as the Goodies, a semi-surreal ratings success on the same corporation that eschewed Python's obvious aggression for more childlike humour. Garden and Oddie were also being hired by the likes of Humphrey Barclay as writers, Garden's medical background also making him a natural for the 'Doctor' series, something that, according to McKenna, Chapman was having none of. 'Graham always felt – which I thought was right – he always wanted to be higher up the scale than Graeme Garden and Bill Oddie. He felt Graeme Garden and Bill Oddie had betrayed it a bit – he didn't like Bill Oddie at all. He always thought Bill Oddie would put in some easy line. He had respect for Graeme Garden because Graeme was a doctor. But he didn't like their scripts. At the same time he didn't feel there was much of a competition, because he felt he was better – particularly better than Bill Oddie.'

McKenna – as with Cleese – maintains that he was very much

the 'nuts and bolts' man when it came to working with Graham, noting his predilection for throwing in lines and ideas and his need to have someone around to facilitate them. Graham's partner, David Sherlock, also wrote with him during this period on some of the 'Doctor' series.

'There was no point in him picking up the pen, the point has to be made, because he couldn't even read his own writing back. And this is the reason why all of the people he wrote with have a memory of being the scribe only, or at least a rather bitter memory of doing all the work. That is producing the ideas, and sometimes Graham would then take a quantum leap into the abyss with that idea and come back with something totally wacky that was from another planet. My mother always said that she was scared of opening her mouth because she knew damn well that some of her phraseology would find its way into, particularly, the characterisations of either the Rosemary Leach character of wife to Ronnie Corbett in *No, That's Me Over Here!* or quotations about the mother-in-law in the same series. A lot of those characters were based on either my mother or Graham's mother or Cleese's mother, all of whom figured to an extent in Python and other things. And so therefore Graham was ticking away all the time, listening . . .

'When I was working with Graham, he could field phone calls in the middle of writing a script. The phone would ring, he'd field two or three phone calls sometimes, one after the other, and deal with somebody coming into the room and then go straight back to the exact same line that he had dictated so fast that I could only get half of it down before we were interrupted, and that line would be exactly the same. It came out almost fully formed as a complete, finished script and usually it was timed precisely to fit the two twelve-minute slots or whatever it was for commercial TV [without the adverts]. That for me was how he worked.

'Some things had a wonderful shape. Something that was as freewheeling as Python was different again, and it depended entirely on how the day started with Python. But in the other much more, shall we say, traditional, old-fashioned style of sitcom-writing, he had an idea of an overall style certainly by the second or third day of working on whatever it was, because many of the scripts were written and finished in one week, which for a half-hour sitcom is a pretty tall order, and like many writers it was not until the eleventh hour that the writing started. It was always under pressure, very much so.'

Humphrey Barclay remembers that all too often the pressure was more evident. 'The hard part was getting him to do the work because he was pissed. If it hadn't been for Barry Cryer and for Bernard McKenna making him actually do it, we'd have never got those scripts in. He absolutely was carried by his co-writers. He would not have managed to do it by himself. You knew your scripts were coming from somebody who was drunk most of the time, and it was jolly tough and thank God for Bernard.'

As Cleese became more and more remote from his first significant writing partner, largely in the sense that he wanted to write with others and in other styles (most predominantly with his wife, Connie Booth, with whom he would shortly write the sitcom/farce *Fawlty Towers*), McKenna's role would become more and more significant, continuing for the majority of Graham's life. Indeed he was himself surprised to find the extent of Graham's dependency on him when he spoke to Graham's psychiatrist. 'The psychiatrist he had, Maurice Lipsedge, who had taught Graham and had taught Alan Bailey once, took me aside and said, "You are one of the stabilising influences in his life." And I said, "What?" And he said, "You're not gay, you're not a sycophant, you work with him – you can help him." And so I entered into this pact with helping him – but not with his knowledge, because if you said to Graham you were helping him, he wouldn't have liked it. So all I did was be very supportive and went round to see him when I could have been doing other things, I suppose . . . but it was interesting, Lipsedge's take on it. He knew that Graham was this void – not to say I was to fill it, but he knew I could help by pushing him along a little.'

By being placed in such a position, McKenna was privy to the most intimate details of Graham's life – something that was hard to avoid chez Chapman. McKenna recalls often witnessing both Graham and David and their numerous house guests wafting around in the briefest of briefs, partly, McKenna feels, as a means to provoke him – Graham once again feeling that homosexuality may well be something that everyone around him needed to own up to, rather than deny.

'From the beginning with both Graham and David Sherlock, it was game for a laugh. Because I was straight, they would walk around in little skimpy pants and things. But I just ignored it. And I think I gained their respect by doing that. I passed the test.'

Humphrey Barclay also recalled the atmosphere in Graham's flat at the times he visited. 'They'd just refurbished it, and I seem to remember it was rather early days, but it was polished wooden floors, and I stepped down and it was all very nice, a little chilly and lacking in character and not feeling very lived in, but perhaps that was because it was new, and I went to a kind of gay party there and I got this impression of everybody sitting around in the early stage of the evening, all these men, I suppose. I have a feeling they were all in dark clothes, and I've got this image of them all like the birds in Hitchcock's movie, perching on wires in rows waiting to pounce!'

This was a period of intense experimentation for Graham. Fuelled by their mutual admiration for the work of Spike Milligan, he was working on a show that was literally breaking down the boundaries of television comedy. Fuelled by his love for David Sherlock, he was embracing a new lifestyle which he was being publicly recognised for.

'As Graham was already "out", he realised there was a large area of material that could be included in Python where you could actually make some sort of social comment on gay issues,' says Sherlock, 'and of course gay rights were suddenly big news from '68/'69 onwards and so it coincided, and since Graham was making no secret of his private life, he then found himself asked to talk about himself to all sorts of groups.'

At the same time, Graham and his partner were relocating, moving from Belsize Park to Highgate, into a new house that Graham's success could now allow for.

Graham was also clearly responding to the open relationship that he and David had agreed on, and both enjoyed. All his co-workers at the time remember many personal visitors to their premises.

'He used to take people back to Southwood Lane and pounce on them,' says Bernard McKenna of their daily trips to the pub. 'He was predatory. But he was very clumsy. He would meet the odd lad, and they would be totally in awe: "This is Graham Chapman from Monty Python" – and then Graham would have his gin and tonic and say, "I only live down the road, you know? Would you like to come and have a drink there? Because I've got to get back, I've got to start cooking." Of course they're not going to say no . . . and so off they would go. And the next day I would say, "So how was last night?" And I'd find out that he had said, "I'll show you the house" – corny! – then take them upstairs and try and kiss them . . . He would take the lads back and either successfully or unsuccessfully pounce on them.'

David Sherlock's own mother would refer to them as the 'lame dogs' that would attach themselves to Graham and would continue to do so throughout his life. Having dealt with his own decisions with remarkable equanimity, Graham was now in a position – slightly fuelled by the good nature that alcohol brought out in him – to see himself as helping others. After all, it was something that harked back to his medical training in many ways. Plus, having come from so strong a family, Graham, realising that his own lifestyle and the times he lived in now precluded such a thing, was often looking for a surrogate version of the same. He first encountered it in the form of two runaways named Brendan and Jimmy. Both were Irish lads, although Jimmy had forged his father's signature on a cheque to make his way back from America to Dublin, his home. Both had hooked up on the admittedly limited gay scene in Dublin so had decamped – underage – to London – imagining a better and more liberal life. What they found was a prison for young offenders, the worst thing that could have happened to them. What they found after that was a saviour in Graham, at least for a while.

'Our social life revolved round a group of friends who were all professionals,' recalls Sherlock, 'either in restaurants, antiques, all of those trendy areas of the sixties where successful professional gays were beginning to make inroads.

'However, one of our friends had a brother who was an extremely left-wing gay political character, and he telephoned Graham and said you're the only person I can think of – there are two kids who have been sent to borstal, and I believe they shouldn't have been sent there because they are being abused, apparently, in the borstal, and there was going to be a big exposé in one of the papers about the general lack of discipline in this particular set-up, and he told us that these two boys were going to have a hearing in court, he was trying to get them bailed, but they had to have somebody with a qualification, i.e. a doctor in this case, who would vouch for them. Therefore the judge might let them off under probation, which is what happened. However, having done so, Graham discovered that there was an added thing to all of this, and that was that the boys were suddenly dumped on our doorstep and that they were coming to live with us. Graham had a couple of phone calls from the court, saying, "You vouched for them, but this means are you prepared to take them on and find them work?" And Graham was in the middle of writing that morning and said, "Yes, yes, anything." So we then had a couple of deeply dysfunctional nineteen-year-olds, with what I would have said was the emotional age of about thirteen and, like many abused kids, they knew all about sex and nothing about life. And because they'd always been manipulated themselves, they tried to manipulate us, and in fact it was terrifying really to be in this situation. Graham suddenly had kids who needed attention, and it was a bit like having two stray dogs that will do anything, like tear up the sofa just for attention, so long as they got it. These kids were a huge problem.'

Graham was always worried about money, partly because he kept everyone around him on what amounted to a form of salary. This was never meant as a slight or to make the people that made up his inner circle feel they were in his employ. For David Sherlock it was what he termed 'pocket money'. Graham was simply the famous one earning the cash and he was spreading the wealth. While there was every opportunity for him to be exploited, those closest to him certainly never did so, and never felt that Graham begrudged his expenditure. He was a facilitator of his life and his lifestyle and the people who comprised it.

Graham, feeling responsible for the two young men he had taken on as charges, fulfilled his personal and court-bound obligation as far as he could, although it did not prove to be a successful case of creating his own family. 'These two boys, for a time, worked for us as cleaners,' Sherlock recalls. 'We virtually had to teach them how to wipe their noses and everything else, so with cleaning, you also had to show them how to do it, so it wasn't much of a job. But anyway they fell out. One of them, Jimmy, left and moved in with a much older guy, fell out with him and decided to teach this guy a lesson. So the guy came back from the pub to find that Jimmy had hung himself from a rotary washing line and had absolutely staged the thing to look dramatic, and Graham was called, by the distraught pal who had fallen out with Jimmy, to come and identify the body.

'Graham said there were two marks . . . he said it was obvious Jimmy had tried to get the damn thing off. So tragedy struck, and we had to deal with a whole year of the other kid who was blaming himself, but had no one else to blame but Graham, and Graham was telephoned at all hours of the morning with this kid saying, "Come and get me, I'm in some terrible club," or whatever. Graham hauled him out of some awful dives which were basically full of dirty old men . . .

'Someone once called Graham an armchair socialist and he never forgot it, so he was trying to live up to this figure, his ideal of how people should behave.'

In light of this, at the time Graham publicly stated, 'I think that one really great reform would be gay adoption societies, or at least the encouragement of adoption by gays. So many unwanted children, so many religious taboos on adoption – it's absurd.'

Bernard McKenna was working with Graham on a daily basis at the time and noticed his fondness for the aesthetic of the younger man, something that Graham himself had said in interviews of the time, blaming the media for any anxiety resulting for any hypothetical dalliance between a 'vicar and a choirboy'.

Graham in turn would regularly interrupt his writing sessions with McKenna to gaze out of the front downstairs window of his Southwood Lane house to watch the boys heading home from Highgate School for Boys. 'We always had to stop at about five past four because the boys from Highgate School would come walking past, and he would go and stand at the window and say, "Ooh, my chickens," and make lascivious noises,' 'chicken hawk' being a common term on the London gay scene of the day.

One of the things that developed from Graham's personal emancipation was a realisation of who and what was available to him on the gay scene, and his open relationship with David.

One person he became acquainted with would prove to be the other love of his life. John Tomiczek was a teenage runaway from Liverpool, who, after the death of his mother, found himself exploring the gay scene in London. He was a strikingly handsome young man who looked older than his years, claiming to be seventeen when in fact he was still just thirteen. He worked as a DJ at the London nightclub Yours or Mine? in Kensington and got to know the clientele, Graham and David included. Another man he became familiar with was a well-known television actor. He had come to know Tomiczek through the clubs they both frequented. When John became ill, the actor, not particularly knowing Graham but knowing Graham had already met John and of his background in medicine, sought him out.

'There was this club and there was a young man who was DJ-ing and helping out and he latched on to Graham and was a great fan of Python and he was John Tomiczek, and Graham was particularly thrilled that someone young, vibrant and exciting had even heard of them,' recollects Sherlock. 'He told us he was seventeen and in fact he wasn't, he was thirteen, and so we realised he was staying with a celebrity who we met at the club, and this particular celebrity telephoned Graham in the middle of the night and he said, "I've got a young man staying with me who has your phone number, which is why I'm ringing." We'd met him once before in another club called the A&B, which was on the edge of Soho and fairly sleazy by today's standards, but a mixed gay club. So we vaguely knew him and he said, "This young man is ill. Can I send him over in a cab because I know you're a doctor and I know you'll be discreet."

'Graham and his brother, John, were both at our flat. John was just on a visit, and this boy was sent round in a cab, and they both examined him and both came to the conclusion that he'd got glandular fever. We knew he'd been hanging around this club, he'd been drinking, but at this point we did not know his age, we thought he was a very young and undeveloped seventeen-year-old. He was extremely androgynous-looking but very attractive and he was quite streetwise, came from Liverpool, had a strong Liverpool accent. He was a very, very attractive young man, and he was packed off to hospital, and we visited him and Graham said, "Look, when you're better, come and stay with us for your recuperation because you must not drink," which was very funny, coming to our place, but, quite seriously, that's what happened.'

'I met Brendan once,' says John Chapman. 'John followed on fairly swiftly after the other two. Obviously John proved ultimately to be a little more tractable and more profitable an investment in time than Brendan did, anyway.'

Bernard McKenna was also present in the first few days Tomiczek spent at Chapman's. 'I was there when Tomiczek first appeared on the scene and that was very peculiar, with Graham pretending he was helping somebody but basically – he had a young lad.'

Having recovered from his glandular fever, Tomiczek was certainly nurtured by Graham initially, with one of his early ideas being an attempt to introduce the young Liverpudlian to what had been one of Graham's life-long loves – mountaineering. Things, however, didn't go according to plan.

'Graham decided we'd all go climbing,' says Sherlock, 'one last stab at his old favourite hobby. We went to climb Snowdon, and John was really a city boy rather than a country boy and did not know that if you're on scree, it'll move if you run, and the scree started moving, took him with it. He was on the edge of a precipice and luckily for him he was hit by a large rock which was moving from above, and it stopped him. Graham shouted, "Lie flat, lie down, don't try and stand up on moving scree," and the rock sort of knocked him down.'

The result was Tomiczek broke his leg and needed to be rescued, which inadvertently resulted in something of a revelation. 'He was then sent to the local cottage hospital, gave his correct name, address and age, and we suddenly realised he was thirteen, soon to be fourteen. His father came to pick him up and turned out to be a Polish serviceman who'd come to live in this country, settled after the war, and he was thrilled to bits to find his son alive, well and happy, but his son said, "I'm not going back, if I have to go home I shall only abscond again, because I want to go back to London and I want to live with Graham and David." So the police said to his father, "You do realise that Mr Chapman is a gay man," although he didn't use that word, and his father said, "Oh yes. Yes, my son's told me," and he said, "I don't care where he lives, so long as he's happy." John's mother had died when he was eleven, from a congenital heart problem, which he had inherited, so John was also an interesting medical case, suddenly.'

Graham was divided by his feelings for John. And his concern with the boy led to him dealing not only with John's father but the North London police, who were suspicious of his intentions. 'When he came down to stay with us,' Sherlock explains, 'the Hampstead CID turned up and interviewed them both. Partly because of Graham's doctoring, the interview went very smoothly indeed, and they said, "Right, off you go . . . We don't approve of this, but . . . " was virtually how they put it. Those liberal ideas seem to have died with the seventies really and they've just gone. Such a liberal reaction. Can you imagine the reaction these days?'

'There was a mixture there,' McKenna observes. 'I think Graham genuinely wanted to help him in some ways, but Graham also always used to say to me, "Ooh, I'm in love with two people at once."'

'It was a verbal agreement with his father, made in the presence of the police,' recounts Sherlock, 'that if he was in London he had to live with us and if he left our care then he must go home. He took one look at our flat and decided he'd stay. So he did! John's father visited us subsequently with his other children and they had some good times.'

McKenna noted the changing dynamic within the household.

'David was, as it were, the reliable wife who would always be there, and John was the wayward child but loved carnally as well. I remember when Tomiczek first appeared on the scene, Cleese rang me up and said, "Have you seen Graham recently? Who's this John bloke that he brings to dinner?" Because if people said to Graham and David, "Come to dinner," Graham would say, "Terrific," and then bring John as well. People would think, "We invited the two of you as a couple and you've brought three." And Graham wouldn't say anything.

Graham thought John Tomiczek was the most beautiful, beautiful creature he'd ever seen and he could just gaze at him all day. And John would burst in on him when we were writing and say, "Oh, look, Graham, I'm just going to go and get some cigarettes, do you want some tobacco?" And get some money and go out. And John had no understanding or respect for the earning that had to take place before he could do any of this. By and large, John was brought up pretty much as a spoiled and often indulged teenager.'

Humphrey Barclay also noted the added presence of John Tomiczek. 'We assumed he was a pick-up and that they were screwing, and it was strenuously denied . . . they were looking after him. Well, I don't care what the details were, but it seemed like we were being fed one story when we could all guess that it was actually another story, but he seemed a charming person, and, you know, who cares? OK, he was a handsome young guy, a pick-up that was very congenial, and he came from a rotten background, and Graham's affection for him spread into wanting to look after him as well.'

Their new living arrangements and Graham's investigation by the local police led to John becoming the responsibility of Graham. 'Graham lived in an amazingly cocooned, totally non-intellectual world,' said McKenna. 'He liked them young –

thirteen or fourteen. He didn't think about the law. I think he thought if they are gay, then that's fine. But I think he played at being a homosexual rather than was homosexual. He used to talk to me about his sex life, how he used to wank John off. He wasn't into penetration. He used to call it the "cross-hand boogies". He was more into cross-hand boogies. He was more into kissing and fondling than penetration. I remember Graham saying to me, "Ooh, I had a great night last night," and me saying, "Oh, up some smelly arse or something?" and him saying, "No, were you up some smelly twat?" He wanted to reduce it all to some competitive thing.

'I never got the impression that he ever experimented with penetration. I think he was in a grey limbo area where homosexuality is on this side and heterosexuality is over here and Graham was in this sort of grey area.'

David Sherlock concurs that this form of mutual masturbation was Graham's preferred sexual activity, even from their first night together in his tent in Ibiza.

McKenna recalls that it was something that would even intrude on their writing together. 'I remember one day when we were writing he said, "I'm feeling very randy," and I said fine, and he said, "Do you mind if I go upstairs for a bit?" and I said no. So he went upstairs and then Anna Yallop, a great no-nonsense New Zealander who also worked with him, came down and said, "Graham's just sent me downstairs. Do you know why?" And I said, "Oh, he's randy and he's just called John to his room." And it was always, "Oh, John, can I have a word with you?" So she and I sat there, and then he came back down with a change of shirt and went, "That's better," and we carried on.'

'Oh God, you didn't need to discuss it,' Sherlock adds. 'It's one of those things that you know.'

McKenna contends that Graham never strove to intellectually better himself, despite his academic background, his grounding in medicine giving him a firm – albeit realistic – view of the world, one that precluded McKenna's fondness for foreign-language movies and Sherlock's taste for opera. 'I did take Graham to the opera once. I took him to *Götterdämmerung*, and there was this wonderful stage whisper in the prologue when the three Norns are twisting this piece of rope, the rope of fate or whatever, and suddenly you could hear the hiss of the Schweppes bottle as it was being undone. His Schweppes bottles were always doctored – a third of the contents was poured out and then refilled either with gin if it was tonic, or Scotch if it was dry ginger. He couldn't be bothered with the bar. There was no intermission not for an hour or three, so people would be going, "Sshh, sshh," like the advert itself. Then suddenly there was a very loud stage whisper, "When's something going to happen?" and then he said, "I think I can see a giant bear looming out of the gloom." So we couldn't take him to the opera.'

The relationship between David and Graham meanwhile was always warm, although fraught at times with arguments, with David one night marching out of the house only to find himself with no recourse but to sleep in a hollowed-out tree on the boundary between Highgate and Hampstead Heath.

Another instance took place relatively early on in their relationship, on a trip to Rome with Peter Cook, the occasion being Dudley Moore's honeymoon with his first wife, Suzy Kendall.

'This was nineteen-sixty-eight in Rome in the presence of Peter Cook,' Sherlock recalls. 'We were in Rome and Peter Cook was filming with Dudley, who'd just got married. She and I got on like a house on fire and Dudley was not best pleased.

Well, it was his honeymoon, but I mean, why sulk on your honeymoon when you've got one of the most beautiful women in London just madly in love with you? And Dudley seemed to me to be another Cambridge person who had no idea how women worked, and that was the problem. And she absolutely knew how we worked because she was so at ease with boys, in fact she *was* one of the boys. Graham and I had an argument one night in Rome, and I broke his pipe. Now that is serious. I did this on an outdoor table, it was a very large restaurant-hotel complex, and Peter heard the noise and came out to see what was going on and rather languidly said, "Oh, awfully sorry," but so did the waiters, and it was very funny because we were being very passionate and very noisy and there were a whole load of Italian waiters absolutely amazed, because we were much more noisy and passionate than they were. Our rows, when we had rows, were nearly always alcohol-fuelled and about nothing particularly. A lot of those arguments were about the frustration of being with Graham who was still pursuing his career, he's out there working, and we had little or no time together for ourselves, and this was one of the major problems throughout our relationship, and that's what always made me angry. He often took me for granted and only very seldom did he actually make special time for us because anything else, anything social that happened was often to do with work; if we went out to dinner it was often with work people. Well, a lot of the time that's interesting, but if you yourself were not involved, it can be very dull indeed. You're just a wife who's taken along for the ride.'

Nonetheless the next day the two were reconciled, with Graham distraught over the anguish he had caused the man he saw as his life partner. David for his part remained a permanent figure in Graham's life.

'Graham had an enormous love of life and *joie de vivre*, and, if you like, the melodramatic moments in his life were pretty damn melodramatic, but that was not the total pattern of his life by any means. For instance we might have a bust-up during the heavy-drinking days, but the next day would be sweetness and light, and possibly for the next week, there'd be nothing. A dark cloud had passed and it was all over. He never forgot anything, but he'd never hold grudges.

'A mutual friend of ours said in the early seventies, "Look, this guy's got a drink problem, if you're going to survive you've got to have separate lives," and other friends said, "Well, Graham chose this style of life." In other words he wanted a surrogate family of his choice and to begin with he did say to me, "Do you mind?" Well, what could you say? But at times one realised it was more and more an extremely difficult juggling act and a lot of the time, I said, "Well, no, I don't want to know most of these people."'

Despite Graham's seemingly strong constitution, Sherlock recalls instances, during dinner parties, of him curling up under the table and going to sleep with their dogs. 'There were times when he was totally out of control . . . and there were occasions when he overdid it, and of course there were also occasions when the paranoia took over . . . I always needed to go out with money in my pocket because, quite often, we would be driven to wherever we would be going, in the days when Graham was drinking, however we went, whether it was by cab or by chauffeur. But during the times when things got really sticky, I always made sure that I'd got enough money because there were many times I had to leave crowded restaurants with Graham shouting incredible details about what he thought of our sex life, what was happening in our sex life.'

For all the differences, the bond between Graham and David

remained strong and in many ways reflective of their era. The conscious decision to have an open relationship ensured there was little animosity between them.

'Graham just could not say no. He was incredibly generous, he was very kind. Then John became as much of a problem alongside Graham, as far as I was concerned, because he was deeply influenced by Graham, and he copied Graham's habits. Graham allowed him to drink; he had exactly the same problems . . .'

'Graham never would talk to me about it,' remembers McKenna, who was still a daily presence at the house, 'but he would say things like, "Ooh, it's very hard being a dad," or a mother or whatever. I knew what was going on, but you can't challenge, you don't want to. Graham could never make out if John was his child or his . . . whatever . . . he deceived himself into thinking he was the child that he wouldn't have.'

'We all kind of knew stuff about Graham at the time,' states Gilliam. 'Nobody pried too much.'

'It was definitely like a marriage,' Sherlock adds, 'as I understand it, with all the ups and downs with kids intervening in between.'

Chapter Six

As Python and its success and influence developed, Graham took time to publicly discuss the nature of that very peculiar beast, even if at times he seemed to be discussing his own way of life rather than that of those around him. 'It's only really possible to write this stuff for four hours a day, so we spend a long time getting round to it. We put it off for most of the morning, then manage an hour before noon. We stay out rather too long over lunch, come back feeling very guilty and get down to it in the afternoon. If a sketch is getting a bit conventional, somehow a pantomime horse creeps in. I never write anything on paper. I find it very inhibiting. I can't spell or punctuate, and my writing is terrible, whereas John is very good at it.

'We consciously try not to bring the same characters in too often, as it's all too easy to get in a rut and rely on the easy laugh. Just as none of us want starring roles. We all feel that too many comedians want to be loved. If you want to be loved, it's hard to make any sort of comment at all.'

Despite the increasing success of Python, John Cleese was already growing restless, in part because of the responsibility he felt towards Graham and his sense of obligation to work with him, when Cleese's original intention with Python had been to an extent to break that bond and attempt to mix things up among the team.

'The problem was you'd think the Pythons were fairly loose and relaxed,' Cleese says, 'but in fact we weren't particularly. People didn't confront each other about things they were not happy about. Graham was late for years, but no one ever really confronted him, and he was fucking up stuff, both on film and in the studio because he couldn't get it together, and I wasn't confronting it, but the other Pythons were quite happy to let me deal with the problem because I was there every day writing with him. I had tried early on to play around with the writing relationships because I thought it would have been enormous fun to split into different combinations, for example Eric and I wrote together "Sir George Head", and "Hitler in Minehead" was written by Mike and me. I was rather excited by the possibility of us writing in different combinations because I thought we would produce different material. This was during the first series, before Graham's drinking was a problem, so I was excited by the idea. Later, as Graham's drinking became more of a problem, I tried to raise the idea once or twice that we could write in different combinations, and by that time people decided that they absolutely weren't interested. I'm not sure whether they were avoiding Graham's problem, or whether they really thought it was better. But it seems to me a wasted opportunity because what we actually wrote in those different combinations, and it only happened a very small number of times, was among the best material.'

'It was probably punishment that John deserved to write with Graham and work with him,' adds Terry Gilliam, 'because I can't imagine what that was like, but maybe it was good because John was able to just babble on and do what he did, and Graham would do the nudge that would push it into something extraordinary, because John was so straight down the line and then Graham would knock it over there. But it was just always "watching" Graham. I always felt it was like watching him from a distance. What's he going to get up to now? What's he going to do now? What's going to happen there? I always had this theory that he was the portrait of Dorian Gray; no, he wasn't the portrait, he *was* Dorian Gray, and all around him there was ugliness and things getting damaged, and he just puffed his pipe.

'Sometimes I used to have theories about him being *the* most selfish in the Python group,' Gilliam continues. 'I mean, John always said of Eric that Eric gives selfishness a bad name. That was one of his best lines. We were all pissed off at Eric for something, and he said, "Eric gives selfishness a bad name." But sometimes I thought it was Graham. Maybe because it was so kept inside, but it was there. There's a smugness about a pipe-smoker that you want to just take a bottle and take their face off, it's that. Because the rest of us are sort of flailing about, but a pipe-smoker, it's just an unnatural resentment. I think pipe-smoking is a very weird thing, I mean, it completes the circle always, and it's infantile, somebody sucking on a tit the whole time, and it gives somebody such a sense of authority and seriousness and maturity. It's almost like him being castrated if his pipe was taken away. I don't know what it is, but it allowed him to be totally insular, I think.'

A few years later (in a series of interviews conducted in 1976) Graham told Ken Levy his own thoughts on the nature of the group, which inevitably led him back to his feelings towards his first chosen profession. 'We were all primarily writers really rather than performers, but it's just that we got angry with performers saying, "No, I won't do that. I refuse to do this because it's wrong for my public image," and we always thought the stuff that we wrote was rather funny. We've been lucky enough to be able to perform it ourselves. It's a thing that we just had to do because in various ways we're all angry. I suppose that's it. Actually it's an interesting thought that the bloke who first started the radio show *I'm Sorry I'll Read That Again* – he's an Australian but that's no fault of his – was a chap called Peter Titheridge, and he first got this group together on radio, and I was sacked fairly quickly, and he'd given up writing because he said, "I'm just not angry anymore, at anything," and I think a lot of the thing with writing is you have to be angry about something; you have to inject some kind of message into what you're saying, even though it's not obvious. You're not stuck for a subject if you're angry about something. That's a very important point, I think. I'm angry about almost everybody.

'I wouldn't go to a doctor who wasn't a drunkard. I really wouldn't. They're the better ones. The ones who are really out of their minds, because they know what it's like to be a human being. That's a really important thing. I know it sounds facetious, but it is important.'

John Tomiczek was now a permanent feature when Python were filming on location, with the crew instantly taking to him. 'Everybody was so kind to this strange child with his heavy Liverpool accent,' remembers Sherlock, who more often than not would absent himself from such events, as he did in many ways from Graham's increasingly active social life.

'I remember the day that he brought John to the studio,' recalls Gilliam, 'and the whole group wasn't sure whether it was a boy or a girl. He was totally androgynous and beautiful, and then John and David adopted him as a ward, but I mean he was this sort of *Death in Venice* boy; he was just beautiful. And then over the years, as Graham just kept sucking his pipe, John got fat. There was a party at Graham's house where Graham threw some people out. They came back fifteen minutes later, knocked on the door, John opened the door, and they slashed his face open. So this beautiful creature was becoming this fat, scarred . . . and Graham just sailed through life sucking on his pipe, and it was just strange. And that's what I thought the selfishness was – that other people were suffering, and Graham glided steamboat-like through life.'

Tomiczek was, however, suffering from a rare congenital heart disease, familial hyperlipidaemia, that had claimed many members of his family. 'Sufferers get severe arteriosclerosis at a very early age,' explains John Chapman, 'and die of obstructions to the blood vessels from atheromatous plaques and things like that in the coronary arteries or the cerebral arteries. Aneurysms and things like that.'

'He did get very, very fat at one time, and Graham put him on a really good diet,' adds Pam Chapman. 'It's a vicious thing. It's not as manageable as things like diabetes. It's a chronic thing that you can't actually cure.'

'Graham would certainly have been concerned about it,' resumes the elder Chapman brother, 'and insist that John had reasonable care and took sensible advice about it and took sensible measures on the advice that was given to him. It may have been that that helped to stem things off for a while, but one never knows quite what would have happened if such and such a thing hadn't happened, what the balance of probabilities is. But whether the management that he had was sufficient to prolong his life, I don't know. It may well have been, because they were taking fairly good care of him at that stage.'

Graham's care of John extended to yearly blood tests, something he insisted on for all his family, as David Sherlock recalls, 'He had always kept his contacts with the medical world and he had the most wonderful man who would come round personally and do blood tests. And this happened right the way through the Python period, and at least annually we would have a blood test as well. It was particularly important for someone who's an alkie or bordering on, as he saw it. So he continued. John Tomiczek had to have them as well, because of his health. Once they'd diagnosed what was wrong with him, they realised they had to monitor his blood, so there's two reasons for the bloke coming round, and so occasionally I'd have it done as well.'

One of the things that appealed to all of the Pythons was film. By now Graham and John had worked – with varying success – on a number of movies that had all failed to make their own personal grade, despite the presence of such performers as Peter Sellers, Peter Cook and Ringo Starr.

Much as the group had viewed film as an arena in which too many people put in too many oars, if they were ever going to be satisfied with the possibility of their work on the big screen, logic dictated that they should stick firmly to the six-strong core nucleus that had already proved itself so well on television.

However, in their first movie they made two big mistakes, both because they allowed themselves to be seduced: firstly by Victor Lownes, the head of the London Playboy club, and secondly by their desire to conquer the American market.

Lownes was a friend of Cleese at the time. Gilliam later quipped, 'He became John's best friend, which I think meant access to Playmates . . . that's the part of America John really aspires to – blondes with big tits.' Bunnies aside, Lownes conceived of the idea of taking the best of Python's TV sketches, refilming them for cinema distribution and taking just such a movie to the US, where, based on the number of college campuses alone that he perceived as being receptive to this kind of anarchic humour, the film's financial success would be guaranteed. For all of the Pythons, it was a tempting idea. Of all the post-war British comedy stars – with the exception of Sellers and, in a different arena, Frost – no one had made it across the pond. If anyone could, the Pythons could, that was certainly Lownes's thinking, and the six of them fell in line.

Thus was conceived the movie *And Now For Something Completely Different*, which, for all those concerned, was anything but. Taking ninety minutes' worth of their best material from the first and second seasons of the show, the Pythons reshot their greatest hits, largely in a disused milk dairy in Totteridge, North London.

The shoot meant early starts for all on cold October mornings in late 1970, for what was, for many of them, the thankless task of performing material that had already proven itself in front of an audience but was now being played out in front of a small, freezing camera crew.

Graham at the very least needed some fortification, and it was during the making of this movie that Graham's friends first became seriously aware of, and worried by, his level of drinking.

As with the rehearsals for the TV show, it had become common practice that Michael Palin would pick Graham up in his car to take him to the location. On one occasion during the shooting of the movie, Palin inadvertently discovered a bottle of vodka in the battered old brown suitcase Graham used to always carry with him when working. A few hours later he discovered less of the same bottle.

'It was some years before I realised that he [Graham] didn't work properly,' John Cleese offers, recalling the same event, 'because he was essentially very clever. He had a very good mind. And I think it was only slowly that I began to see how disconnected he was emotionally. But in those days male friendships in my experience were rather old-fashioned – people in brogues and sports jackets calling each other by their last names. Graham and I always laughed together, and at moments when we laughed there was a genuine contact between us, but after the moments of laughter I think there was a kind of retreat. I'm not sure when it started, but I do remember during the shooting of *And Now For Something Completely Different* we went down one day to shoot the "Upper-Class Twits" and we couldn't find a script, and Michael said, "Oh, Graham's got one, I saw him put it in the case this morning," and he went to a little suitcase that Graham used to keep things in and opened it up and took a script out and did a double take and almost blanched, and I think somebody said, "What is it?" and Michael looked at this bottle of vodka, which to my surprise was inside the case and said, "That was full this morning." My recollection is that this was about ten o'clock in the morning and there was a lot of vodka missing, and that was the first time that I realised something was going on over and above the fact that some people drink a bit too much.'

By now Graham, David and John were firmly ensconced in their house in Southwood Lane in Highgate, just a short walk into Highgate Village itself, one of the most pleasant and desirable of all of North London's small, almost self-contained communities. The house needed some work when they'd moved in, and Graham and David took to repointing and decided to paint the exterior of the house completely white, in part to hide the work they had had to do to it. It soon became known by the locals as 'the White House' – it was also known as a place that saw a large amount of traffic, much of which came from the numerous local pubs.

The domestic side of the White House was often in a state of flux, something that echoed the number of people who passed through its doors. 'Every now and then I would say, "I'm fed up doing housework; it takes up too much time,"' Sherlock remembers. 'Every now and then we'd have a blitz. Graham would also very much do his part, but as everybody does with housework, you get bored and you go back to what you're better at. So we would usually have people recommended by Marty and Loretta Feldman, who were my mentors and, to a certain extent, Graham's, but Loretta dealt with all practical things. She knew the best builders in North London, for example – she knew absolutely everybody worth knowing and said so frequently. But she was great fun and I learned a lot from her, and so we used this cleaning agency they went to, and we had a succession of extraordinary people, some of whom were persuaded to live in, because Graham said, "How much do you make in a week?" They said, and he said, "Right, I'll pay you that, and you can live here rent-free and just be." But often I found they ended up as sophisticated dog walkers. And one of our live-in people was somebody who started off as, in my case, a quick fling, then I realised he was somebody who needed a great deal of re-socialising and, since at that time Graham seemed to have lots of "pets", humanistic ones, all sorts of people who I didn't have much time for, I thought, "Sod it! We'll have this guy as a cleaner and I'll teach him." He'd got a job cleaning houses anyway, and I said we'll resocialise him, I'll teach him to read and write, stop him being too aggressive. So we took him in and we gave him one of the rooms in the house as his own, and he had his cat and his fish tank, whatever. This guy was a sort of Dave Joe Cockney thug, or that's how people saw him, but he'd had an extremely tough life. He was barely literate, and he'd got a string of kids by a gay girl who was happy to have the family but didn't want him to live with her, and we *did* resocialise him. He was the same age as Graham but emotionally very young indeed in some ways.'

Graham became a regular on the local scene, particularly favouring the Angel pub where the landlord, his wife and all the regulars knew him and knew to often expect outrageous behaviour from him.

'I knew he drank heavily,' recalls Bernard McKenna. 'I wouldn't actually say it got worse, it just regularised itself and that's how it was. I think he was very shy, and, as happens with a lot of extroverts, alcohol liberated him, it freed him up in that it let him be silly. He would go and put his dick in people's gin and tonics in pubs. Sometimes I would be fairly appalled, but then the people would go home and say, "Graham Chapman stuck his dick in my gin and tonic."'

Graham's celebrity did indeed make allowances for his outrageousness, but he was not the only like-minded soul in the village. Others soon followed suit or were attracted there by his presence, McKenna and fellow writer David Yallop (whom Graham knew from the *Doctor at Large* series) among them. The three of them once marched through the streets of Highgate, just after Liberal party leader Jeremy Thorpe had been forced from power following a controversial homosexual incident, yelling, 'Get behind Thorpe.'

Another time, Yallop and his wife Anna bolted out of the Angel completely naked and ran around the centre of the village. This was for charity, but as McKenna wryly notes, 'I think once again drink had been consumed.'

Although he too was drinking heavily and regularly, David Sherlock preferred to distance himself from this wilder side of Graham's life. 'He was an alcoholic and a workaholic. I was a morning person, he never was, not until the last years of his life when he kicked the booze. The problem expanded in those days in that somebody like Graham, who was as generous as he was always, had a huge entourage of boozing pals. Basically people from the pub who you just couldn't get rid of. I insisted that I had my own sitting room, as I called it, simply because I did not want to be part of all the rest of his crowd.'

John Tomiczek, however, was only too eager to join in, slowly moulding himself on Graham as he made his way into his feelings. In light of this Tomiczek had also begun to drink heavily, something that his medical condition should have precluded, but Graham was always one for letting people do what they thought was best for them.

Sometimes, of course, such activities would lead to things getting out of hand. When Dave Yallop, fresh from his naked dash through Highgate, ended up with a gashed lower lip, blood streaming out, he and McKenna made their way to Dr Chapman's house.

'He'd arrived at mine at about nine, ten o'clock at night and he just arrived at the door – again everyone was always dramatic in those days. I opened the door and blood was pouring from Dave's face, and I just sat him down and got this bottle of brandy and this glass, and he said, "That's nice," and I said, "No, it's for me." '

Mrs Yallop, it transpired, had sent him out into the night in his Mini on some errand. McKenna explains, 'So we went out and got into the Mini and we went up to Highgate, Southwood Lane. Dave parked the Mini, and one window of the Mini came out, and he put it on the roof, and I got out and I thought the roof was covered in ice, and I wiped it and the whole window shattered all over the street, catching Dave in the mouth. And he said, "What the fuck are you doing?"'

They found Graham and John at home, along with the

painter, appropriately named Peter Painter; all in there had had more than a few. 'We went in, and Graham took one look at Dave's face and he cleaned it and said that he needed to have it stitched. He lived near the Whittington Hospital and the Royal Free in Hampstead, but he decided we should go to Bart's. John [Tomiczek] was his driver at the time and he was drunk – everybody was drunk – but we got into this car and set off down the Holloway Road. It was an icy night . . . and we're halfway down Holloway Road and John is pissed, driving, and to avoid a coach he slammed on the brakes and we hit a traffic island, knocked the car sideways. It's now nearly twelve o'clock, and we're going down Holloway Road sideways – we're all going, "Fuck – this is it!" But John managed to bring the car under control, and I said, "Look, the police'll be here. Go down the next side road and put the lights out." And we all sat there.'

Graham sat quietly in a Zen-like way, eyes closed, repeating his somewhat selfish mantra, 'Numero uno. Numero uno.'

'Good mantra! I couldn't believe somebody had given him that! Then we got out and examined the damage, and the front side of the car had buckled in on the tyre, and so somebody said what we need is a four-foot piece of scaffolding, and one of us got out and said, "Right," and climbed over a fence. We heard an alarm go off, and he came back with this four-foot piece of scaffolding, and we tried to move the bumper back out . . . but it wasn't working; we needed something heavier. So we went down this side road, and we found a heavy metal cross-wired *Evening Standard* rubbish bin. So we got that and we're walking along, and this police car pulled up and said, "What are you doing with that?" and we said, "We're just going to fix a car. We slightly skidded and we're going to fix it." And they said, "What are you going to do with the bin afterwards?" and we said, "We're going to put it back where we found it, Officer."

He said, "OK, carry on." And we said, "Thank you, Inspector" because it turned out he was an inspector. Then another police car pulled up, they leaned out, said, "What's going on here?" and we said, "We fucking told the inspector," and they went, "OK," and they drove off. We drove back and Graham's still saying his mantra. We fixed it, took the bin back and set off for Bart's. Graham went into Accident and Emergency – with his pipe and his pint of gin. They said, "Oh yeah, that needs stitches," and they took Dave in. And me and Graham at the time were writing a "Doctor" film that never happened . . . and Graham said, "I'll show you the outpatients' area," and a Hattie Jacques-like matron appeared and said, "Oh God, I remember you as a student here," so we went back to collect Yallop, and the young student doctor who was assisting said, "Are you Graham Chapman? Weren't you president of the bar here? Did you know you can have the bar opened any time you want just by demanding it?" It was three o'clock in the morning, so Graham sent for the current president, who arrived in a kilt and no shirt. And opened up the bar – which had only closed an hour or so before, so others were still around, and Graham was ordering drinks for everybody. And I remember stealing a bike and cycling round the quad and into the building. That was an evening and a half.'

One of the other figures Chapman used to socialise with during this period was Peter Cook. It made sense of course that they should be friends: after all, they were both Cambridge graduates, had been in the Footlights, lived in the same part of North London, were generally regarded as two of the finest comedians of their era, and of course both were heavy drinkers. The relationship, established during *The Rise and Rise of Michael Rimmer*, developed significantly over the years, with Cook even coming to David Sherlock's twenty-first birthday party when the couple were still in Belsize Park, despite Cook having broken his leg and having to traverse five flights of stairs.

'In the early days I think Graham was really a bit frightened of Peter and Peter's abilities, because he was quite something,' recalls Sherlock. 'Graham was still a student when people like Cook and Moore and Bennett and Miller were all doing their thing. They were great heroes, and Peter was a great hero of Graham's and then became a friend.'

Cook was a frequent visitor to the house in Southwood Lane, often phoning up during the middle of one of Graham's late-night dinner parties and being invited round for the dessert course. Cook would promptly hop in a taxi and arrive on Chapman's doorstep shortly after.

Then again, it was a very busy house. 'It was a house where there was always lots of booze,' states Sherlock. 'Graham would like to have been thought of or referred to as a *bon viveur* and he certainly was, but of course it's quite a step being an "out man" at that time when most people weren't, plus just walking into the BBC bar, heads turn. I've been used to negative comments all my life, and luckily one gets fewer and fewer of them, but you still have to deal sometimes with total confrontation in the street, and there were a couple of times when there were incidents coming out of some little gay club at four in the morning or something. I must admit I was fairly flamboyant myself – the sixties and seventies were the height of flamboyance, and so at times we looked fairly extraordinary.'

Although drink clearly fuelled their lifestyle and certainly had an impact on their relationship, Graham did occasionally try to take a break from it. 'Graham would decide every now and then it was time to stop altogether and dry himself out and give his liver a bit of a holiday. It never lasted long,' and soon the party was rolling along again.

'We had an open relationship, which was a very sixties thing, which meant that we had other partners and we made no secret of that. I think a lot of people have probably forgotten that that was the case, so people talking about me may have a very different view of our lifestyle, but that meant also that Graham, being a shy sort of person, had to deal with a lot more than people who were, say, going home to a wife and kids, and it was a totally different lifestyle.'

Graham would sometimes repair to the Angel pub not to make an exhibition of himself but to sit quietly with a group of regulars and do *The Times* crossword. On other occasions he would taunt the odd seminal punk band who showed up at his local. 'Graham did cause a bit of a stir when he had a go at the Sex Pistols when they all turned up at the pub. He challenged them to be abusive and blasphemous and pointed at this guy and said, "Are you frightened?" And said, "Shout at this one as if you've been struck by a thunderbolt!" and they just couldn't do it!'

The majority of his socialising lifestyle, however, still included a great deal of clubbing on the gay scene, which provided many opportunities for Graham to meet other celebrities, even if he didn't always recognise them. 'Early in the seventies we went to a gay club and the table that we had booked was double-booked, and we were at the table first and then David Bowie and his dear wife, Angie, arrived at the same table, and she said to Graham, "Do you know who we are?" and Graham said, "Do you know who I am?" and I was kicking him under the table saying, "David Bowie and Angie," and he'd no idea who they were. It was wonderful and we kept our table. Anyway, some years later they were on tour in Glasgow at the same time as Bowie, and they met up and became quite good pals really, and of course then the last time they were together was on

Yellowbeard when Bowie just happened to be staying at the hotel, so they gave him a part as a shark, which was funny.'

Throughout this period Graham still managed to conceal the extent of his drinking from the majority of those around him, more than likely also from himself, although some were becoming increasingly aware of it, and more and more concerned. 'His parents would often come down to visit us, and I'd be taken out in the garden and quizzed as to how Graham was and whether he was drinking too much or not,' says Sherlock.

For his work colleagues the extent of the problem was beginning to dawn on them. 'He would have a few too many and he would probably get quite aggressive,' recollects Cleese, who had become aware that Graham's drinking began as a substitute for breakfast. 'I realised that when he came or I went up to work with him and he would drink these big grapefruit juices in the morning that had vodka in. It took me some time to realise that too. And I can't remember when it really began to affect him each and every day, but I would have said that it was during the second series . . . That's when it was quite clear to me that there was something going on, but two or three of my friends have had drinking problems, and it is the hardest thing in the world to know whether to do something, and usually you chicken out.'

Clearly Graham's dependency on drink was beginning to affect his work on camera. As well as girding his loins with a few before he went on, shots of gin or vodka would be positioned behind the sets, for Graham to grab a quick hit between set-ups.

By this time Alan Bailey was working as a doctor for the BBC and saw a good deal of Graham, although he took Graham's state of health in his stride. 'I worked for the BBC in

1972 for a year as an occupational physician,' says Bailey, 'and I saw a lot of Graham because he was always there because Python was there. So I saw a lot of him. Went to all the performances and everything. I was a supporter then in any way I could be.

'I think there's this perceived wisdom that pressure makes you drink, but it's not true. There's definitely a genetic component, there's definitely a personality component, there's definitely a component about pressures, outside pressures, and how you cope with them, because it's a coping strategy, a bad one probably.'

For Cleese, however, it was a sad sight to watch, even if he and his colleagues were unwilling to do or say anything about it, largely because they didn't really see the breadth of the situation, as Palin explains, 'I knew he was a heavy drinker, I didn't know he was an alcoholic, certainly not. I didn't know that he was an alcoholic until he gave up drinking and he told me he was an alcoholic, and I said, "I just thought you drank a lot," and he said, "No."'

'I remember in the first series how good he was as a performer,' continues Cleese. 'I'd always thought Graham was particularly a wonderful actor. In the first series if you see him doing that sketch about the father who's the playwright and the son has gone down the mine, that performance, which I think was one of the very first shows, I remember looking at him and thinking how good he was. And, as he began to drink, he got progressively less good and not only was he more confused and less focused and in a sense lazier, he also used to start having a few drinks at the bar before the show to give himself a bit of courage, and we got to a point in the third series when we did a sketch, something about a sculptor – he was sculpting me, and there was a line, which I think he'd sculpted me very well, except my nose was much too long, and I was very hesitant to criticise the sculptor, and he said, "What do you think?" and it was this perfect sculpture with this long nose, and I said to him, "Do you think . . . ?" and he got quite irritated and said, "What, what, what?" and I said, "Well, do you . . . I'm not sure from this angle," "What, what?" and I said, "Do you think the nose might be . . . ?" and he got very upset and said, "No, no, the nose is fine. What are you talking about? The nose is absolutely all right!" and I said, "Excuse me a moment," and got a little chisel and knocked about six inches off the end of the nose, so it was the proper length, and then he looked at it and said, "Oh, yes, you're right, it is better, yes," and I produced the immortal line "I may not know much about art, but I know what I like." Now I don't think that sketch ever went out, because when we were recording it in the studio, Graham couldn't get anything right. And we went again and again, and Ian MacNaughton, you could hear him upstairs going spare, because Ian was not someone who controlled his emotions that easily. And in the end we abandoned the sketch because we literally couldn't get it on tape because Graham couldn't do the lines.'

'There were certain recordings where he just couldn't get the line out,' Palin concurs, recalling the same incident, 'and there would be that awful tension – is he going to get this right? Is he going to get the next line? And when you actually look at some of the recordings you can see that slight glazed look in the eyes and a slightly weird way of talking, and all I can say is that because of Gray and his particular talent and his ability to act, he would get away with it most of the time, but not always. There was one sketch that just got abandoned, about a sculpture. Graham was the sculptor sculpting various people making outrageous errors, making their nose about ten feet long, and people would say, "Excuse me, is that . . . ?" "Ssshh, I'm doing this. You think you can do that job, you do it." A good character, but the sketch never worked.'

Graham himself recalled the incident differently in an interview with *Time Out* magazine: 'I remember one instance where the studio audience was so pleased when a particular line was got right that there was a cheer, so you had to cut that and do it again. By this time you're forgetting your lines like mad, and so then there's another cheer when you get it right.' (He added in the same interview, ' . . . Alcohol, yes. It seems to work for me.')

Although Graham's lifestyle was causing some tensions within the group, the impact of the show itself was being felt far afield. As well as representing the BBC at Montreux, they were called on to perform in such locales as Munich and Coventry. The former saw the Python team jet off to Germany for what turned out to be two hour-long specials of original material for German television, the first show having them perform the pieces in phonetic German; for the second edition they stuck to English.

For once this was an opportunity for the group to spend some time together as a whole, not just break and settle back down to their constituent parts or partnerships. Eric Idle was amazed that, after what he had always seen as fairly shoddy treatment by the BBC, they were flown out to Germany just to explore the country for writing ideas.

Among the cultural opportunities on hand was the chance to visit a Second World War concentration camp, something that Graham clearly took in his comic stride. 'They were going to show us this concentration camp memorial at Dachau, and first of all I think we were quite surprised as we drove there that Dachau was still a place where people lived – quite a nice suburb with quite pleasant houses,' says Palin. 'I think we all thought they would have changed the name because it was so notorious.'

It was a cold and rain-soaked trip and the group initially got lost, finding that when they stopped to ask directions, many of the locals would deny the camp's very existence. When they finally found it, it was closed.

'They said it closes at five,' continues Palin, 'to which Graham sort of stroked his sideburns and said, "Tell them we're Jewish," it was very naughty at the time, but just a wonderful joke.' And one that worked, as it got them admittance.

Given the opportunity Germany afforded the troupe to spend some time together, inevitably it was Graham – with partner David in tow – who would disappear the most often. He had a guidebook to the gay areas of the city and was determined to explore and experiment, often regaling the others the next morning with tales of the previous night's exploits.

'The best moments of Graham to me,' recollects Gilliam, 'were the mornings after when he would sit around and tell his tales of outrageousness.'

'We were just finding our feet socially or anti-socially and filming based in Munich with a director who was also incidentally gay,' Sherlock remembers. 'He realised we were gay after four of us came down to breakfast, rather than two, in this nice little family hotel run by an extremely Munich-style hausfrau, and she was not amused. She was deeply tight-lipped, so the director said, "I think you should go to the Deutsche Eiche," which was the German Oak, which is one of the places where Adolf and his pals used to go for drinks parties when they were actually forming the party. And it was now a gay bar with rooms and it was a funny place.

'While we enjoyed the experience, it was a most extraordinary thing for Graham to have dialect coaches every morning for German practice. The lines of course were learned parrot-fashion pretty much, because Cleese was the only one with any German and everyone else had to learn it. But Graham evolved a theory that German sentence construction is a little like Latin and because of that you can't have the subtlety of humour that you get in Britain, and therefore an awful lot of jokes are much more like banana-skin prat-fall type stuff, which of course the Romans also loved.

'It was fun and some of the locations were extraordinary. To be tramping round Bavaria through glorious settings, it was a bit like *The Sound of Music.*'

'We had time to wander round Munich,' Palin recalls, 'and we used to go to this strange club called the Why Not? and I seem to remember all the girls were men, and these British lads were quite fooled some of the time. Graham thought it was a pretty good place.'

Part of the filming took place during the Oktoberfest Beer Festival and Graham was reportedly absent for several days as he partook of the festival's delights.

'There was always something separate about Graham and myself,' Sherlock says, 'and we always had these international gay guides which would tell you where the best restaurants in town were, and quite often we found ourselves at one of these and there were these celebrities from the BBC, and whether or not it was because they'd got a guide, I doubt it, I think it was just because they knew it was a good restaurant, but as a result we found ourselves eating substantially better because we could actually get fresh vegetables, which seemed to be not very popular with most of the German restaurants we were taken to. I can remember Mike and myself commiserating over the fact that you could not get a salad for love or money, and after two weeks of filming one was dying for something fresh and green.'

Palin recalls the German experience as one of group solidarity. 'On the German show I think a good time was had by all, because we were all together and we all went out there, and I can remember having a great time and John got very silly. I remember one evening John got quite tiddly and was chatting up the wardrobe mistress, and we were having a little sort of garden do, and he leaned against this hedge and he just fell into it because it wasn't as substantial as he thought, and then later in the evening he and I went off to try and find the red-light district in Munich and it was closed! So it was a very good time, and this was usually when the group was taken out of the home context and shipped off somewhere else . . . when we came back to England, I think then that the groupings tended to split apart because people also had different kinds of friends, different projects they wanted to do.'

The Python team had all cut their teeth on the stage in revue format, but had never worked together as the team they now were in the arena of live performance. An invitation to perform in a late-night slot at an arts festival in Coventry soon changed all that and afforded Graham and the others the opportunity to find a means of taking Python to the people first hand, on what would turn out to be a global scale.

Eric Idle was instrumental in putting the show together for the Coventry Arts Theatre, mining their TV shows and previous stage work for material that would play well in a live setting. It was during this brief run that the Pythons became aware that their material was now being perceived in a rock 'n' roll kind of way – their audience weren't there to see anything new, they wanted the hits.

'I remember going to Coventry and being surprised at the inventiveness of the audience,' says Palin. 'They were dressed up, all the front rows had people with knotted handkerchiefs on their heads, and you realised that you don't really know, very often, how an audience is exactly responding to your show. You do your show, you do your programme, we're based in London, we see audience viewing figures, something like that, we get some letters, we read reviews in the paper, but they don't really give you any clue as to exactly what people are picking up on. And that day, when we got to Coventry and saw the people queuing outside and then saw them in the theatre with the knotted handkerchiefs, was something totally unexpected. The fact that they'd picked up on this particular aspect of Python and this particular character was something that the audience did for us, and we just didn't know anything like this was going to happen. And I think this was the first time that we were aware of this almost fanatical following.'

'The audience reaction to their three nights at the Coventry Festival was very exciting,' Sherlock concurs. 'It was the first time they realised that people knew every word, which was a bit scary, because if anyone forgets their lines, there's a whole front row who can prompt you immediately. So two years later when they went on tour in Britain, they were being treated like pop celebrities.'

Following their success in Coventry, Graham and some of the others took time out to meet a literary hero. 'The next day we went to visit J. B. Priestley, which was an extraordinary little outing,' Sherlock recollects. 'He was living just outside Stratford at the time, and we all turned up and went to see him. Cleese, Chapman, myself, John Tomiczek and Barry Cryer. Barry virtually invited himself to tea, and J. B. was so flummoxed and amazed that anyone should want to come and see him. It was an extraordinary thing because he was extremely shy and rather gruff, but because Graham smoked a pipe and so did Priestley, they struck up this sort of rapport, talking about the technical thing of tamping down the tobacco and what sort of mix and everything else. It broke the ice, and he relaxed and talked a little bit about the politics of the day and how he thought it was a mess. He knew who Python were, which was quite extraordinary. Graham and I later adopted the two white mice that were used on stage in the "Mousaphone" sketch. They were real mice and we actually named them after Priestley and his wife – we called them Jack and Jacquetta: Priestley's wife was Jacquetta Hawkes. The mice had quite a good life with us.'

When Monty Python subsequently toured the UK two years later – followed by Canada – it was indeed akin to a rock and roll tour. No comedy group had ever gone out on that touring circuit before, whereas nowadays it is commonplace. George Harrison opined that he felt the spirit of the Beatles had passed on to the Pythons once the Mop Tops split, and subsequently they hit the road and brought the spirit of rock and roll to the comedy tour. Modern British culture was being rewritten.

'On tour it was more interesting watching Graham,' states Terry Gilliam, 'because Graham was always having adventures, and he was the constant surprise. We were in Wales, in Cardiff, it was a very narrow backstage, and we had to get from one side of the stage to the other, and in one of the shows, Graham, I don't know if he was getting a hand job or what by some young guy backstage in the middle of the show! It was like, "GRAHAM!" '

Gilliam also recollects a moment that took place on their flight to Canada that particularly amused Graham. 'We were on the plane, and I was looking out of the window, and I said,

"Look at that! There's a great big bunch of water down there." And Graham got on to that one and was for years on that one, "a bunch of water", which at a certain point I would then start doing that all of the time just to make him feel good, that I was a fool, and I would keep inventing things. I don't know if they knew I was doing it purposely or not, but it was, again, them being performers and me not as such. It was just always this difference going on.'

It was also the fateful British/Canadian tour that, in many ways, sewed the seeds for the group's future, in that Cleese decided he had had enough, and he also decided that Graham had had too much.

As with any high-functioning drunk, Graham had got away with an awful lot. 'We just accepted Graham's condition, because that was the way it was really,' offers Palin. He had kept it together under a huge amount of strain – writing for at least three shows at any one time, juggling the egos of his fellow Pythons alongside his own and living the life of an openly gay man who really did put considerable efforts in to justifying his view of the world – by helping others (as well as himself) and by trying to break down barriers he saw as inhibiting and useless. Alcohol was his crutch – on tour it became his only mode of transportation.

The first nationwide Monty Python tour opened in Southampton, followed by Brighton, and then on to other towns round the country. It was not an auspicious occasion for Graham, who, drinking to allay his nerves, let alcohol get the better of him. For once the others, Cleese in particular, were not prepared to let Graham's behaviour go.

'The first show was in Southampton, and we had an unhappy time. Graham drank too much in order to compensate for his nerves, I think,' Palin states, going on to elaborate on how this turned into an unprecedented situation between Graham and the rest of the group: 'The only times I've ever seen a real row about performances and behaviour within the group was really when we did our stage tour and Graham was so drunk the first week he could hardly get through it,' Palin recalls, 'and I remember John gave him, publicly, a real big bollocking about that when we were in Brighton; it was just not good enough and it was selfish. And so there were dark moments then when people would get very, very upset and angry. It was done among all of us – it wouldn't have been wider than that.'

Palin noted in his diary of the time – March 1973, 'Upstairs in the restaurant, ate salad and drank champagne, there was just enough to create the feeling of occasion. Graham and Eric reached a point of explosion, and Eric threw down his napkin with a rather impetuous little flourish and left the restaurant. Later Graham, Eric and John had "full and frank discussions" at which John told Graham straight out that he had performed very badly in both shows and if he went on like this every night, there was no point in continuing on the tour. For my own part I feel that Graham's condition was the result of a colossal over-compensation for first-night nerves and he's clearly gone too far in his attempt to relax. Maybe now the first night's over he will no longer feel so afraid.'

Graham's drinking was so out of hand at this time that he would sometimes miss his cue to go on stage, with either Idle or Cleese going on in his place. Chapman was furious when this happened.

(There was indeed at times some kind of unspoken animosity between Graham and Eric, something that John Tomiczek – then attending art-school classes – picked up on in his attempts to keep Graham pleased. 'John would come home with drawings of Eric with arrows and daggers in him and show it to

Graham to approve,' says Bernard McKenna. 'And Graham would say, "It's very good – this picture of Eric with a knife through his head," because John, being very young, had misread professional frustration with hatred. Graham would say, "Eric's fucking on about this and that," but all Eric was doing was carving out his own niche in the Pythons.')

Nonetheless the tour ploughed on, Graham got his act together, and it proved to be a great success, so much so that the team decided to take their act to Canada, where the TV programme was already an established hit. It was on this trip that Cleese dropped what was surely a bombshell for the group, but more so for the more dependent Chapman. Cleese had had enough of Python and would not be back for a proposed fourth season. Given that for many he was the face (and certainly the legs) of the group, this was a potentially devastating blow, especially when it was dropped in at 30,000 feet over Calgary.

'I was very happy to do the second series, although my enthusiasm was waning a bit because I felt we were repeating ourselves, and I was not keen to do the third series. My complaint is they never listened to the reasons for my not wanting to go along with this . . . so when I finally decided that I just didn't want to be involved any more and they were just going to go ahead with the fourth series and not really hearing me at all, I said, "OK, well fine, go ahead with my blessing. Graham and I had written some material . . ." And I went off – when was it that I took that decision? I think it was on the plane to Canada that I told them.'

For Graham the loss of his writing partner was something of a blow. It was the kind of moment from which he could rise or sink. As it happens, he just meandered along, still working with McKenna on the 'Doctor' series and, in many ways, handing over the reins of Python to Jones and Palin.

'The other reason I didn't want to go on doing the television, which was hard for him,' recalls Cleese, 'was because it had taken over so much of our lives, because in addition to that was the stage shows, the records and the books, and Python was kind of ten months of the year, and that was the point when I thought to myself, "I don't want to do Python ten months of the year," so for those various reasons I remember that I summoned up the courage to leave.'

Cleese had other reasons to sever his writing partnership with the man he saw as being largely dependent on him. A recent financial investment in a gym had collapsed when the health instructor Cleese had invested in died from stomach cancer within a month of the club opening. Cleese found himself financially strapped and looked to Humphrey Barclay, among others, to offer him script work, material he chose to write alone, much to Chapman's disappointment.

'Chapman was very possessive of me, and when I needed this money because of this investment, it was rather sad actually . . . I'd paid some debts that I wasn't legally liable for, but I was morally liable for; in order to earn that money I wanted to write these shows, and I didn't want to halve the money with Chapman, because Chapman didn't provide fifty per cent of the work and I needed that money. But Graham was very cross with me that I went off and took work and wrote something without him. He kind of felt that in a sense he owned me, I think, and that I was letting him down by going off and doing it. And that was what I found oppressive about Python, the fact that some of the members at that time were trying to stifle any ordinary individual freedom in the name of the group. It was certainly true of Chapman to some extent in those days and of Terry J.; I don't think it was ever true of the other three . . . I wanted it to happen, and there was a resistance to it. Of course one of the other problems was as Graham got more and more into his alcoholism, the others wanted less and less to work with him.

'I think that Graham loved being a Python,' Cleese elaborates, 'because Graham was never in the engine room. Graham was always on the outside lobbing very good ideas and very good lines in, but he was not someone who could pick the ball up and run with it. You needed to have other people running it, then he would make a very useful contribution. So I think Graham was totally happy to be a Python and at that point not a great deal else, although he used to supplement his income by going off and joining people like Barry Cryer and Bernard McKenna and doing other sitcoms, he would fit that in. But the others, I think, once the initial excitement was over, wanted to go off and do other things. I think Michael did, I think certainly Eric did, and Terry J., who has probably done the widest range of all of us since Python became less than a full-time activity, was more in the Graham camp. I think he felt really happy when he could be basically the director, the one who stayed on at the editing sessions after everyone else had gone and because of his tremendous energy he was probably, I would have said, the most dominant figure in the creation of the programmes, and I think that he and Graham were the ones who resented it most when I said I just didn't want to do it anymore but I found it had taken my life over in a way that I hadn't anticipated. And I remember, I think, Terry referred to me as, I can't remember what the word was, but some kind of harsh word for letting the Pythons down, but I remember thinking, you know, we were just going to do television together, we weren't getting married, I remember thinking that.'

Ultimately the whole experience made Graham angry, and anger he tempered with the bottle. 'I think he was angry because the BBC thought that Cleese was Python and without

Cleese Python would not exist,' confirms Sherlock, 'and he was angry for the short-sightedness of the BBC and that Cleese had, he thought, packed up and was ready for off as soon as something got boring for him. However, of course, in the meantime as far as Graham was concerned, Cleese was more interested in chasing all sorts of commercial ventures which Graham didn't consider were artistically very meritorious at all.'

According to Palin, however, Cleese's imminent departure was something that Graham had been aware of ever since the group began their third series on the BBC. 'There became an imbalance in the amount of material, and John and Graham weren't writing quite as many absolute solid-gold class-A "bankers" as they were in the first couple of series. They did write some great stuff, but it wasn't as consistently strong as they'd done in the first one, so we all felt perhaps a little wobbly that perhaps the material wasn't as good as it should be, but we were still having great fun doing it, most of us.

'I think Graham must have been aware that it wasn't as smooth for him and John as a writing relationship in the third series as it was in the first. And I think they would probably have spent less time together. Graham always had his court, a little group of people that he hung around with anyway, and so I think a little bit of a split widened between John and Graham. I'm sure he felt upset that they weren't writing stuff quite as well as before.'

Following the Canadian tour, most of the Python team decamped for a brief sojourn in Los Angeles (to appear on *The Tonight Show*, minus Cleese, who years before had also abstained from *Cambridge Circus*'s appearance on *The Ed Sullivan Show*). Graham stayed at the Hyatt Hotel on Sunset Strip, affectionately known as the 'Riot Hyatt'. It was *the* rock and roll hotel in town, with any band that was anyone opting to stay there while on tour. Legend had it this was the hotel where Rolling Stone Keith Richards first iconically threw a television set out of a hotel window. Needless to say, such a hard-drinking environment suited Graham to a tee. He was at this time becoming something of a fixture amid a core group of rock stars, key among them being Keith Moon (whom Graham had met at a Python-related charity football match). The drummer with The Who had a reputation both for alcohol and public exuberance that made Graham look mild by comparison. 'It was all cherry bombs down the toilet from Keith Moon, etc.,' Sherlock recounts. Graham would often visit Moon in his home in Beverly Glen, and they would do old Python routines together (occasionally Peter Sellers would join them and the three would recall and enact *Goon Show* moments of yore).

Graham and Moon, now fast friends, often discussed trying to find a project to work together on, a notion that would eventually result in *Yellowbeard*, a decade later and several years after Moon had died.

Additionally Graham was often hooking up with Ringo Starr and Harry Nilsson. An acclaimed singer-songwriter, Nilsson had enjoyed a fair degree of success over the previous few years, scoring big with a cover version of Fred Neil's 'Everybody's Talking', which served as the theme to the Oscar-winning movie *Midnight Cowboy*, and with the worldwide success of the ballad 'Without You'. He knew all the right people and was also a notorious drunk. Indeed all of Graham's rock and roll friends were united by their passion for booze. Most of them would not outlive that passion, although Graham did find himself involved with Starr, Moon and Nilsson on the big screen in Nilsson's unique take on the vampire mythology 1974's *Son of Dracula*, a project for which Graham corralled the writing skills of

Cambridge graduate – and Python fan – Douglas Adams. (Graham and Adams also worked on a one-off TV special for Ringo Starr, entitled *Our Show for Ringo Starr* that unfortunately went unproduced.)

'Graham was asked by Harry Nilsson to do rewrites on his *Son of Dracula*,' Sherlock recalls. 'This was about summer of 1974. Harry had an idea and he installed an editing machine in our dining room, which was also Graham's office when it wasn't a dining room. So Graham sat in the dark the whole summer trying to dub Ringo Starr – they wanted to rewrite the ending of *Dracula*, so Graham was dubbing the voice himself, doing Ringo impressions in the dark, trying to lip-synch to already existing film, which was an extraordinary process. Sadly that project failed. However, that's an indication of some of the bizarre projects he worked on and the way in which he was prepared to work for an old pal.'

Back in London Graham continued to temper his life of excess with his genuine desire to help others. For all the examples of him sticking his privates in somebody's drink, he would also often recruit people from the pub for other reasons, counselling them in essence. However sozzled he was, he was always aware that his situation had afforded him a remarkably easy transition into his current life. He outed himself without losing his career or face and managed largely to avoid the prejudiced attitude that was still prevalent to homosexual men at the time. As well as financially aiding the launch of the *Gay News* newspaper, he would take up issues on a one-to-one basis, helping people he met who were both confused by their sexuality or overly dependent on alcohol. It's fair to say that at times he fell into both categories but was reluctant to register such things in himself, in many ways was possibly transferring his own feelings to the waifs and strays he set out to help.

'He had a huge insight into both alcohol and sexuality,' says Alan Bailey, 'and he tried to help other people, and he knew he had an alcohol problem long before he stopped drinking. We told him he did. We all had a bit of an alcohol problem in those days.'

Graham also spent time with young women dealing with unwanted pregnancies, going so far as to pay for one woman's abortion, when she could not afford it herself.

When questioned on how Graham came across these people, Sherlock succinctly replied, 'Search me! They and their boy-friends would be in the pub in Belsize Park or in Hampstead or in Highgate or wherever.'

All of these activities were of course kept extremely low key, and, despite his fame, it was still important to Graham that he lived in relative anonymity in public. 'I wander about smoking a pipe and looking fairly aloof and find that I am not recognised much. None of us are, except John. He suffers because people will keep saying, "Hey! Do your silly walk." People sometimes half recognise me and come up and talk, which is pleasant unless they start saying, "Have you heard this one?" I can't laugh artificially so I have to point out that I don't like jokes.'

'He loved the anonymity,' Sherlock concurs. 'Conversely what was exciting, I think, was going shopping, something as prosaic as going shopping in Harrods for a new cooker and meeting Una Stubbs who also happened to be looking for a cooker at the time, and this sort of mutual-admiration society or at least recognition that here were two people doing something really quite ordinary and yet wasn't it fun and also wasn't it fun to be shopping in Harrods and be able to afford a decent cooker?

'He loved to tell the story of how, when he was working with

John in Basil Street, they would go to Harrods to the juice counter, the health-food counter or whatever it was, and drink carrot juice, and in those days there was this extraordinary wheatgerm called BMax, and they were stopped outside Harrods by a vox pop group who wanted vox pops about BMax, and John Cleese said, "Oh yes, I eat BMax every morning and I sprinkle it on my cornflakes," and then suddenly choked on camera and fell backwards with a prat-fall to the ground, and Graham was with him and told me about it. Graham loved the fact that he was becoming known, but curiously lots of people did not recognise him until much later in his career, and even then he continued absolutely to do just what he wanted. He would not be restricted by so-called publicity people who said, "Oh gosh, you can't do this."'

Back at work Graham's drinking continued to be an issue and, without Cleese to rely on, the balance of the show shifted in Python's fourth and final series for the BBC. 'What happened when they did the series without me,' states Cleese, 'and I heard this, I certainly didn't observe it, because I wasn't there, but before, Jonesey and I had sort of locked horns and then the others could jump on one side or the other and balance it this way or that way. But Jonesey on his own, because he is a bit of a control freak (I mean we all were, but I would say that Jonesey and Gilliam are as control freaky as anyone, which is why they went on to become film directors), Jonesey was kind of unmatched by someone who could balance his commitment, so he probably got his way, one of the members told me, more often than was good for the show. But there was a lot of feeling about that, but also what I felt about Jonesey, because I did lock horns with him a lot, was that he could never let go. We'd decide at quarter to six – we were hoping to leave at five but there'd be an argument going on at quarter to six – Jones would finally concede that all the other people thought it was better to do it in way B and he was finally going to give up on way A. The moment you assembled the next morning, as you were making coffee, he was, "I was thinking last night, I really, really do think way A is better because . . . " and you'd be off into this thing that you thought you'd finally decided the previous evening. Chapman and I certainly used to agree on the enormous amount of time that was wasted because Terry felt intensely about everything. We all feel intensely about something, but Terry always felt intensely about everything.'

Graham did, however, try to stand his corner, although he always seemed to feel he needed someone else in that corner. One of the people he turned to during this time was Douglas Adams.

Terry Gilliam clearly remembers Adams's arrival in the once closed-shop group. 'Originally they thought of me as this interloper. That's what's so funny – years later, when Douglas Adams was helping Graham write, my attitude was like them "Who is this interloper trying to worm his way into Python?" '

Cambridge graduate Adams would work with Graham for the next few years, including some time spent co-authoring Graham's book *A Liar's Autobiography* (an on-off project for Graham begun in 1976, published four years later), before throwing in the towel and admitting he could no longer keep up with Graham's drink-imposed work schedule. He formally severed the relationship in a letter stating, 'Our phone seems to be not working at the moment due to a little misunderstanding with the Post Office, and, as it won't be working again until tomorrow, I thought I'd drop you a line instead. I gather from Jill that once again you feel unable to work for the rest of this week. This situation had been carrying on for so long now and

David Sherlock on the beach in Ibiza, soon after he met Graham.

David Sherlock back in Ibiza in 1971, where he and Graham always had a good time.

raham catching some un.

Graham is a picture of boredom as he works on *A Liar's Autobiography*.

John Tomiczek, Graham's young friend who moved in with him and David Sherlock.

A now sober Graham and Terry Jones take a break during the filming of *Life of Brian*.

Graham as Brian.

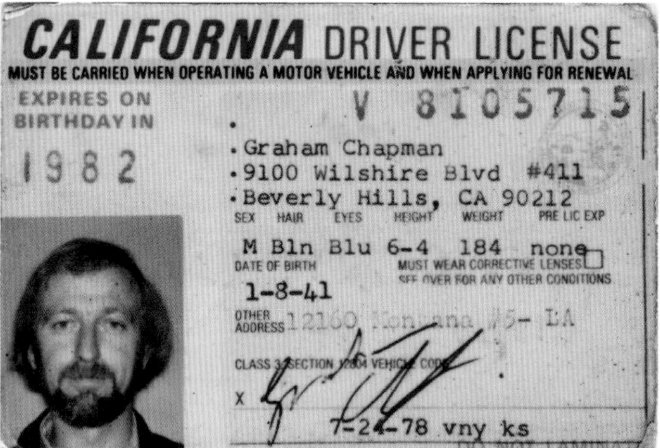

CALIFORNIA DRIVER LICENSE
MUST BE CARRIED WHEN OPERATING A MOTOR VEHICLE AND WHEN APPLYING FOR RENEWAL

EXPIRES ON BIRTHDAY IN 1982

V 8105715

Graham Chapman
9100 Wilshire Blvd #411
Beverly Hills, CA 90212

SEX	HAIR	EYES	HEIGHT	WEIGHT	PRE LIC EXP
M	Bln	Blu	6-4	184	none

DATE OF BIRTH 1-8-41

MUST WEAR CORRECTIVE LENSES ☐
SEE OVER FOR ANY OTHER CONDITIONS

OTHER ADDRESS 12160 Mon ana #5- LA

CLASS 3 SECTION VEHICLE CODE

X

7-24-78 vny ks

Enjoying the life in Los Angeles, where Graham moved to get away from taxes and his old drinking haunts, and to experience a very different lifestyle.

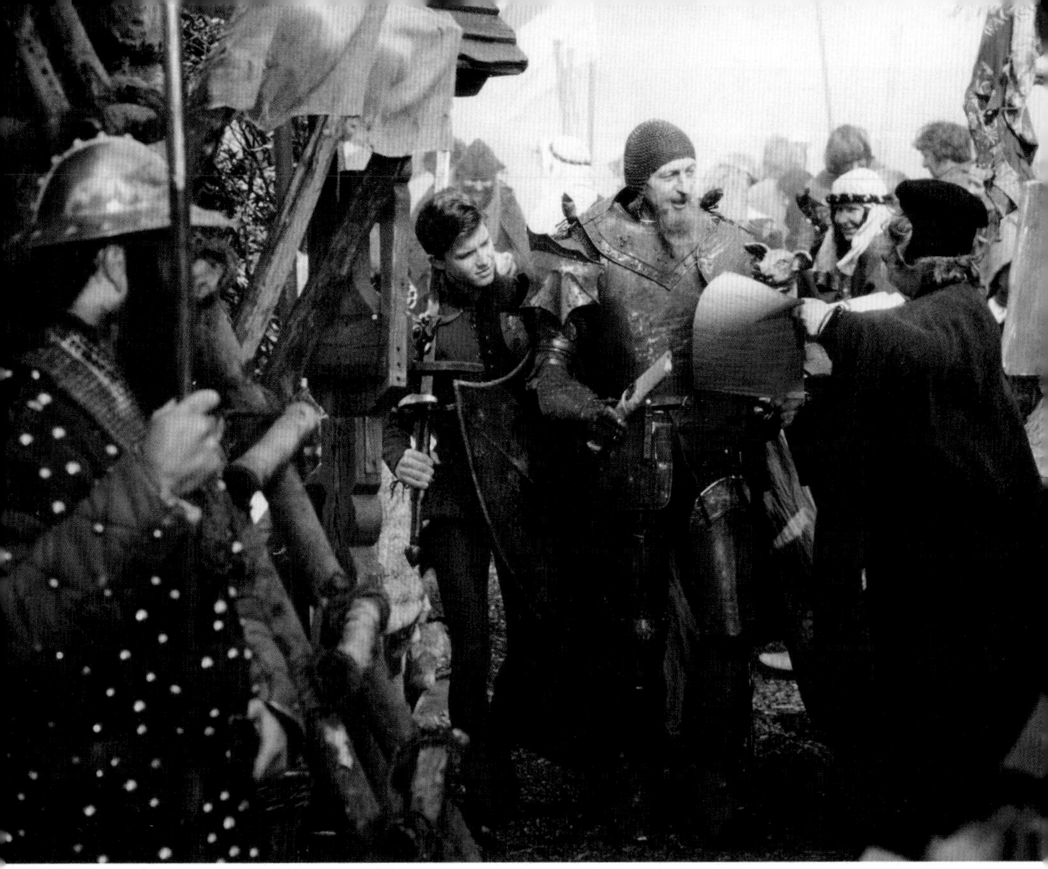

Graham in action during the filming of *Jake's Journey*.

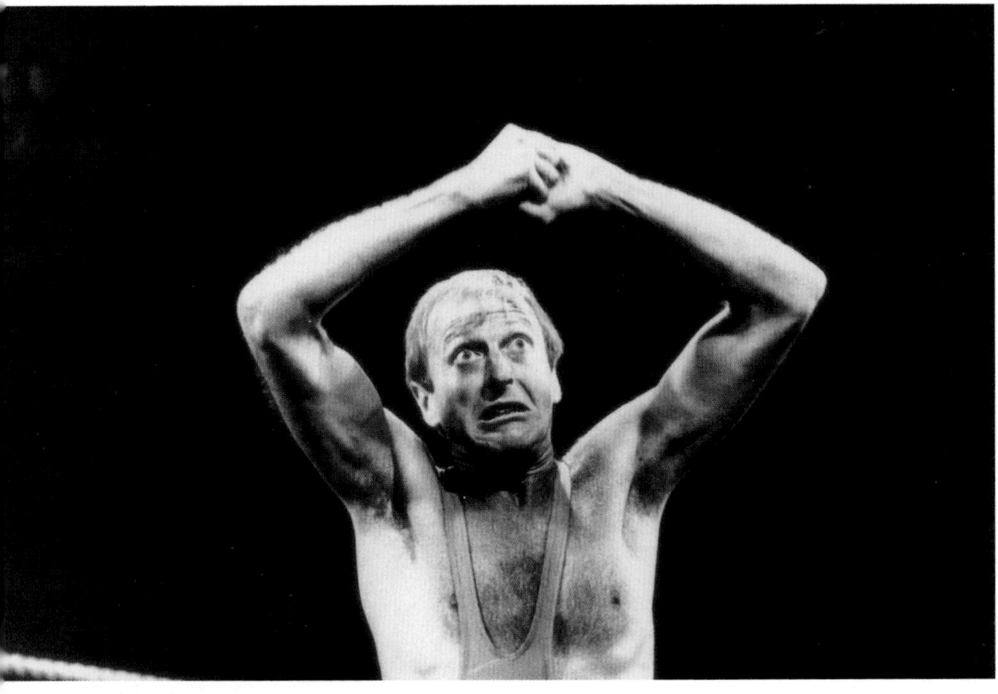

HUMPHREY BARCLAY

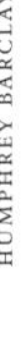

One-man wrestling, as developed by Graham.

COLIN C PRIOR

John Cleese, Graham and Michael Palin during a break in the filming of *The Meaning of Life*.

Graham returns to his medical roots in *The Meaning of Life*.

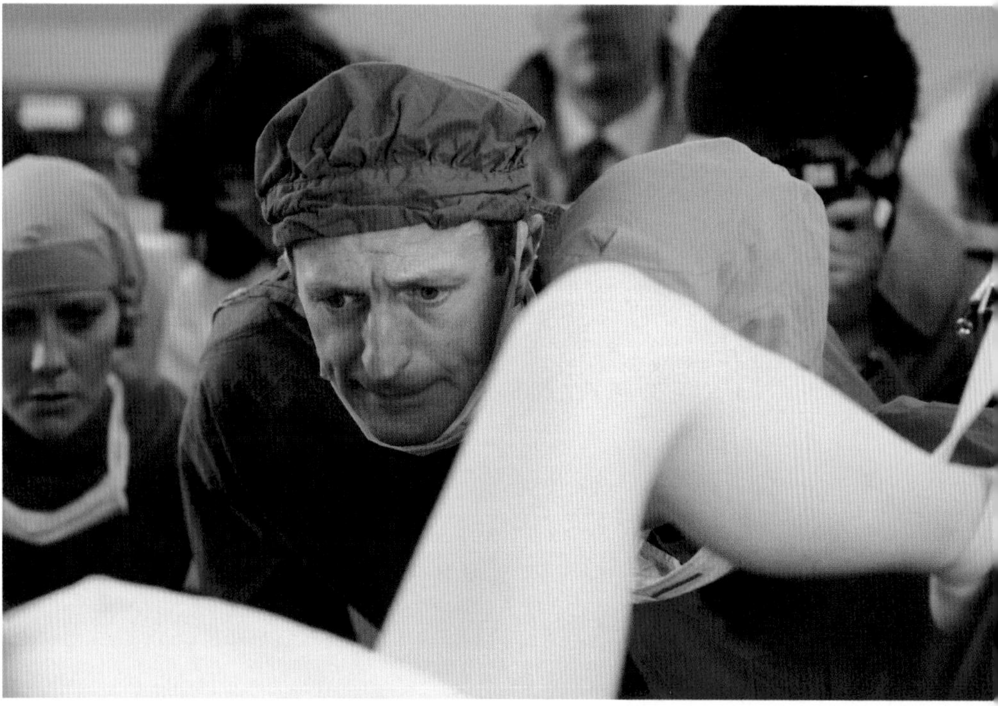

PYTHON (MONTY) PICTURES

Graham goes riding on the snow at St Moritz as part of his link with the Dangerous Sports Club.

Raising money for the Maidstone Hospice in 1988, where Graham would eventually die less than two years later.

Mountaineering was one of Graham's passions.

John Tomiczek, Graham and David Sherlock at home together in the late 1980s.

The last photo taken of Graham, in his house in Maidstone, before his death on 4 October 1989.

so very little has actually been achieved that I can only assume that the book project comes very low down on your priority list. Since it has become totally impossible for me to believe you when you say we'll start tomorrow or we'll start next week or at any time at all, I've had to commit myself to a job that I couldn't afford to turn down, which strangely enough involves guarding members of an Arab royal family for about sixty hours a week for the next two months. I'll have the occasional day off, which I will be prepared to spend getting raw material down on tape with you, which I can then work over at home. If that doesn't suit you, then it'll have to wait till September – I know that's late, but I've been ready and willing to work for a very long time and nothing's got done. At the same time I'm trying to launch my own career and the constant frustration and anti-climax of endless cancelled or wasted days makes this very difficult to concentrate on . . . '

Having opted to become a bodyguard for an oil-rich Arab family, Adams did go on to launch his own career, penning *The Hitchhiker's Guide to the Galaxy* for radio, print and just about any media going. (The big-budget movie version was released in 2005.)

Graham meanwhile tinkered away at the book, co-opting whoever happened to be around, including David Sherlock, who recalls their mutual typist, another indication of Graham's life-long trust in the police, inspired by his father and his growing up. 'We found a typist who was available to decipher my scrawl; as we were working on other sections we would bring it through to her, and she was a wonderful woman who worked for Kilburn Police Station, and we said, "Some of this stuff's a bit racy, you may find it a bit difficult." She said, "When you've typed up what I've had to type up and you've seen what I've seen, nothing shocks you," and she was such a prim and proper lady that we were a little worried by that, but she was actually wonderful.'

Graham's drinking was still if not escalating, then certainly constant. Following Cleese's public admonishment of him back on tour in Brighton, everyone else seemed reluctant to confront him over it. Except one.

'The one person who had the guts to say something was Humphrey Barclay,' Sherlock recalls, 'who was working at the BBC at the time on something else and mentioned it to Alan Bailey, who of course he knew slightly anyway from doing revues at Bart's Hospital, and he mentioned it, he said he thought Graham was drinking too much and could he do something. Alan sat Graham down and talked to him about it, and Graham absolutely hit the roof and said, "Nobody tells me what I should and shouldn't do. I'm a doctor myself and I know, I'll deal with it." And it caused quite a lot of friction. But the others sort of would say something, but it was nearly always a comment to somebody else and not directly to Graham.'

Ironically, as Python appeared to be breaking apart, the show which could easily have been labelled anti-establishment (or at the very least designed to lampoon the establishment) found itself and its constituent members held together by business. Early on the group had formed Python Productions in an attempt to control their destiny outside of the BBC. All had previously worked for commercial television and/or movies, so their view of the BBC as being all-powerful and in control of their destiny was wisely never an issue for the Pythons. Consequently whenever they toured, produced albums (that were slowly finding them a following in the US) or books such as the blue-covered *Monty Python's Big Red Book* or *The Brand*

New Monty Python Papperbok – both huge bestsellers in the UK – the income came directly to them and their company and was split equally six ways. In fact these offshoots – the very elements that Cleese resented as helping take up ten months of his year – were earning the Pythons more money than their TV series, which had now come to a close.

Invariably the team would regroup for regular business meetings to divide up royalties (sometimes as little as a £19 cheque each for album sales) and discuss offers and the future. Graham would often turn up late and, as Palin noted, 'fortified', and then argue against the others in favour of making an appearance on *The Russell Harty Show*, Harty himself at the time being a closeted gay Northerner.

However, this ongoing business side did afford Graham the opportunity to continue his working relationship with Cleese, as Palin's diary entry states, 'G. C. and J. C . . . gave out cheques for £800 each from Charisma, advance from the LP made last May. But as soon as we got to point one: General – what is planned for the year? the gloom set in again. No universal consensus on anything. John has a full year of writing but is prepared, indeed rather anxious, to supply material for a book. There was a glimmer of pleasure for Graham Chapman when John agreed they should write together on the book.'

In late 1973 there came the offer of doing an extended run of the stage show at the Rainbow Theatre in North London, a very rock-and-roll venue that would have cemented that side of their appeal to their audience. Instead, and against the wishes of some, it was decided to stage a protracted run at the Comedy Theatre in Drury Lane.

'There's a discussion about Michael Codron's offer of six weeks starting at Christmas in the Comedy Theatre,' Palin's contemporary diary recounts. 'Eric and John are very keen.

Terry G. less keen, myself very anti. For some reason I find myself in the rare position of being out on my own, although Terry J., I think, feels the same but is keeping tactfully quiet to avoid accusations of a blocked vote. Briefly I see it as six more weeks of a show which I find very dull, and here we are going to the West End, forsaking our Rainbow pop following, which John says "scares the shit out of me", for the £2.50 circle and front-stalls audience with a show that seems to be full of old material, some of it done in the West End before. What's become of Python the innovator? Graham arrives, I think a little fortified, and from the stage show the talk goes on to accounts, blah, blah, blah . . . '

Having recently apparently left the team, Cleese was already back in the fold, working towards their live show in Drury Lane. The show once again proved to be a huge success artistically, even if for Chapman it was further evidence of his decline and his increasing inability to handle himself and his work, which resulted – once again – in the occasional missed cue and culminated in him knocking himself unconscious one night before his famed one-man wrestling routine.

'They were doing the show live at Drury Lane,' Sherlock recounts, 'and Graham actually knocked himself out, and I was dressing at the Opera House and I would put the first act of the ballet on, then run all the way from the Opera House – they had no idea I was moonlighting – into the stage door at Drury Lane, get Graham out of his first-act costume and into his second, his second being the wrestling match, and he knocked himself out and came offstage.'

The Drury Lane run, however, was a huge success, despite Graham's occasional unconscious moment. To those around him, Graham appeared to be keeping everything together – and indeed he was. He was a fit young man, holding his own and holding whatever it was he chose to imbibe. Yes, there were moments, but everyone around him was prepared to forgive such moments. They were, after all, the moments one would attribute to a young man about town, with a certain degree of fame and a certain degree of wealth to back it up. There was almost a gauche nobility to it all in a post-sixties world, a hedonist who could still walk the walk (even if when he talked the talk it might be slightly slurred).

His immediate family were aware of a certain degree of his excesses, but that's all they were. Nothing much to worry about.

'He would always turn up late,' recalls his elder brother, John, of family gatherings, Christmas and the like. 'He'd usually go to the pub in the village beforehand and then come down.'

'But he was a young guy and that's what young guys do,' adds John's wife, Pam.

'I was aware that he liked a good drink,' says his brother, 'and, like me, he was capable of being a bit indiscreet from time to time and going a bit over the top, but not that it was a daily problem, as it were.'

'Drink helped him to open out and relax a bit,' Graham's sister-in-law elaborates. 'But he'd be very capable of coming here. He'd perhaps be only here for three or four hours, and half of that time he'd have his head in a book or newspaper and not be communicating with anyone. He was shy. It came over as shyness, being reserved. Also he got on very well with our children. He loved them. He was very capable of communicating at their level . . . They all idolised him of course, having an uncle who's on television. And he was extremely generous with presents. His Christmas presents were just amazing, like a washing machine for me, that sort of thing. He was aware of what we needed as a struggling young family and he would come up with things like that. Yes, he was very, very generous and very sensitive too.'

Late in 1973 Graham was offered a shot at redemption. It was a chance to keep the ethos of Python alive, another chance to write with his closest of partners, John Cleese. It was a chance for them to exorcise the demons of past movie excursions he and John had made together and finally to get it right. Monty Python were going to make a movie. Graham was going to become the King of the Britons. They were searching for the Holy Grail. All Graham had to do was keep it together.

Chapter Seven

It's a cinema in Leicester Square, London, in March 1975. One of the Goons' few forays into film, a surreal short, 1956's *The Case of the Mukkinese Battle-Horn* is playing. The audience is laughing at this well-chosen supporting feature, all dressed up and eagerly anticipating the main attraction – the premiere of a major new British comedy movie. All except one man in the middle of the crowd, who is unexpectedly making rather a lot of noise. It is Graham Chapman, star of the upcoming feature, *Monty Python and the Holy Grail*, and he is freaking out. Loudly and noticeably. Maybe it's the amount he's been drinking, maybe it's the fact that he's sitting there about to be compared with his comedy idols, the Goons. Or maybe it's the fact that it is slowly dawning on him that he has the lead role in the film about to unspool. The weight is in many ways on his shoulders. If he fucks up – and he has come to realise that on occasion he is more than capable of fucking up – he will have let everyone down. It will be his responsibility. He is not taking this thought well. But no one seems prepared to deal with him, they are trying to ignore him, hoping he will go away, or maybe even just pass out.

'One of the most frightening moments for me was the opening of *Holy Grail*. Graham completely lost it and started to gibber at the screen during the gala premiere,' his partner,

Sherlock, also in attendance, recollects, 'and his agents just looked along the row at me and hissed, "Can't you do something?" A whole bloody cinema, and everyone at this time is going, "Ssshh!" and Graham's saying, "Argh, urghh, fucking hate this film!" and so on. This is one of those public moments which is one of the worst-nightmare scenarios to be in. Nobody else moved to help Graham or do anything, they just pointed a finger and left it to me. My fault. Myself, John Tomiczek and Graham were in the middle of a whole load of extremely important people and we were in the middle of this row and Graham just flipped. They were showing the Goons' short, which was not a good idea before the screening of the Python film. But of course they had mortgaged their houses to the hilt; it was the scariest thing, and Graham realised only at that moment when he got into the cinema how fearful he was and it was all resting on his shoulders. He is King Arthur, all the others had said, "Oh no, we want all these little wacky character roles, we don't want that role," and I don't know whether any of them had seriously thought that whoever plays this role has got to carry the movie, and that's the moment when Graham realised. It was absolute panic, and that's where the alcohol came in, that's why he had secretly had so much, and nobody had been aware. John Tomiczek had no patience with Graham in this situation and said, "If you don't slow down and quieten down, I'm going," and so he left, and Graham got worse, and everyone around us got worse.'

In the end it was down to Graham's ex-girlfriend, Lesley Davies-Dawson. 'I went and got Lesley Davies-Dawson, who was sitting on the back row with her new husband and was the only person I could think of who he'd respond to. I said, "I can't handle this, I don't know what to do." She said, "I do," and dragged him off to the bar.'

Here, the recently married Davies-Dawson set Graham up with a large gin and tonic and made him down it in one. Then she got in a few more rounds, each time unbeknown to Graham lowering the amount of gin and increasing the amount of tonic. Graham was ready to rejoin the crowded premiere for the last two minutes of the movie and its final battle scene. He was relieved, however, to hear the applause and realise that the Monty Python team had made the movie they had set out to make.

'That was when I really knew we were dealing with alcoholism in the raw,' says Sherlock, 'and that I was on my own.'

Afterwards Graham went back to Highgate where he got the landlord of the Angel pub – who had been in attendance – to open up the pub so he could placate his nerves (and those of the people around him) even further.

The Python team had wanted to crack the movie market almost from their inception, *And Now For Something Completely Different* only proving to them that using their television material was not the way to go. They were confounded by narrative, but in the retelling of the story of King Arthur and his Knights of the Round Table, they hit upon a formula that worked for them, although it took them some time. Originally the movie was set equally in Arthurian times and modern day, much of the modern-day material having been penned by Graham and Cleese, involving scenes set in the huge department store Harrods in Knightsbridge, which Cleese had lived near in the late sixties. It was Terry Jones, now a noted historian, who suggested they all but abandon the modern-day material and focus on the time of King Arthur.

'*And Now For Something Completely Different* hadn't done that well,' Jones recalls. 'John had wanted to do that because he thought he was going to make a lot of money and, when he didn't, he was less keen on doing another film. I was very keen to do a film, and eventually we persuaded John that we should think about a movie. Then we sat there to talk about what it should be and Mike had got this beginning of King Arthur and his apprentice Patsy doing coconuts. We all suddenly thought, "That's a funny image and why don't we do a thing about King Arthur?" And so we all went off and started writing King Arthur. I went off and tried to do a bit of reading – Arthurian legends and things. Then we came back with various bits, and in the first screenplay there was a lot of this stuff set in Harrods and modern day, which John had written. I was a bit disappointed, so I said, "Let's do it for real and do a real Arthurian legend." That's partly because I was into the Middle Ages, but I said it won't be what's expected of us. The thing we've got at the moment is more like what you expect; it's a sketch show, and it would be much more interesting to do a narrative thing and keep it in the Middle Ages. To my surprise, people agreed.'

It was this inspired idea that led the team to write of their search for the Holy Grail. Although the film was conceived as a fully functioning narrative tale, its structure allowed the group to function as they always had – in that individual teams broke off to write their own parts. Each knight was given his own segment and adventure, which were then woven together, so each section of the film was written as if the team were still writing sketches, just linked by a unifying theme. These were then corralled into a screenplay, which was to be shepherded to the screen by co-directors Terry Jones and Terry Gilliam, both men eager to move behind the camera and assert some degree of creative control, if not creative harmony.

For Graham it was an opportunity to exert his ambitious side, something he generally downplayed in the presence of others, but something at least one of his writing partners was aware of. 'He loved to be able to say, "I've just written this,"' says Bernard McKenna. 'He loved the arrival rather than the journey. The journey was always very painful. Cleese rang me once and asked me, "How do you work with Chapman?" because he was having problems with him writing Python. And I would say we book it in – like "Monday, ten o'clock." Then Graham would say, "Got to finish at one because Cleese is coming round." So I'd get two hours and have to go. Cleese never went to the pub and drank and I suppose I did . . . I think he just loved to line it all up and say, "I've written this, I've written that, I've done this, I've done that . . . "'

The Pythons' notion of debunking Arthurian mythology was financed in a most unusual way. As well as investing their own money – which in some cases involved remortgaging their houses – the Pythons cemented their relationship with the rock and roll fraternity by having the likes of Led Zeppelin, Pink Floyd and Elton John chip in to finance their film, which came to the then whopping sum of £229,575. (Admittedly at this time in England income tax for the very rich – i.e. rock stars – was somewhere in the region of ninety-three per cent, so most of them invested as a tax dodge, fully expecting the film to die a death at the box office. They were pleasantly surprised by its success. Graham would later return the favour to at least one of the bands when he compèred Pink Floyd's show at Knebworth in 1975.)

'I don't remember much about writing,' Terry Gilliam says. 'I just remember there was this whole scene in Harrods that John and Graham wrote and that's gone. That scene in Harrods may have been the first thing that got us on to the medieval thing, because ideas were just being thrown around, ideas were being dredged up from the bottom of drawers, old material: "Oh God, what can we do?" Everybody did their research and started writing funny sketches. And then we started stitching them together, so it looked like there was a story there, but luckily the structure allowed for it – the gathering of the knights; we get them together, then we split them up and we have to get them back together. This is a perfect vehicle for sketches.' It perhaps wasn't as easy for six to draw together a narrative structure.

The lack of a vast amount of funds led the group to come up with inspired ideas as to how to make an epic movie on a relatively minuscule budget. Much of the writing took place during the Drury Lane run, with daytimes devoted to the movie and night-times devoted to the theatre. One of the first ideas that set the tone for the film was the realisation that they couldn't afford horses for the knights – hence the use of coconuts to replicate the sound of hooves. 'The coconut gag was the original gag that sparked the whole thing off,' states Jones. 'We did talk about having horses at one point and then we quickly dismissed it, because we thought it would be funnier not to and because we couldn't afford horses anyway.'

'There was an awareness that we were going into new territory,' Cleese recalls of the writing period, 'but I don't think we knew a great deal about how to do it. I really don't. One of the problems is this: if you're trying to write you can write easily with two people; it is possible to write with three; it is impossible to write with four. If you have four people in the room, there will always be one of the four who doesn't like the latest suggestions. It's strange but that's just the way it is. When you're doing a movie you really need to craft a central story, and if two of us had gone off to craft the story, it might have been better. As it was, the story was crafted by the six of us in the room; it was therefore harder to find agreement. If you add to that the fact none of us had really written movies before and we didn't really know anything about story and that kind of thing, then it was very much a question of just putting together a lot of sketches and trying to make a story out of them, rather than starting from the story and working out from that. And it worked really quite well in *The Holy Grail*.'

'It quite skilfully managed to combine sketches into a narrative story,' concurs Palin, 'but I think what really worked was that the events in the story could be broken down into an old university-revue format – ten sketches and three songs – and we also managed to join them together rather well. There were little bits of sealant that kept the narrative watertight, but in fact it was all a bit of a con. It wasn't really a story in which everything began at the beginning and ended at the end, it went off in all sorts of different directions and everyone had their adventure, which is very much like the Arthurian legends. The way they were written, after everyone had their little adventure, they all went back to the table and talked and then went on to the next adventure. So it suited Python really very well.'

'I was very intrigued by the idea of us starting to try and work in film,' recounts Cleese. 'I didn't understand film. It's amazing, if you look at the first draft of *Grail*, how little of that appears in the movie – it's about ten per cent of the first draft. But I remember Mike and Terry reading out the coconuts thing, which gave us a key to a certain approach of how to do it.'

Despite his occasional lapses of responsibility, it was decided early on that Graham would take on the lead role – perhaps this was a nod to the others' respect for him as a performer, or perhaps it was because they wanted to take several smaller, but funnier, roles for themselves, it holding true that certain members of the team write characters with a view to playing them.

'It's hard to remember why Graham got the lead,' states Palin. 'I'm not sure that anybody else particularly wanted to do Arthur because it was a very straight part, not a lot of laughs. I think Graham volunteered. He had that dignity and this wonderful saintly long-suffering look. I think also it was quite a selfless thing to do because it cut you out of a lot of other sketches. Otherwise casting was determined mainly by who'd written what.'

'Just as Graham would have played Arthur better than I would have done,' Cleese continues, 'I would have done the Black Knight better than Michael would have done. If you write something, I believe you probably have a deeper understanding of it than someone who comes to it from scratch. I think it was obvious that Michael, Eric and I would probably get most of the laughs and King Arthur was a slightly straighter character around whom the insanities occurred. It was just so obvious that it would be Graham that I'm not so sure there was ever much doubt about it.'

Directors Gilliam and Jones spent two weeks scouting locations and settled on Scotland. 'Once we decided it was going to be about King Arthur and the Grail, it seemed the perfect vehicle,' argues Gilliam. 'You gather the knights together and you've got a structure that most people can understand: a quest. Terry and I were great medievalists and couldn't wait to get in there. What was interesting about the start of the movie was how traditional we wanted to be. We wanted to make real movies, not Python movies, not the crap that we did. *Real* movies. If we'd had the money we would have had real horses. What was wonderful was the limitations put on us by the budget. We couldn't do all those things so we had to get clever and thank God, because the coconuts saved our ass. We would never have got through that movie with real horses. It makes a wonderful leap because with that opening shot you accept the kind of lunatic logic that's there. Arthur is incredibly serious, never a blink, and then in the background you've got all this stuff going on.'

Despite some problems with castles not being made available for filming, the troupe descended on Scotland in mid-1974 for six weeks of what proved to be gruelling principal photography. Graham had contemplated staying sober for the run of the film, an idea he quickly abandoned, as Gilliam recalls of day one of shooting: 'Graham was a drunken sot! He couldn't say his lines as Arthur. He'd get through a sentence and then he'd blank out, that's what was going on with Graham. This great, dignified character is actually blotto and he's struggling to get through his lines.'

On that first day on location in Glen Coe, Graham – as Arthur – was requested to run across a rope bridge that had been built for the production by mountaineer Hamish McInnes. 'Graham was a mountaineer,' Gilliam continues. 'He became a member of the Dangerous Sports Club; he was all of these things. We come to do the Bridge of Death and he couldn't go across it. He froze. He just completely froze. So Gerry Harrison, the assistant director, had to put on his costume and double as Graham going across. What's so funny is that you're up somewhere on a mountain and all the truth suddenly comes out – Terry and I don't know how to direct and Graham can't go across a bridge!'

Palin also recalled the first day of filming: 'We were all in chain mail and we were driving up into the great grandeur of the Pass of Glen Coe in our van dressed as these knights. I can just remember people going by on the other side of the road, because it's quite a tourist spot, and just doing *the* biggest double takes of all time; necks would snap as they saw these knights driving their Ford transit van up Glen Coe. And then of course it was a tricky morning, because Graham was very uncomfortable up there on the side of the mountain, and it was the crown and the chain mail and all that sort of stuff, and it took an awful long time just to get the shots done, and I remember thinking, "Graham's a mountaineer, he's always on about climbing, and here he seemed to be stricken with terror," and I think it was dear old Gray with first-day nerves and he'd probably drunk a bit before he'd started, I don't know what had happened.'

'Graham had been our adviser on mountaineering and everything because he used to go off mountaineering,' Jones later admitted. 'We were going to shoot this, but Graham just wouldn't go near the edge and was shaking from head to foot. He was in a terrible state. I couldn't understand it, I thought he was afraid of heights: "That's not like him; he's supposed to be the mountaineer!" It was only later that I realised that he was getting the shakes; he'd taken himself off alcohol in order to play King Arthur and that was when I first realised this about him.'

Graham later admitted to suffering from the DTs on that first day. He was acutely aware that he was letting himself down and his friends, and in some way he would later claim that this was the moment when he resolved to give up drinking, although it would be several years before he made good on that promise to himself.

'Our first day's shooting was high up in the Pass of Glen Coe,' Graham recalled in a magazine interview at the time. 'Hamish McInnes, the mountaineer, had built a rickety rope and plank bridge, "The Bridge of Death", over a seventy-foot chasm no less! The last shot of the day was to be me in full armour, dashing across. I was tired, cold and shivering with fear and I chickened out. The assistant director did it for me.

'Nice and early next morning,' Graham continued, 'I had to kneel and pray while they threw a dead sheep at me. Now this sheep had been dead three weeks, and although disembowelled, the stench from the carcass was nauseous. By the fourth take I was retching in shot. Then I had to run up some castle steps while they threw mock human ordure at me from the battlements. It wasn't real, but it was very cold and very unpleasant indeed. It was at that point I decided I really didn't want to do the film at all.'

Not that problems early on were solely to do with Graham and his performance. 'The first day, the first shot, we're up on this side of the bridge,' recounts Jones, 'and not only was Graham having the heebie-jeebies and wasn't able to go anywhere near the edge, but also the camera on the first shot sheared its gears and so, suddenly, when the cameraman opened the camera, all the cogs fell out! We only had the one synch-camera, so Terry and I went through what else we had to do and the only stuff we could shoot mute was on the other side of the gorge. We tried to work out what we could do, but there was nothing really we could do on the side that we were on, and to get to the other side of the gorge it was an hour's walk all the way round. I was trying to persuade people to go across the bridge so that we could actually keep shooting and people wouldn't. I don't blame them, with equipment, but even if just the cast had gone across, we could have started rehearsing or something over the other side. In the end we all had to jog around the long way.'

'On my very first directorial shot the camera breaks!' adds Gilliam. 'So what do we do? We do all the wrong things. We somehow manage to get another camera going and we shoot close-ups, which we could shoot in anybody's back garden. We're standing in the most magnificent scenery and we're doing close-ups. It was just madness. But we learned how to make a film in a very short time.

'At the end of the first few days,' Gilliam continues, 'Terry and I are just trying to keep this thing together. Graham got drunk and was just howling at us about how useless we were and what assholes we were, useless fucking wankers, whereas Ian MacNaughton (Python TV director) – he knows how to do things. Once again Graham wasn't exactly right.'

'I was going round and my motto was "Don't panic",' adds Jones. 'This is before *The Hitchhiker's Guide to the Galaxy*. Everybody was in this suppressed state of panic, all of us. We'd chosen this location which in retrospect was crazy, although when you go and look at the place now, it doesn't look very far from the road, but you can't get the equipment up to the point where you're shooting, so we had to carry it and it was half an hour's hike. So it was a crazy place to be filming.'

'The two Terrys – that particular relationship didn't work,' adds Palin. 'It wasn't a particularly good way of making the film, because if someone had a criticism, they would play one director off against the other and say, "Well, Terry would never have asked us to do that." And because they were both called Terry it didn't help either.'

Graham wasn't the only one to express reservations about the filming of *Holy Grail*. Given the wet, oppressive weather, the extremely tight budget (that saw the Pythons hiring locals and visitors to double as extras for a pittance per day) and the increasing animosity between the two directors, both of whom had very clear ideas of what they wanted to do, even if the other one didn't agree, the rest of the cast and crew felt initially that they'd signed on for what might well end up being a huge disaster. It didn't help that they weren't able to view 'dailies' (the footage shot the previous day), as the film had to be sent away to be processed and took nearly a week to come back. Sensing this among the crowd during that first week, Graham threw a small party in the hotel bar, the drinks were on him, and everyone suitably relaxed, a mood that was buoyed even further the next night when the first set of dailies finally arrived. They were screened in a converted hall, and everyone could finally get a sense of what they were making. The two events combined cemented those making this movie into a team that really wanted to see the Pythons succeed.

Not that it was plain sailing after that, Graham admitting later that he had no idea what he had left himself open to. 'The appalling thing is we never think we're actually going to have to *do* these things when we are writing.'

Now that the crew had seen at least part of the result of the work being done, the filming proceeded with good will, something that Graham took to heart, as Palin's diary of the time reveals: 'Graham ended up being seduced by an Aberdeen gentleman on a fishing holiday. Graham resisted evidently but was well pissed and woke me about one o'clock, banging on my door, saying he was Ethel de Keyser. On Monday night he woke me again, and just after I'd dropped off I heard him in his room saying he was Betty Marsden very loudly in a variety of silly ways. On Tuesday night, however, he was kind enough to be content with putting a note under my door with "Best wishes, Betty Marsden" written on it . . . '

Yet slowly but surely, a real performance began to emerge from Graham. His innate ability as a performer came to the fore, and though he was rarely sober, he delivered one of the most accomplished – and more importantly, sustained – performances of his Python career. He was the crucial centre that was needed to elevate the film from the ranks of sketch comedy writ large.

'The thing was we were so pissed off for so long about his drinking and his fumbling performances,' Gilliam concurs, 'but he was a truly brilliant performer, if you look at the stuff when he was on form, and I mean the idea of him playing Arthur was such a brilliant idea because it was such an unlikely idea in a strange way because it was like, "Well, he'll be the straight man," and nobody else could have done it and so we suddenly realised we had our leading man in Graham.'

Within a matter of weeks shooting on *Monty Python and the Holy Grail* was complete. The Python boys had made a movie that they considered to be a 'proper' one. Palin recalled the end of shooting in his diary entry on 1 June 1974: 'Got the sleeper to King's Cross. I'm almost too tired to fully enjoy the elation at the end of the day when the filming, or my part of it anyway, is completed. Want to leap up and down, but can't, so just stand there looking out over the Scottish hills all grey and dusky and hazy as evening falls and feel wonderfully free. That night, back at the hotel, have a drink with Tommy Raeburn, other chippies and drivers – hard men of films, who nevertheless reckon the chances of the film's success to be very good. Roy, the art director, says he wished he had money in it. There's a warm and genuine feeling of communication which comes from being part of a team who've all worked as hard as each other. Three large gin and tonics and a bottle of red wine floored me early on, however, as the Rosses finished serving up a special five-course meal with a jokey *Holy Grail* menu complete with "mud sorbet à la Palin". I began to feel my legs getting wobbly and my vision swung out of control. At about 11.30 went up to bed thirty-two days after we'd first clung to the side of the Gorge of Eternal

Peril in Glen Coe. Thirty-two days since the first shot when the camera broke and all that seems as far away as the first Python series. I hope in all the hard work of the general rush to complete we haven't lost any of the performances. Certainly tonight there was a good deal of optimism around.'

The film was finished, then began the laborious process of distilling it. This involved a series of screenings, often for the rock-band investors, during which the Pythons seriously thought they had got it wrong. The movie they had laboured over was initially providing few laughs; its verisimilitude (Gilliam said it was visually inspired by the work of Pasolini) was perhaps overwhelming.

'In the evening we had an investors' preview of *Monty Python and the Holy Grail*,' Palin recalls in his diary of the day. 'Arrived feeling fairly buoyant with three large gins inside me. Tony Stratton-Smith was there and Ali and Brian Gibbons, the financial wizards behind Charisma. A lot of beautiful people, presumably Pink Floyd and their wives, also Maggie, Carol Cleveland and Helen, who had never seen the film before. A total of about a hundred and fifty people. [Producer] Mark [Forstater] had to make an announcement before the film explaining it was not yet finally cut . . . there is definite bad feeling among the Terrys and Julian about rushing this screening, but the result was even more disastrous than I thought. It was one of those evenings when Python flopped. There was some laughter and there was some enjoyment and there was polite applause at the end which felt like a spear in the guts, because it was clear that the audience had been, by and large, disappointed. [Producers] Michael White and John Goldstone wouldn't speak to us, but then again they never do. White walked out at the end, giving Terry G. a brief and non-committal pat on the shoulder . . . I didn't, I must admit, immediately look to technical faults to explain away my acute discomfort through most of the showing. I just felt, through looking at it, that there were not enough jokes there . . . None of the investors seems anxious to shake us by the hand or even tap us on the shoulder . . . Terry J. clearly felt that what was wrong was that there was too much animation and too noisy a soundtrack, both faults of T.G. Poor T.G . . . he's been working eighteen hours a day on the film. Helen and I went on to a meal with Eric and Lyn. Eric had walked out halfway through the viewing. Not a great night for Python.'

'We showed our first cut of the film and people hated it,' Gilliam adds. 'There were walk-outs. I think Graham or Eric walked out. The sound was wrong, and there was such expectation and tension within the group, and they thought Terry and I had just completely fucked it up.'

The music was changed and the movie was screened in various forms (re-editing taking place after each screening) up to a dozen times before its Leicester Square premiere. Finally the Python boys got it right, and the film that premiered – Graham's angst aside – went on to become a major worldwide hit, significantly breaking the Pythons in the American market, where their show had finally been picked up, playing on the cable public-broadcast channel PBS.

If *Holy Grail* had been intended as a last hurrah for the Pythons, it ended up being more of a rebirth, one that ensured the Python empire would keep rolling. Nonetheless the first recourse for its members – following promotion for their breakthrough movie – was to take time to establish themselves as individuals over the next few days. Cleese hit big first with his deliriously wonderful sitcom-cum-classical farce *Fawlty Towers*, co-written with his then wife, Connie Booth, who had been a constant presence during the Python years. Eric Idle took

Python's love of satirising the medium that gave them life and created his own television station – and its output – via *Rutland Weekend Television*. Gilliam looked to movies, resulting in *Jabberwocky* a few years later, while Palin and Jones reverted to the 'Boy's Own' adventures of their youth in penning *Ripping Yarns*.

Graham meanwhile looked after his family, enjoyed the lifestyle that movie stardom afforded him and thought about his next move.

'Graham felt that he still had some useful things to say via Python,' Sherlock states. 'He also wanted to take the surreal element of Python humour and develop it further, having got an audience who, if you like, had been re-educated into extraordinary aspects of offbeat humour, for want of a better word. He reckoned that you could take it even further and *Out of the Trees* was Graham's riposte to Python. It was very Python in style, and he wanted to continue in a vein he thought was still worth mining and Cleese didn't. And he was very angry about it, I do know that.'

Out of the Trees was Graham's initial stab at solo television, which ended up being a one-off pilot programme. Co-written with long-time faithful compadre McKenna and recently arrived Douglas Adams, it was a half-hour show that captured the surreal nature of Python and attempted to embellish it. It was originally intended as a series, but the BBC threw it away, when it was broadcast in 1976, scheduling it opposite *Match of the Day* on a Saturday night, effectively killing it in the process.

However there were still a few pieces of business to attend to. The first was a stage show, organised by Cleese, originally titled *A Poke in the Eye (with a Sharp Stick)* and later retitled *Pleasure at Her Majesty's*.

'Amnesty International came to me,' Cleese recalls, 'and said,

"We need to raise money – do you have any ideas?"' Thinking of the quickest way to motivate those around him, he suggested a stage show. It was also an opportunity to combine the strengths of Python with those of their immediate antecedents, *Beyond the Fringe*. 'To me that was the easiest thing to do. I had a bit of a think about how to go about it and I got Jonathan Miller to direct it, so we were pretty safe there. Then I made it my job to get everybody involved. In other words I was the producer. Staged in February 1976, it was called *A Poke in the Eye (with a Sharp Stick)* and it was us, the *Beyond the Fringe* group and several others who were around and available. The show was a great pleasure because these were all people who were comfortable together. I think it was a huge success because everyone enjoyed themselves so much.'

Indeed they did, the first show offering prime opportunity for all those involved to go out of their way to crack each other up on stage, none more so than Cleese and Palin during what may be the finest rendition of Chapman's 'Norwegian Blue' ever performed. It was certainly a meeting of comedy minds, even if Graham wasn't always in his at the time.

Shortly after the initial show (and before the Amnesty shows transmogrified into a series loosely based around the title of *The Secret Policeman's Ball*, initially overseen by Cleese), the Pythons once again took to the stage, this time launching themselves in America, beginning a run at City Center in New York that – building on the success of *Holy Grail* – finally firmly established them in the US.

Terry Jones – as he recounted in his diary of the time – having just done the Amnesty shows, was less than enthusiastic. 'In the dressing room I realised I was going to miss the mixture when we do the show in NY and it's just Python again . . . thinking back to the buzz I got out of the Amnesty show, I suddenly realise (yet again!) what a corrosive effect the group is having on me – particularly John Cleese. In the same way John undermines Terry G., he has started coming up to me and giving me notes on everything. John's reactions are very strange – his total acceptance of everything Mike does or says and his hostility to Terry G. and me. Again maybe I'm being oversensitive to this at the moment. I'm sure Mike would say I'm making it up, but then again I write it down because I don't realise it most of the time.'

Despite tensions within the group, Graham enjoyed being the centre of attention in a foreign land and the New York run proved to be a huge success. He was in fact given the Freedom of the City by the NY chapter of the Gay Liberation Front, allowing him free access to any gay bar or club in town.

'It was much more rock 'n' roll,' Cleese recounts. 'I remember on the opening night getting this huge reception as I said the first line, then playing the sketch more or less to silence and thinking that it wasn't working or that we were screwing up or that I wasn't doing it right, and then doing the punchline and getting this huge reception again. I came off and said, "What is this?" And a stagehand took me to the side of the stage to watch the audience. I watched them and I could see all the people in the front rows and their lips were moving; they all knew the material. He said, "You have to understand this is a pop concert. They've come here for the experience of being with you. They're not going to laugh, because they know all the stuff better than you do." And he said, "They love being here and are having a great time, don't worry."'

The American audience took to the shows in growing numbers, so that from signing a few autographs at the beginning, they soon needed to take limos back to their hotel to avoid the crowds.

'The sketch where we did tend to let our hair down a bit,' recalls Jones, 'was where I do something about rat pie and Graham comes in as my daughter. He'd corpse me by putting on his lipstick in a terrible way sometimes, it'd be all across his face and he'd do it just to make me laugh.'

The New York shows confirmed the Pythons as global stars. It featured former Beatle George Harrison, noted fellow drinker Harry Nilsson (both in the chorus for Palin and Jones's 'Lumberjack Song' – at various times) and opened the door to subsequent work for all concerned.

Graham also found the time to travel uptown to Harlem, as he recounted to Sherlock: 'It's a good example of his totally fearless attitude to life as this was in the days when Harlem was not a place you went on your own and you were advised not to if you were white-skinned, but Graham quite happily went off to Harlem on his own, having been warned not to and had a whale of a time. He really enjoyed himself and he said, "If you treat people as you wish to be treated, why should they be different from anywhere else?" '

Graham took Python's recent on-stage success in his stride, but was becoming more and more concerned with the group's earning abilities. Money had always been an issue for Graham, probably because his overheads (Sherlock and Tomiczek included) were constantly increasing. After all the work they'd done – from TV to albums to books to – now – movies – he felt there should be more cash flowing. And took action when he realised there wasn't.

'Graham went elsewhere, so far as his accountancy was concerned,' Cleese recalls, 'and at that time nearly all the Pythons were having their financial matters looked after by two people – one was Anne James, the other was Steve Abbot. And what would happen is every six months a new set of accountants would approach Steve and Anne saying we represent so and so, and we want to get very clear and accurate figures on the following matters because we feel he's not being paid properly. And this happened every six months – he would give them his version of facts, Steve and Anne would have to spend a certain amount of time trying to convince the accountants that there hadn't been any skulduggery. Graham's accountants would then become convinced that Graham had not been cheated, would go back to Graham, at which point he would dump that set of accountants and go to another set of accountants who would set off on exactly the same quest. He was looking for the right answer. And that went on for some time, and it was very hard for Graham because he very much wanted to be a star, probably more than most of us. He wanted the trappings of stardom and he also wanted the lifestyle, but of course he never really had a success after Python and Graham was always hoping somehow that the money existed somewhere that would justify the lifestyle he was after, but it was an absolute fantasy.

'I guess that was because we didn't start making any real money until *The Holy Grail* became a success in America, and *Holy Grail* became a success in America in '75, and that's when, all of a sudden, we started to have a lot of money because up to that time, and the figures are quite interesting, we were earning astonishingly little. A friend of mine called Tony Hendra, who'd been at Cambridge with Graham and me, and he and Graham had gone off to the Royal Court, visited me in London and was watching one of the early Monty Pythons and laughing a great deal and afterwards, when we started talking about what we were paid for it, I told him and he laughed even more than he'd done at the show and fell off the sofa. One of the few times I've seen someone literally do that. And that was when I told him I was getting £240 a show. So, although we were young and it was a long time ago, it was still, by American standards, hilariously small. The first film, which was *And Now For Something Completely Different*, was round about a hundred thousand. And I think that the *Grail* was round about £240,000, and my recollection is that we got paid £4,000 each for writing and performing. But then we were informed that we were only going to get £2,000 and they were going to pay us the other £2,000 at the end. At which point John Goldstone called me about a week before we went up to Scotland and asked me if I would mind sharing a hotel room, which I'm afraid I refused to do.'

'Graham was absolutely certain that money was being sidelined away from him,' states Sherlock. 'Graham was furious to the point of apoplexy that while he was later away in America, the Pythons decided to use his name to launch their company Prominent Features in Camden Town, and he thought they were using his name to advertise the launch without asking him. They didn't ask him, and Graham was very, very angry. He was absolutely certain that there was a lot more money in the kitty and it wasn't coming their way. He never changed that opinion. Absolutely not. He died thinking that somewhere along the line money had been stashed away and found its way to the vast number of people who seemed to be supporting the industry. Graham actually thought that some of the people who were working for them were bent!'

Money would remain a major issue for Graham. By the late 1970s he would decamp from England and relocate to Los Angeles, largely to avoid British income tax. He was amazed at the free-flowing amounts of cash that were paid out during his American sojourn, taking a role on a US television show and, later, lucratively touring American college campuses as a speaker, largely recalling the highs and lows of Monty Python.

However, in the meantime Graham had set himself one more thing to achieve. His feelings of disappointment with himself and his level of performance during the making of *Holy Grail* had given him serious food for thought and he had decided to get sober. Having had the odd spell of sobriety before, he opted not to seek help but – ever the doctor – to do it all himself. He chose a festive moment to do so. It was Christmas 1977 when Graham Chapman opted to go cold turkey. Christmas, traditionally a time to make merry, was a far more sober occasion in the White House in Southwood Lane. Turkey was carved but bottles remained unopened as Graham began his move into sobriety.

It was in part brought on by his desire to play the lead role in Python's next movie, *The Life of Brian*, but more than anything, Graham wanted to know he could do it. He had already admitted to his lover, David Sherlock, that he personally felt he was not long for this world: 'He was slightly drunk at the time of his thirtieth birthday, but he actually said to me at the time that he didn't think he'd live long, and I thought, "Oh yeah, well, that's the booze talking."' Now he was determined to prove himself wrong.

Chapter Eight

His body twitched, his mind ran circles, the desire for a drink was strong, but the need to beat it was fiercer still. For the first time in his adult life, Graham Chapman had determined that he could function without the always-near-to-hand pick-me-up. It was a shock to the system, but his system's unwillingness to accept it proved that he was right. He lasted three days over the Christmas period . . . and then he keeled over.

'He didn't write about it accurately,' Bernard McKenna argues in reference to Chapman's own account of his collapse in his *A Liar's Autobiography*. 'He'd been off for more than three days. He'd announced that after Christmas he was going to stop. Strangely enough he took no medical advice, just cold turkey stopped. He rang me – he used to ring me and say, "Ooh, do you want to come up and have some lunch?" and I wouldn't really like to because he definitely became – not boring – but there were lots of silences. He asked me up one day, and I rang Jane Maud, who used to be his secretary, and I rang her and she said, "He's asked me up," and I said the same and said, "Let's go together," because neither of us could face it. So we got there and the room that he and I had always written in had bottles and optics in one recess where you'd expect to find books . . . And she said, "What do we do about drinking?" And I said, "We won't have a drink, no alcohol." When we got there, we could see he was very pale, very shaky. And he said, "Have a drink," and we said, "No, no, we're fine," and of course he spotted that and he thought, "You don't have to do this, you can have a drink," – "Come on, Mrs McKenna [as he used to call me to wind me up], have a brandy," and I went, "OK. I'll have a brandy." He got Jane a drink, and when he went to get mine his hands were shaking and he couldn't handle the optic. And I don't know what was going on – he couldn't pour the drink and he just went into a seizure, and I then leapt forward and he took me, and all the optics and the two of us ended up on the floor, with everything all over the place. And he wet himself. And bumped his head on the fireplace. He was much heavier than I thought because he fell on me and I was holding his weight and he took me down with him. Then John Tomiczek came running in and I was saying to get an ambulance.'

Graham's brother, John, confirms the extent of the problem: 'This is the way it was put to me subsequently; he decided that he had to stop drinking in order to get through *Life of Brian*, in order to learn all his words and be able to perform properly. And of course the fact that he decided to stop dead provoked the acute reaction, literally the delirium tremens and he was in hospital for a time with that, really, really very acutely ill, and we went to see him in there briefly . . . he had to be in shape to go through the rigours of the filming process. He cut himself off completely and within forty-eight hours he was in delirium tremens, the classic situation of an alcoholic stopping drinking. He went for complete cold turkey and brought this upon himself and he really was in an absolutely desperate situation. But he saw it through . . .' There were other things, other stresses in his life at that time. Old friend Alan Bailey wasn't able to be there in person, but he ensured that Graham was taken to the nearest hospital.

'Graham never went to AA. He did it all himself, and he had his fit three days after Christmas. He'd been dry. And Dave rang me up and we got him into the Whittington because it was an emergency and you can die under those circumstances. He was quickly admitted and then a psychiatrist friend went to see him, and gave him a talk and Graham had already decided, had made up his mind that he was going to stop drinking.

'You get withdrawal symptoms when you drink three bottles of gin a day. To suddenly stop you get withdrawal symptoms. They're worse than heroin withdrawal. Alcohol withdrawal can be much worse than ordinary drug withdrawal and on about the third day he fitted and that worried Dave a lot, so we got him into the Whittington and we made sure he didn't die. The psychiatrist gave him a lecture and Graham stopped drinking and that was it. I don't think he had any other support.'

Following his stay in hospital Graham committed himself to getting in shape – admittedly not in the most direct manner. 'It's very typical to have a *petit mal*, as it used to be known, or a mini-fit,' recalls Sherlock of Graham's post-Christmas collapse, 'which is a clear indication that you are alcoholically dependent, so you can have these once you're truly hooked, and in fact he was aware that it was about to happen because he was actually reaching to get himself some alcohol fast when he collapsed and took a whole shelf of booze with him really. It was about three days after he'd quit, so it was true: "on the third day he rose again" and all of that. It was quite frightening of course at the time, and as soon as I spoke to his pal, Alan Bailey, he said, "Oh thank God for that, now we can do something," and that was when he did start to do something, and also Graham was seen by a shrink who was actually someone [Maurice Lipsedge] who was called to make some assessment of the person's mental abilities and deal with any confusion they had. He was also the same guy who Graham sent Keith Moon to see some time after he'd stopped drinking. He spoke to Graham after Graham had been taken ill and he told him straight, he said, "If you ever touch another drop of alcohol again or you go back to drinking, within a week you'll be back to exactly where you were before and you will not survive."

'Graham's liver-function tests were so appalling that he should have been dead, and (although his liver-function tests returned to normal very quickly, as the liver is an organ capable of regeneration, so that the damage that had been done was rectified apparently and therefore Graham knew that, or thought that, he might survive longer) he was basically given a year to live if he did not change and even then, with the damage that had been done, it was touch and go. And of course after *Brian* they all had to make their wills before going to New York in case someone took a pot-shot at them, given the controversial nature of the film.'

Having made his decision after twenty years of persistent drinking, Graham found himself able to keep his addiction at bay (where it would remain). He was eager to aid his self-prescribed recovery by distracting himself with work, which once again took the form of a movie with Graham cast in the lead. It might have been about Jesus – then they (wisely) decided to make it about this other bloke that people had mistaken for Jesus.

'It was actually on the Canadian tour,' Palin recalls, 'that Eric had come up with the *Jesus Christ – Lust for Glory* title, which we all fell about at, but we'd probably had several gins and many brandies at that time, and red wine and grass.'

'I thought it was at a lunch in Soho,' Cleese recalls,

contradicting everyone, 'having a chat, and he said that line, which I thought was very, very funny.'

'*Jesus Christ – Lust for Glory* came out of promoting *Holy Grail* in 1975. We were in Amsterdam on a pub crawl one night,' Gilliam says – always contentious – 'and I remember Eric sitting down and coming up with *Jesus Christ – Lust for Glory*, and we fell off our chairs, it was just so funny. That was the start of it, so we just knew that was good, and that got us going on the idea of doing something about Jesus and Christianity.

But Python's take on Christianity was still in its early stages – which given everyone's individual plans didn't make things any easier. 'The availability of people to write on another movie was by no means a foregone conclusion,' Palin admits. 'John had done *Fawlty Towers*, which was a success and had moved him into another league, and Terry and I were doing *Ripping Yarns*, Eric was doing other things, Terry Gilliam did *Jabberwocky*. There were lots of different paths branching off from Python at that time. On the other hand, because we had a business, that kept us together, kept us at meetings, and at meetings there'd usually be a bit of banter, some jokes, some ideas being thrown around. Python could always be kick-started by some jokes or some good, funny ideas, however much everyone else was preoccupied with their own things. Someone just had to come up with an idea like *Jesus Christ – Lust for Glory* or something like that, to get us all giggling again and laughing, and that's why *Brian* began to move on.'

Graham meanwhile – now sober – also wanted to move on with his life and career (given the relative failure of *Out of the Trees* – not viewed as a successful venture given the work of his fellow Pythons). He wanted – according to co-scribe Bernard McKenna – to hit it big with a solo movie. For that he chose McKenna's old Ronnie Barker script *The Odd Job*. Graham helped McKenna rewrite it – and by that he took a thirty-minute, very decent piece of work and tried to expand it to feature-film length – and not content just to write it and star in it, he also wanted to cast a good drinking buddy of his in the joint lead role – Who drummer Keith Moon. Graham would play an abandoned suicidal husband, Moon would play the hit man he hired to kill him – then can't convince not to go ahead with the 'odd job'.

'Graham wanted to be the first Python to go off and be the star of a movie,' McKenna says, 'and he didn't pay much attention to the script. And Pink Floyd were involved in the financing as well, and he loved all that, getting on to the Floyd and Keith Moon, and all that, while I'd be saying, "Yes, but there's a script here, and we really should address the structural problems . . . " *The Odd Job* was made after he got sober and *Brian* was straight afterwards, because we were in Tunisia shooting it when *The Odd Job* came out.

'While I'd had great success with it as a half-hour, Graham was determined to produce it as a film. I was going through a divorce.' (McKenna's first wife left him the night before he began writing the screenplay with Graham – the first scene involves a man's wife walking out on him.) 'He came to me and said do you want to make a movie of this? David Frost had approached me, and Graham hated David Frost and Graham wanted to get in there.'

While McKenna was happy to go along with Graham's animosity towards Frost, he was less sold on casting drummer Keith Moon as the man who is hired to kill an errant husband, the latter role Chapman had taken for himself. Then again, neither was anybody else.

'He couldn't pass the acting test,' McKenna relates. 'Keith came and auditioned, which was very sad. Graham wanted

Keith because he was his new rock and roll friend, even though he'd never been to a Who concert or bought a Who record . . . we read it with him, and Keith had a fantastic personality but he was just crap. It was all grotesque, it was a lie – how he'd behave in a pub as opposed to how you'd behave in front of a camera.

'Then Keith had to go after the audition and Graham walked out to the car with him and as soon as he went [director] Peter Medak turned to me and said, "No fucking way," and I said, "I agree with you." Then Graham came back and said – and this was typical – "Oooh, I think that went very well." But he would also do that when he was drunkenly writing scripts with me – he'd say, "That's a very good scene." And I'd say, "There's just three lines in this scene and they're not particularly great." It was all after he quit drinking and he didn't show any difference in his approach to his writing; it was always lazy.'

David Jason, a regular from *Do Not Adjust Your Set*, was soon cast in the role Graham had hoped Moon would play. 'David Jason was already established as a good actor,' adds Sherlock. 'But David Jason had certain acting traits that Graham wasn't crazy about, and Graham was so understated as a comic actor and in his early days David Jason was anything but understated. But there were other people at the same time who Graham thought, as a comedian, fitted a similar mould. I think as time went on Graham was far less bothered by such things because he was no longer working with them but he felt that certain types of comedians were known for mugging, and he wanted somebody with a particular feel of menace about him. Keith Moon would possibly have been able to show that, if he'd been directed by Graham. Graham felt that he could get the performance he needed, whereas other people wouldn't at all have been able to get it. And also, heaven knows, you could have only got Keith Moon if he was in some way clear of alcohol, at least for his medical [standard insurance policy on any film], to work on the film. And this is something that's got to be remembered about Graham's collapse. That's what he was doing. He knew he was an alcoholic by then, even though he probably wasn't totally going to acknowledge it, because that's part of the deal as well. But he knew that he would only get the medical for *Brian* if he started to clean his act up well in advance. And by then he knew he was going to play the lead in *The Odd Job*, even though he wanted somebody else to do it because he wanted very much to direct, but it wasn't going to happen.'

'I didn't like the script,' says co-writer McKenna. 'Graham supposedly co-wrote it with me, but when they started shooting he did stuff and I didn't want to know. I don't think Graham knew how to write a screenplay. I didn't probably.'

These feelings were reflected in the movie that emerged, a failure both critically and with audiences, and surely something that Graham – having set himself up as a leading man away from the security blanket of the Pythons – bore the brunt of.

Graham, experiencing sobriety for more or less the first time in his adult life, was really throwing himself in at the deep end – taking the lead role in not one but two major movies back to back. It was the kind of hard work that could turn a man to drink – but, much in the style of his next major character, Brian, Graham turned the other cheek and embraced the fact that he felt deserving of such work and prominence.

Riding on the tail of the success that was *Holy Grail*, Python's next opus had a lot to live up to. The writing of what was to become *Life of Brian* was in many ways a protracted process, not just because all team members were busy off working by themselves, but also because all of them wanted to be true to the spirit of what they intended to discuss, dissect and make fun of.

Following Idle's off-hand comment vis-à-vis *Jesus Christ – Lust for Glory*, the team decided to eschew Christ himself and focus on what they really wanted to have a go at – organised religion and all that had been done or said in the name of Christ – without his blessing. It made perfect sense, after all, all six of them were university-educated men who had grown up in a time when religious doctrine was taught as part of general academia. Rather than accept everything that had been told to them, they had a few questions – by being funny about it, they thought they might get some answers more quickly. They were right.

'*Life of Brian* was going to be about the thirteenth disciple and how he always turned up late,' says Cleese. 'Of course the funny thing is that if you turn up five minutes late for a miracle, you might as well turn up two and a half thousand years late. So he'd missed the Last Supper because his wife had invited friends around and he was going to come on afterwards for a drink. I thought it was really funny, but that got dropped quite early on.'

'I wasn't that keen on the idea,' retorts Jones, always the antithesis to the Chapman–Cleese relationship. 'I think mainly because I'd gone to a Church of England primary school and my idea of the Holy Land and pictures of that period were these people in long, shapeless robes walking around. I never liked the costumes, I wasn't driven by the idea of it. But the first thing we did was read the Gospels again and, reading the Gospels, I started getting into it a bit more.'

All the Pythons began to take their comedy more seriously than ever before, with Graham particularly immersing himself in reading around the subject to know it better. Gilliam had once thought about becoming a missionary, and each of the Pythons, in their own way, was steeped in some level of religious education. Now it was actually time to sit down and think hard about what they really thought about such things.

'I remember it being quite hard to get the right tone,' says Palin. 'We all agreed we'd read up on the Bible story and that period historically and see what we could get out of it. Then of course up came ideas, particularly the idea of there being Messiah fever in Judea at that time. That was really the key to it and gave us the theme, so we could create this character who wasn't Jesus but led an almost parallel life, was almost his next-door neighbour.'

'Very quickly we came around to feeling that Jesus was okay, we weren't going to take the piss out of him. He was genuinely okay, so that's where "Brian" got created; he was a parallel,' adds Gilliam.

It was Palin who made the breakthrough the rest of the group had been searching for. 'There was a hugely important moment when Michael read out the Pontius Pilate stuff and I remember we all said, "THAT'S IT!"' Cleese recounts. 'At that stage we knew we had the story. It was an extraordinary script meeting and I think it was the last one of the first session. After that we put it all together, went away for a bit and thought, "That'll work."'

Although it wasn't all smooth sailing, partly due to Graham, who despite his sobriety, was – as has been said – not always there (as Terry Jones's diary recalls): 'Another Python meeting. Graham was an hour late because he got the day wrong. He also revealed that he thought yesterday was a day off. John had also obviously not been writing. Eric had done a good deal and got out his order. I'd lost mine so we started discussion based on Eric's. Terry G. arrived just before lunch. I seem to have got a bit better at meetings – for example I kept quiet about my order, but by the end of the day it had come round anyway. Meetings are certainly a lot jollier than they used to be – my worry is that we're all taking it too easily.'

Gilliam puts it even more succinctly: 'We went around and around about how to do it – having taken on chivalry in the Middle Ages, then what better than to take on Christian religion? That night we were going round with the idea of a guy pretending to be the Holy Ghost, he'd knocked up Mary: "Don't worry I'm a messenger from God." And Mary goes home and has to deal with Joseph: "He said he was a messenger from God." It started on the basic stuff and then we made the leap to doing it obliquely by inventing the guy who was born in the stable next door at the same time. In a strange way we were being very cautious about not being blasphemous, by being totally blasphemous, but about another guy. My mother, an avid churchgoer, saw it, but she didn't have a problem because it wasn't about Jesus.'

Unfortunately not everyone saw it that way. Mere days before Graham was due to head off to Tunisia to begin filming his titular role in *Life of Brian* in early 1978, Bernard Delfont, the man whose company was financing the film, actually got around to reading the script. He didn't take it well. He, and many who followed him, couldn't make the leap that the script was actually about religion and not Christ. He felt it was blasphemous and not the kind of thing he wanted to be behind.

Around the same time, Ken Levy asked Graham if he was worried about getting *Life of Brian* widely distributed. 'We had trouble with the last one being released because EMI didn't want to know about it. They wanted to know about it since we've earned the money, they sure did, but they're a load of twits at the top of that organisation. No, it was EMI, they released it but they didn't put any money in and they didn't want to know about it, but we did it anyway because of nice people like John Goldstone and Michael White . . . We found the money separately from people like Pink Floyd and Led Zeppelin, who put up the money and we put up some money as well and that's the only way we managed to get it made because there was no company that would give us money then. They're all falling all over themselves now to do so. Fuck 'em still.'

'I heard that Delfont was worried because one of his brothers had financed the life of Jesus, the Robert Powell one,' recollects Cleese of 1977's *Jesus of Nazareth*, directed by Franco Zeffirelli and produced by Delfont's brother, Lord Lew Grade, 'and had got a lot of prestige out of it and suddenly thought he would be compared very unfavourably to his brother for producing a parody of it. So he withdrew and paid us compensation and there was a secrecy clause and we, as Pythons, naughty little things that we were, always pointed out with great delight that there wasn't a secrecy clause about the secrecy clause. So we lost the finance and we were a bit crestfallen because we really thought it might not happen. I remember that [producer] John Goldstone did the rounds of Hollywood studios, and two or three of them were prepared to put up a certain amount of money, but they were interested in buying the American rights, and they weren't prepared to put up enough for us to be able to raise the money necessary to meet the budget. And then really out of the blue, Denis O'Brien [who would shortly become the Pythons' manager] appeared on the scene, and Eric, I believe, had shown a copy of the script to George Harrison, who was a good friend of Eric's, and George read it and said, "Ah, you know, I want to see it," and said he'd put the money up and so Denis came forward, and all of a sudden it was all happening.'

Thus was born O'Brien and Harrison's Handmade Films, one of the British film industry's most successful boutiques of the day. Meanwhile, early in 1978, mere weeks after Graham had stopped drinking, the Pythons had opted to go abroad, decamping to Heron Bay in Barbados (staying at a house once frequented by Winston Churchill), an idea instigated by Eric, who was there anyway. It was a notion that was thoroughly enjoyed by all, as well as Keith Moon, who happened to be around and was due to play a role in the film and who would hang around outside their villa, essentially asking if Graham could come out to play. (The unlikely combination of Mick Jagger, Jerry Hall and Des O'Connor also showed up one night to play charades.) Meanwhile the now more disciplined Pythons kept strict nine-to-five hours. One of the key decisions that was made during their Barbados sojourn was to award the now sober Graham the lead role in the movie.

'The big decisions were taken in Barbados about what scenes were left out and the thing about the casting,' states Cleese, who had a vested interest in the casting, in part because he felt he had never played a lead role in a movie at that time. 'I put myself forward [for the role of Brian] in Barbados and I remember going for a walk up the beach afterwards feeling mildly aggrieved and then seeing, fairly soon afterwards, that [Graham] was much the best decision. But we put it together in Barbados, and it was hugely successful because you can just think about it all the time and you don't have wives or children or people who have to go to the dentist or anything like that. It's a very good way of writing.'

Palin concurred: 'There was a bit of worry about Graham as the lead, and I think that's why, when we were doing the casting, John actually volunteered to do Brian himself, but it just seemed a colossal waste really of all the other things that John could do. The idea of John playing Brian wasn't felt to be right. There was a quality in Graham that he'd shown as Arthur that I remember thinking would be just right for Brian. I know he wanted to play Brian. It was probably the best way of dealing with it because he'd just have to sober up, he'd have to be prepared to do this. John, I don't think, saw it in such sympathetic terms; he just thought that Graham would be a disaster because of his drinking. Drink was going to affect everything he did, so whether he was Brian or not, or other characters, he would still suffer. So there was some argument over that. Most of us were generally of the feeling that Graham would be best and that he needed to sort himself out and would sort himself out. It was not ever discussed really that Graham had a drink problem when Graham was there. You didn't say that. We would have the normal discussion about casting Graham and the issue of whether Graham was best or not to do it would have been a side conversation probably, like a phone call later that day or something like that, that's the way things used to happen. John felt that Brian, being the core figure of the whole film on whom the whole film depended, had to be played by somebody who was absolutely reliable, so in a way John was making a bit of a sacrifice. I felt if Graham was going to be in the film, it was better if he was given something of substance to do, to really force him to get right, than be shunted out and do lots of little parts.'

Sherlock was also worried about the fact that Graham was decamping to Barbados so soon after getting sober, and asked Alan Bailey of the possibility of him reoffending. At this time, after all, Graham had been clear of alcohol only for a number of weeks. Sherlock also voiced his concerns to Bailey about his own health at the time and his feelings of possibly being left behind now that Graham appeared to be so adamant in moving on in his life and away from his lifelong habits, to which Bailey replied, 'Have a good stiff drink, old man!'

Cleese was also aware of the changes in Graham: 'He's supposed to have fallen over and gashed his head on a fireguard or fender and was taken off to hospital, and he just decided "this has to stop" and he linked up with someone who helped people get over alcohol dependency and by the time we came to shoot *Life of Brian* he was in great shape . . . he had about eight months ultimately to get himself sorted.' But at times Cleese still found it hard to forgive past indiscretions: 'He was sabotaging, no, that's a stupid way of putting it, he was ruining stuff when he was drunk. I remember feeling, "What's the point of writing these sketches if he's going to fuck them up?" and there wasn't any way he was going to suddenly stop fucking them up and he suddenly got his act together and became very healthy and much more present. My recollection was probably that . . . I was running with the ball most of the time when we were writing . . . that was the period when it was worse. But he and I were coming up with very good stuff, but when I think of the stuff we were coming up with, it was more my kind of stuff, like the Latin lesson, because I was quite good at Latin and I taught for two years, you know. Maybe I assumed that I was running with the ball most of the time.'

Palin later termed the writing of *Brian* as 'our last really good group experience in writing terms', commenting further on how the change in Graham was reflected in that 'Graham had suddenly come out of a long slumber. He became much more concerned about the small detail of writing, which he would probably not have bothered with before that, in his drinking days. It was nice to have Graham back concentrating.'

With the producers showing concern over the potentially blasphemous nature of the script, Graham opted to show it to a friend's father, Canon Fisher, one of the Queen's canons, to ensure that the moral stance they had taken on the script was the correct one. He loved it, saying there were things in it he had wanted to say publicly for years.

That first draft of the then titled *The Gospel According to Saint Brian* is credited solely to Chapman and Cleese, with a handwritten note from Graham on the cover insisting that all six Pythons be credited, obviously an oversight in the first place, as it bears a very strong resemblance to the film they eventually made, a film that many consider to be their finest moment. In 1976 Graham told Ken Levy what the film was about: 'At the moment it's *Monty Python and the Life of Christ*, which we think will offend everybody, so we'll try and do that.'

He also used the interview opportunity to expound on his association with the rock hierarchy of the time. 'It's very odd actually because we're all roughly the same age and all that, you know, born round about 1941, 1942 or just before then. It is odd that that should be such a rich era in terms of people who are now round about thirty-five. I don't think that's the only reason that we happen to like each other, but we do seem to have a lot of common projects in hand at the moment, like I hope to get a television show together for Ringo.

'Also The Who. We're involved with them, and I'm writing a film for Keith Moon at the moment [*Yellowbeard*], not just for Keith Moon as a performer, although he will be in it, I hope . . . So as far as Keith Moon is concerned, I'd like to say that he really is one of the nicest people in the world, and unfortunately mad, but he's very nice. I love him!'

The conversation turned back to *Life of Brian* and how he saw the nature of the Python group. 'The earliest it could be filmed would, I think, be the spring, but it may be summer of next year. I don't worry about it being big, I just worry about it being good. So you take your time and you do it properly.

That's all. I mean, it would be easy to do a rip-off job, do another quick film, which we could have done obviously, but I don't think that's the right way to work. You've got to have the right ideas. I mean, it's got to be written properly. That's the most important thing. And there are bound to be ups and downs, and also in terms of production and direction, there are bound to be ups and downs; we're a group. You get something like the Beatles, for instance, to use a parallel, which is a ridiculous one, but still, I think George Harrison went off his head at one point doing all these silly Indian things. He's a very good musician, he's a fine writer, as well, of music. John Lennon's still off his head but he's all right. They're all off their bleeding heads, they're still good at the thing they do, but when they were best, they were a group, they were together. We're going through that stage now . . . We just do our work and we do it right. We write and we perform it. We'll never have the sort of success that will make us feel odd or different . . . This is the way groups break up.'

Graham wanted three things from *Brian*: a chance to get sober and put at least some of his past behind him; an opportunity to prove himself as an actor; and an occasion that allowed him to reacquaint himself with his original chosen profession. Rather than picking up a few bottles of duty-free gin, when Graham finally travelled to Tunisia in 1978 to begin filming *Life of Brian*, he took with him instead a suitcase full of medicine. Having in theory healed himself, he seemed determined once again to do the same for others and made himself the on-site/on-set doctor for the duration of the shoot, essentially holding court each day to look after whoever needed looking after. He acquitted himself admirably.

Terry Jones was privy to Graham's choice of supplies. 'Before we went, Graham showed me his case. It was full of medicines and I remember thinking, "That's a bit silly, isn't it?" I thought it was a bit over the top because he *really* had a suitcase *full* of medicine, but of course it wasn't over the top at all, it was absolutely the right thing to do. After a day's filming Graham would have quite a big queue of people coming to be treated, so it was a very sensible idea. Graham was great.'

Graham himself took a more humorous approach to his notions and potions. 'Terry Jones is a fanatic about filming,' he told the BBC at the time, 'and I have to fill him up with little pink pills so he can direct.'

'He did it properly,' Bernard McKenna – who took several small roles on *Brian* – confirms. 'He didn't fuck about. If he saw somebody with a cut on his face in the street, he'd go up and say, "I'm a doctor."'

Old friend Alan Bailey was also of use to Graham during the shooting of *Brian*. 'I was on the end of the telephone in those days. If he was worried about somebody, he'd give me the symptoms over the phone, so he was ringing me up about things. But he kept up to date with medicine.'

David Sherlock meanwhile felt that the essence of Graham's performance in *Brian* stemmed at least in part from his experience of dealing with the young runaways, Jimmy and Brendan, he had looked after years before. 'In a funny way it was like a big, very long rehearsal for his role as Brian because for Brian he actually drew on all of those things. Nobody really knew quite where that character came from, but Brian's quite a definite character and he's been thought through.'

Graham's recent decisions didn't, however, preclude him from letting others have a good time, no matter what time of day it was: 'When we were doing *Brian*,' recalls McKenna, 'one morning we were all asked to wait in the hotel because of the weather – they weren't sure whether we were going to film or not. And Graham came down – this was about half ten – and said, "All these long faces? It's Bloody Marys all round." We should have been on set at eight – but Graham got the bar opened – he was on cola himself.'

On location McKenna noted another form of abstinence on Graham's part. 'When we were out in Tunisia, there were gay people working on the film who literally had swing doors put in because there were so many people going in and out. But Graham was so focused on the part that there wasn't any real hanky-panky going on, because he was sober and focused and they had a good project. It was the best acting he'd ever done.'

For Graham, *Brian* was very much a process of liberation, one that would come to influence and determine the last years of his life. Atypically, having once been the drunken extrovert, he chose to do it quietly, looking after those around him, possibly compensating for the way they had been looking after him for the previous few years. Admittedly (on screen) he did flash his genitals to the waiting hordes, but that was about as wild as it got, despite the admiration of cohort Terry Gilliam. 'For him in *Brian* to do the nude thing – the others would be hard-pressed to do it – but he did it and he did it brilliantly . . . It was all these guys who were trapped in their upbringing and he was just trying to be free.'

(Graham's new-found sobriety even extended to old friend Keith Moon who he tried to help get sober, going as far as saying to The Who, 'I'll stay with him every moment of the day if you want,' and recommending him to his own psychiatrist. Sadly it was to no avail as Moon died a year later.)

Not everyone was completely enamoured of the new Graham, however, as old friend Alan Bailey noted: 'After he stopped drinking and I was still drinking, I found him a bit boring when he drank three pints of diet-whatever, and I had three pints of beer. A lot of that was catching up and saying what's new in this and what's new in that and what's this new drug he'd read about, because he was an avid reader of the newspapers and he was very up to date on what was going on in the world.'

For David Sherlock, though, Graham's new-found sobriety and, in particular, *Brian* represented a time of Graham moving on, and the possibility of him leaving behind what once was. 'In many ways I feel Graham had had – and this is how it appeared to me from what he had to say about his parents – a rather cold upbringing,' David Sherlock recounts. 'That's not to say that his parents didn't care for him . . . people did not show emotion in those days. And what Graham absolutely needed was the security of real warmth and affection. And I think that that was the key to our success . . . we made one promise to each other when we first met, and this was when we decided that we wanted to live together forever, and that was if we met someone we liked better at any point, we'd sit the other one down and talk about it and decide what to do. But generally speaking, because we cared for each other, we would let the other go. But after he got sober, I read up on the "co-dependent" syndrome, and what is nearly always very classic of it is that in my case I had a minor breakdown, and Graham started to get better so during the whole of the filming of *Brian*, I was feeling that. I spent just one week living in Tunisia during *Brian* and that's all. I was angry. Incredibly angry, angry at all that wasted time. And there was Graham happy and me miserable as hell! Think of all the famous alcoholics who have got better, supposedly, including George Best, he's a very good example, and they're off with a new partner. New life, new world, leave the rest behind. So what do they do to the co-dependent? They dump them. And that's exactly how I felt.'

David responded to his reaction to Graham's new-found sobriety – and the pressure it brought to their relationship – by having an affair. More than that, he found himself becoming seriously involved with this other partner, something which despite the 'open' nature of their relationship had never been an issue before.

'The affair happened and once it happened I was full of the guilt of that, and it's probably only that I was in such an emotional turmoil that I reacted as I did. However, the fact remains that I felt I'd reached a crossroads, and in doing so Graham declared to me that he no longer wanted us to actually sleep together, and suddenly that was an incredible slap in the face. And from that I was sent into a complete spin.'

Nonetheless Graham still wanted his partner to remain his partner, despite the presence of John Tomiczek. 'In reality all parties knew it wouldn't work,' Sherlock says of his affair, 'Graham particularly. I sat Graham down for the talk as to what we did about the situation, in Los Angeles, a year after *Brian*. He knew all about the affair. I confronted Graham with the fact that I wanted to give this new relationship a go, to see if it would work. Graham responded in kind. He said, "OK, give it a go for a year and see if it works, and if it doesn't, come home." That is Graham to the core. Faced with that ultimatum, which wasn't an ultimatum, how could I leave?'

It was in many ways typical of how Graham viewed many of his relationships – it was key to him to have a family and a home. Somewhat like the one he had grown up in, but also very different from that in relation to the way his life had developed. He was in many ways paternal.

'I don't know how he was as mature as he was as early as he

was,' Sherlock says, 'but there were loads of people right the way through his early life, and I think at Cambridge and Bart's, who were solid and down-to-earth and I think that's one reason why he didn't necessarily think that showbiz and its glitter had that much to offer him. Yes, he would go along with the interviews and publicity that needed to be done for things, but once that was over, he'd rather go somewhere dead ordinary with ordinary people.'

Chapter Nine

Monty Python's Life of Brian incurred the wrath of just about everybody it was quietly designed to offend. However, it wasn't offensive, just controversial, and achieved everything it set out to do. For Graham and his compatriots it was a justified success, and in certain ways the fulfilment of what they had wanted. It also resulted in death threats: 'We were surprised but we weren't that scared,' says Cleese, 'because the people protesting were fairly obviously a bit silly. They were saying things like, "Monty Python is an agent of the Devil," which I remember was a lovely placard.' It was also banned in various places: 'It was banned in Norway,' Jones recalls, 'so the Swedes advertised it as "The film that was so funny it was banned in Norway!"' – all of which was compensated for by bigger royalty cheques than had been previously experienced by the team.

Graham personally was very pleased with the money . . . but also worried. Given the extreme taxation laws in Britain at the time, coupled with the fact that he had just starred in two movies back to back (*The Odd Job* came and went, *Brian* came and stayed), he was forced into the position of having to become a tax exile, or face bankruptcy. If he left his native country for a year, he could survive financially.

Then again, so much had changed in Graham's life in the last few months that a change of location was almost inevitable. He chose to move to Los Angeles in 1980, the City of Angels, to complete his hoped for redemption.

'It was a total remake going to the States,' Sherlock recollects, 'because Graham didn't have time to think to himself, "Who the hell am I?" before *Brian*, but it was happening simply because he'd stopped drinking. Going to the States was like going into chrysalis form and then re-emerging all over again. It happened very quickly in the States, of course, but then in Los Angeles you can be whoever you want; you tell your publicity guy and then they promote you accordingly. But he did have plenty of time to really relax for the first time, and on the strength of the reaction to *Brian*, he just seemed to suddenly have people wanting to work for him and promote him and be his publicity agent and God knows what. Graham went to the States on his own and found himself a house and everything else, and we stayed back in England.'

Although Graham initially went to Los Angeles on his own, John Tomiczek shortly joined him in his new life; David Sherlock followed after a few months. Graham was, more than ever before, following the success of *Brian*, being fêted as a star.

'Graham had finished drinking,' Sherlock states, 'and with most alcoholics they have a total change of lifestyle once they stop. They make conscious choices, not realising that for many years they haven't made choices in the same way, and Graham particularly had to. I tried to change some of the aspects. For instance I made him cut his hair, because he was thinning on top but he was still clinging to his old-fashioned idea that if you liked having long hair you should still have it styled that way. I said, "You're going to America, you're part of a whole new lifestyle, you have to really smarten yourself up: the first thing you can do is change your hairstyle completely," which of course I'd done regularly, to his horror and shock because he hated me with short hair, because I suppose we'd both grown up knowing each other in what was just before the hippy days. However, he did and it changed him radically, visually. He was changing anyway . . . he seemed to be peppier, perkier, much more on the ball. Within a very short time, he was thrilled to be alive. He was ecstatic about everything that was happening. In a way it was like he was reborn. He was waking up every morning and saying, "My God, I feel good," and bouncing down and having breakfast. Well, breakfast for Graham was a large gin and tonic in the old days. And the only way you deal with someone who is an alcoholic is to say, "No, no, no, stop," and if there is abuse, whether it's verbal or physical, then that must not be allowed at all, and the partner must get out of the relationship or in some way distance themselves. I was very lucky in that even in the seventies when things got really bad with Graham's drinking, and this is what the Pythons talk about, particularly the tour of Canada, during that period, this is when the proverbial hit the fan. But after that Canadian tour, that was our first introduction to Los Angeles. It was not pleasant.'

After the excesses of the years before at Riot Hyatt, when Graham returned to Los Angeles in exile years later, it was still very much a party town, the party now being based around the *drug de jour* – cocaine. Graham indulged at times but never to excess (he'd already done excess). Besides, Graham was in some ways more enamoured of another insidious white powder – sugar.

'I really noticed it in the States,' says McKenna, 'he was more addicted to Dr Pepper than cocaine. Wherever he went, there was one of them in his hand. The cocaine was take it or leave it. Graham knew the medical limits of stuff – he certainly didn't know it when he came to alcohol. But he did get more into coke, more because all these people surrounding him were offering it to him all the time. I noticed when I'd been in LA for three months, I'd had cocaine every day and I actually stopped myself. I sat down and had a talk with myself and said you don't actually have to do this. And I stopped and I've not had any since. I thought this is fucking mad – there were so many stars coming by – and people are saying, "You want a toot?" – and you associate it with "isn't it great I'm hanging around with these guys?" But you could hang around with these guys and not have little spoons of stuff.'

At one point Graham invited his parents, Walter and Edith, to join him in LA to enjoy the now very obvious star trappings of his glamorous new lifestyle. He also took the time to invite Ron Wood, Ringo Starr and Harry Nilsson, among other celebrities, to their welcome party, proving perhaps that while he had at least curbed his fondness for gin and tonic, he still knew how to arrange an interesting room full of guests.

'I don't think he realised what he put them through,' McKenna recalls. 'He had this big party in LA once, and there were all these famous stars and Graham's dad, Walter . . . and various people went off to toot right, left and fucking centre – but he invited them out because he wanted to show them that he lived in Brentwood, he had this big house with a big pool and a big car.'

Graham didn't mean to put his parents – particularly his father – in such an awkward situation; indeed, he always exhibited a huge respect for his parents, as McKenna recalls from another incident: 'Once we were walking down the road and we were smoking a joint – I still had one in my hand – and we saw a policeman coming, and I went, "Oh fuck," and he said, "Why are you frightened of policemen? I've never been frightened of policemen." And I said, "I've got a joint in my hand – they might sniff it." But what he was saying was "They're friendly."

In a strange way for someone who was anti-authoritarian he believed in the authority of the police. He admired his father, he really did.'

What Graham also did in LA was to try and rebuild his family – the stability of which, even if it did at times involve more than one partner, was important to him – and focus on his next two projects – one of which involved Pythons; one of which involved pirates. And, in spirit at least, the drummer from The Who.

Keith Moon had long been enamoured of Long John Silver. As far back as the mid-1970s he had come up with the idea of him playing Silver and Graham writing the script. It briefly became an idea in which numerous fictional heroes – Superman and Co. – would co-exist, but on a practical level – copyright laws being what they are – it was never going to happen.

'*Yellowbeard* came about because of Keith Moon wanting to do an adventure film,' says McKenna. 'I was in a pub one day with Graham and Keith – we'd been in a hotel where we crawled through the foyer, and Keith said he wanted to do a movie that had all the superheroes in it: Superman, Spiderman, all that. So – voice of reason here – said the rights on that – you could start now and we'll make it in twenty-five years.'

Graham prevaricated and once again called him Mrs McKenna.

'Keith had always wanted to play Long John Silver,' McKenna continues, 'and so Graham suggested making a pirate movie. Then they said to me, "How much would you charge for coming up with a short outline?" – we were in a pub in Baker Street – and I said, "I suppose a grand or something." And Keith had his minder with him, and he had a briefcase and he went and opened it and he gave us a grand each from this briefcase, in notes. This was around 1976.'

Keith Moon went back out on tour with his band; Graham and McKenna toiled over the script, after some delay, and finally hit pay dirt. 'After *Brian* Graham shot off to America, for tax purposes,' states McKenna. 'He then rang me and said, "I've met a producer and he's interested in our pirate film idea." And I said, "That's all it is – an idea."'

At that time all they had was a twelve-page outline, but they pitched it to Warner Brothers, who bit, and so the writing began, largely in LA, where there were many distractions to divert them. 'There was one time when me and Graham were writing *Yellowbeard*,' McKenna recalls, 'and we got to the stage where I said, "We're never going to finish this. I'm going home, I'm tired." And he went, "No, no just a bit more" – this was when he was sober. But I said, "I'm exhausted. I have to go home to bed." And he said, "Would you like a little something?" And I said, "What?" And he said, "Cocaine." And I said, "Yeah, okay, that'll do it." And I worked and we finished it in an hour, and he said, "OK, shall I get you a cab to go home?" And I said, "No, I'm going out now."'

Meanwhile, on the performing side of his life, one of the things Graham did during his sojourn in LA was to take Python back to the stage. Following the success of *Brian*, they were in huge demand and were offered the opportunity to play the Hollywood Bowl in 1980.

'Python was once again a rather tempting prospect for a theatre promoter,' Palin says 'and it was suggested we play somewhere in LA. In keeping with our new-found status and the cult thing of Python and the potential of really getting a large number of people together, the Hollywood Bowl was proposed. There was just something about performing at the Hollywood Bowl that I think tickled all of us, because we were all brought up on LPs of people "Live at the Hollywood Bowl", whether it was Sinatra or Errol Garner or the big bands that played on the stage there. It was an iconic venue. And we said, "Yeah, okay, we'll have a go."'

For Graham, newly resident in town, it was the full confirmation he needed of his star status there, as Gilliam recalls: 'We were like rock stars. If the audiences weren't on their feet cheering before we went out, we wouldn't go out. And they knew all the lines, so it was like a sing-along . . . But it was a pop concert. Seven thousand people out there, huge screens on either side, and people were all in Gumby costumes.'

'We had a lovely backstage area,' adds Palin. 'There was food and drink and hospitality, and people like Mick Jagger would arrive, Harry Nilsson and Ringo and others who hung out at that time, and John Belushi and the *Saturday Night Live* boys came along. So it was definitely a "celebrity ticket", that one. So it was our time, our Hollywood-celeb time.'

Naturally, on the strength of such adoration, Graham took to life in LA, largely because of the people he always seemed to have around him. 'Graham was a home body,' explains Sherlock. 'He didn't mind travelling so long as he could take everybody with him. Graham absolutely loved being at home and being domestic as well as everything else.'

He spent a fair amount of time with the British ex-pat community in LA, helping to found a newspaper entitled *True Brit*, for which he – very briefly – wrote a column entitled 'Monty Python's Flying Column'.

Graham's new-found lease of life was accompanied by a renewed eagerness to work, and to work in a much more focused way. When he returned to England in 1982, after his time as a tax exile: 'He came back with really quite a different attitude to life, but he was determined that if he could live in a similar way to the style he'd been living in Los Angeles, he would, and he did his best,' Sherlock explains.

He formed Seagoat Productions (named in part for him being a Capricorn, with himself and John Tomiczek listed as company directors) and started to raise financing for *Yellowbeard*, to an extent something of a dream project for him, in that he hoped it would establish his independence away from Python in the way that the others had already managed.

Not that he was separating himself completely from the old team. In 1980, following their pleasurable experience at the Hollywood Bowl, they reconvened to begin another film project, inspired largely by cash and the desire to repeat the success of *Brian*.

Cleese recalls how the decision to resume work together stemmed from an offer from their manager, Denis O'Brien. 'He told us that after *Life of Brian*, if we made another movie immediately, we wouldn't have to work again. That would have been a nice prospect, if it had occurred. But for that reason and that reason alone we sat down to start writing the next movie without having a fallow period, which I think would have been much better. That was a major problem. A second major problem was how were we all going to sit in the same room and develop the script?'

Indeed Cleese was initially adamant that he didn't want to be involved, so the writing continued for many months without him. Graham reassured the others that he was sure he would come back on board. This working period proved to be very protracted, with all concerned unable to really decide what it was they wanted to do. However, when it was ready to go, Universal Pictures gave them a sizeable budget and the option to not deliver the script but to sell the movie on the back of a poem instead, which began:

There's everything in this movie
There's everything that fits
From the meaning of life and the universe
To girls with great big tits.

Truth be told, there really wasn't a script in place. Trying to emulate the success of *Brian*, the group once again decamped to the tropics, this time to Jamaica, to try to knock their loosely bound ideas into shape.

'We tried so many different ways of trying to get the story together,' states Palin. 'We wrote a huge amount of material that was never used. It was much more of an uphill struggle getting *The Meaning of Life* going. It's very, very hard to know where you go after *Life of Brian*. In fact I can remember us thinking that – where do we go next? And I think the seven ages of man – birth, life, death – that idea, the really big one, was seen to be the only way you could cap *Life of Brian*.'

Graham took some time out from the writing process to experience the local nightlife. 'He went to see *The Robe* on Good Friday in Kingston, Jamaica, and he was the only white face in the audience,' Sherlock recollects, 'and he said it was magic. He was fascinated to see what sort of reaction there would be and he loved it because whenever Pilate came on, it was like panto – he was booed and hissed and people threw things at the screen, and whenever Jesus appeared, of course, he was cheered, and so he thought it was wonderful and he had a great time.'

When Cleese finally came back on board, he and Graham renewed their partnership and ended up writing a good deal of material. However, all felt that it didn't really hang together and almost considered abandoning the whole project. It was only when the title was decided – *The Meaning of Life* – that things began to come together, even though the writing process was still broken down into disparate groups, with Gilliam joining Graham and Cleese.

Gilliam wasn't very happy about this arrangement. 'I remember being in Jamaica, sitting down and having to write with Graham and John, and thinking that was a really cruel and unusual punishment because I've never seen three people who are working in such different rhythms. Eric, Mike and Terry were having a wonderful time, and I'm like, "I want to work with Mike and Terry," but Eric was too clever; he got in with them and stuck me with John and Graham. By then Graham was just down to sucking on his pipe and uttering about one word every five minutes, John was busy trying to talk everything to death, and there was me just wanting to bang through some of it. It was just a very strange time.'

Cleese later commented on the dynamic of group writing and the part that background had played in it: 'I think intelligence played an enormous part, but I don't think education was very important. For example, two of the brightest people I ever met were Frank Muir and Denis Norden. I don't think they had vast formal education. They were hugely intelligent and on the whole in those days I think you could say that the most intelligent people had been to university. You could sometimes, when you were talking to somebody, have a shrewd guess whether they'd been to university or not. It wasn't true with Denis or Frank or, I would have thought, with Galton and Simpson, but it was quite clear that some of those guys were enormously bright, even if they hadn't had a very prolonged formal education. With others, like Johnny Speight, you always felt that there was tremendous talent there and a terrific understanding of the language, but you didn't feel there was an enormous capacity for abstract thought. Which is probably what the university training strengthens. So there were some writers who you would always expect to grasp these subjects easier.'

By now, however, it was becoming apparent to all the team members that they had simply moved on, and their desire to forge ahead with their individual careers made their experience with group movies more disjointed than before. Essentially a collection of sketches (and a short film by Gilliam – working largely in isolation from the others) meant that *Meaning of Life*, while still very funny, was an indication that Python was less and less what its individual members wanted to do.

The film was eventually shot and released and proved to be a success, even if for Graham it was something of a dissatisfying process. 'John and Graham found it particularly frustrating not to be able to write on *The Meaning of Life* with the same success rate as they had done before,' Palin recalls. 'I remember them bringing in things that just didn't quite work. They seemed to be putting a lot of hard work into it, but it just didn't have that light, funny, spot-on feeling of being both well written and essentially as funny as some of the other stuff they'd done for *Brian*, and that was quite demoralising . . . I don't think the writing or the relationship was as good as it could have been.'

Graham was in many ways more concerned at this point with his other project, the piratical comedy *Yellowbeard* for which he had begun working on the screenplay with Bernard McKenna (Keith Moon, who died in 1978, no longer being around to work on it in any form).

'I'd written the script with Graham,' McKenna says, 'and then they wanted a rewrite and they didn't have any money, so I said I'm not writing for no money.'

Work could have ceased there, but McKenna also happened to be writing with Peter Cook at that time on a one-off TV special titled *Peter Cook and Friends* – by virtue of a chance meeting after two different lunches in two different Italian restaurants in the same part of North London, McKenna bumped into Graham and Cleese on their way back from lunch, and on his way back to Cook's. They all descended on Cook's – at first pretending to be Italian waiters – then Cleese found himself a role in Cook's show (a very fine Joseph Chamberlain) and Chapman found himself another writing partner for *Yellowbeard* – one (in Cook) who would (initially, at least) work for free.

So Graham began another draft with Peter Cook, who was scheduled to play a role in the film and who wrote another part for himself based on the actor-manager Donald Wolfit, which was eventually cut from the final draft, indicative yet again of the disjointed writing process that was to be reflected in the resultant film. Graham, Cook and McKenna tried to tie down what proved to be a very elusive script over a drink in the Hampstead pub Jack Straw's Castle but could never really agree on what it should be; the main decision they made being that McKenna should come with them to the location shoot in Mexico, in case they needed his help.

Part of Graham's ultimate dissatisfaction with the film resulted from the fact that – as they say in Hollywood – 'what he really wanted to do was direct'. He had also wanted to do so with *The Odd Job*, having watched both Terrys Gilliam and Jones branch out from their writing/performing careers. But those financing the films seemed to think – in part due to his having taken ostensibly the lead role in both *Holy Grail* and *Life of Brian* – that Graham was too important an element in front of the camera.

'Graham felt he had the burden of the whole thing,' McKenna adds. 'He felt it was his production.' So directing remained a desire he was never to fulfil.

'He couldn't talk to me about it later on,' McKenna continues, 'because I'd say how can you be disappointed when we knew it wasn't working well? This happened twice – with *The Odd Job* and with *Yellowbeard* – in that the production was rushed into when there was nothing to rush into. The script hadn't been settled. It doesn't matter what the idea is – because you can have the most simplistic ideas – but the script has to be settled.'

Graham was joined on the film by an all-star cast, including his old partner John Cleese, as well as fellow Python Eric Idle. Filming was divided between the UK and Mexico, with the former proving to be the easier leg of the journey. 'When they were filming in England, some days were tremendous fun,' Sherlock recollects, 'because it was full of people like Eric Idle, who wise-cracked with the crew, and the moment they arrived they were on: bang! It was wonderful. I always found John Cleese's attitude was the studious one of head down, come out of your caravan just minutes before shooting perhaps, manly stride across to where the crew were, couple of quips and then bang into the shot. And then stride back to the caravan, very often, and not be seen until next take.'

By the time they arrived in Mexico, Graham and David were sharing a hotel suite, but with separate bedrooms, indicative of their relationship. Indicative of the production was the fact that things weren't going as well financially – partly because of the nature of filming on water – with Graham taking the brunt of the responsibility.

'Sometimes there wasn't money to feed the crew at lunchtime,' Sherlock adds, 'and there would be this last-minute extraordinary situation whereby the director would have to fork out from his own pocket for the lady Mexican cook, who was brilliant, who produced the most incredible food in vast quantities for a shitload of people, but there were some hairy moments when she said, "I'm sorry." '

Graham realised the extent to which the production was in trouble when Sherlock, who was working on the wardrobe side of the film, informed him that one sequence was being completely changed on the wishes of the producers due to budgetary means – and they hadn't informed him.

'I alerted Graham and he had to get in a cab and then go out into the night to try and find the producers, who'd all gone out to dinner, and wrestle with this thing about how the filming for the next morning was going to be done, because they daren't tell him what they were going to do.'

Though it wasn't all rough going, as Graham and others discovered on an evening sojourn. 'There was very little really to do in the evening except for the local brothel,' Sherlock explains, 'which was an open-air place with tables and chairs where you could go and have a drink and the local girls, and by girls I mean girls as opposed to young women, would come and join you or ask to come and join you. That was the only place where you could go and get a spliff . . . but it wasn't discovered by Graham; he was told about it. So this was the place to get a roll-up or two.'

Filming off water also proved problematic, often being based in a large unventilated warehouse where – due to the humidity – bales of hay were brought in which were then filled with blocks of ice for the cast to cool off between takes. Hardly the most salubrious of circumstances.

The filming of *Yellowbeard* in Mexico was ultimately marked for Graham by meeting David Bowie on location, while driving out late one night to the local red-light district with a drunken Peter Cook (who would on occasion do his famously rambling E. L. Whisty character while standing in the hotel pool), and casting him in the film. It was then tragically marred by the death on location of long-time friend Marty Feldman, who passed away in his hotel room from a massive heart attack on 2 December 1982. Graham and Sherlock were filming late that night and returned to hear the news. It coloured the film and its subsequent life. Cook later described it as 'a great script which was damaged . . . '

Nonetheless Graham still felt very proprietorial when it came to *Yellowbeard*, even if it didn't go the way he wanted ('He was very, very angry about the way he was stitched up on *Yellowbeard*,' recalls Sherlock), but he knew not to speak out of turn when it came to promoting the film, knowing full well that that was something you just didn't do, not if you wanted to keep working, which now more than ever he did.

Having now returned full time to London, Graham was ensconced in Highgate and ensuring that his home life was secure, even if his house was as busy as during his drinking days, with Tomiczek's friends now constituting many of those who made use of Graham's abode.

'They were an odd mix of people,' states Sherlock, 'you would have thought, for Graham to want to relax with, but he did and very happily. And they played snooker or just watched awful movies on the television and just had a good time and Graham loved all that.'

Having given an interview to the British newspaper, the *Daily*

Mail, discussing his old mountaineering days' desire to visit the Andes, Graham found himself being approached by David Kirk, chairman of the Dangerous Sports Club. Rather than offering him the opportunity of travelling to the Andes, the club asked whether he would like to try hang-gliding over live volcanoes in Equador. Always up for a challenge, Graham accepted the offer, spent a week with the group sizing them up, although he did initially feel in his own words that he might be there as a 'useless mascot' to help them raise awareness/money for their group.

Much like Dachau several years before, the volcano was closed (or at least not open for business), but he did later join the club again for a charity event in London's Hyde Park, Sport Aid (organised in part by Bob Geldof, to emulate the success of the earlier Live Aid charity concert). Graham agreed once again to represent the Dangerous Sports Club and be catapulted into the air. His final event (and you had to perform three) to fully join the club was a proposed bungee jump which on the day he didn't deem to be safe enough, and so that alliance was severed.

It was also at this time that Graham found a new voice for himself in many ways, as he was invited to do a lecture tour in America, generally playing college campuses, which proved highly successful, and while it did often dwell on Python-related anecdotes, he did also establish himself as being separate from the team that now had no real plans to work together.

Although Graham seemed fitter and happier than he'd been in years, his regular blood tests showed a high cholesterol reading, as they did for Tomiczek. 'That was actually the first indication that there might be something wrong,' Sherlock recalls. 'They thought he looked very drawn and very gaunt. Which he did.'

Graham swiftly formulated a new diet for himself and John, realising that the stress of the previous few years – especially his feelings over *Yellowbeard* – had taken something out of him. Sherlock sees it now as a more long-term issue. 'When he survived his fit and then was drying out and all of that, he knew that he was on borrowed time, and I think he even thought he was on borrowed time long before that. It does beg a question: did it eventually get him in the end? Did it all build up? He had enormous pressures and if you are under such enormous stress without the same sort of releases that he had before, it might have contributed to his final illness.'

After his brief shock, Graham relocated his family to a farmhouse in Maidstone in Kent. In some ways it was an attempt to replicate the grandeur he'd grown accustomed to in America, in other ways it was an attempt to establish a family home, one free from the waifs and strays of earlier abodes.

He talked about his move to the *Record Mirror* in November of 1985, in many ways revealing his recent changes in attitude. 'I got fed up with having my car vandalised in London. The countryside and a bigger house seemed rather pleasant. I can't be bothered with dealing with money. And I'm bored with being ripped off a treat. There must be a simpler, fairer way of organising the tax system.'

He also found time to discuss his working relationship with the Pythons and his own feelings about the pressure of performance. 'What's happened is that we've gone solo for our sanity. So we're spending time on our own films and projects. I personally found performing the sections in the TV studio a strain. It was a major contribution to me hitting the bottle. John Cleese used to have to go and lie down on a settee because the whole regime became just too much for him. Sometime later he joined a therapy group.' (He also took time to write two books with his therapist.)

Chapter Ten

'He was fighting, fighting, fighting. Right the way through the eighties, fighting for survival,' Sherlock states emphatically. 'After *Life of Brian* he had all these new projects and he thought he'd arrived and he was determined to enjoy his career, but he was also determined to enjoy life more than he had. People started taking Graham seriously after *Life of Brian*, but if he hadn't gone to the States he wouldn't have had that much broader a view of what he could expect . . . but it meant he pulled away and was able to see the whole Python thing with more perspective really.'

Graham's time in America did mean that more opportunities were now available to him, one of which was a recurring role on an American television show titled *The New Show* and produced by Canadian Lorne Michaels. Michaels was extremely influenced by Python, having had the opportunity to watch it relatively early on in his native Canada. He took some of the spirit of it and applied it to *Saturday Night Live*, possibly the most influential comedy show in the history of American television. A few years later, by the early 1980s, he wanted to take the essence of his hit late-night show and transfer its sensibility to his new project on prime-time TV, essentially reinventing the variety show along the way. Star names hosted, and a regular team of supporting players filled in in between. Graham was one of the latter and ended up using a number of his old comic standbys, including his earlier 'wrestling-himself' routine.

Post-*Yellowbeard* though, Graham toiled away on other projects, struggling to get them kick-started. One of these was a television series, set (in part) in ancient England but determined for American TV. It was titled *Jake's Journey*, co-written with David Sherlock in 1987 and loosely based on Mark Twain's *A Connecticut Yankee in King Arthur's Court*. Both authors quickly decided to abandon certain elements of Twain's book and opted instead for a more free-wheeling, time-travelling adventure.

'Within a very short time we'd decided that the Mark Twain book was basically turgid,' remembers Sherlock, 'while the idea was good so we'd keep the very basic thing of time travelling and also time and space travel. So we thought of alternative worlds and universes and particularly, from Graham's point of view, we started to think that we would make the role of Sir George [eventually played by Graham] this sort of Merlin character to the young Arthur and he therefore, in a rather impatient way, becomes his mentor. We wrote the medieval stuff first and I think that shows. That was the stuff we were interested in and that's what sold it. Graham went and pitched the whole idea to CBS, and within twenty-four hours we had written half the script in a hotel room in Los Angeles. We hammered out three major scenes, and Graham read the whole lot in character to them and they were bowled over and said, "Yes, whatever you want." We couldn't believe it, but at the time the money for that was something in the region of certainly one and a half million dollars, just for the pilot.'

Designed to be produced in England (and to provide another opportunity for Graham and Peter Cook to perform together, as it did), but made for CBS in the US, everything looked good and a pilot was shot under the rather notable direction of Hal

Ashby, the man behind such seminal seventies movies as *Harold and Maude*, *The Last Detail* and Peter Sellers' finest hour, *Being There*.

The network, however, prevaricated over the show and, although further scripts were commissioned, it was abandoned and never aired – a big blow for Graham, who had come to embrace America in many ways.

There was another even bigger blow to follow in late 1988. Graham went to his dentist who, when examining him, found something he didn't like the look of in the back of his throat.

'I remember the exact moment when we realised something was seriously awry,' Cleese states. 'We had a meeting and Gray as usual turned up late, nobody took any notice of that. We were all chatting among ourselves and suddenly this high-pitched strangulated voice spoke, and I remember all of us turned round, and it was Graham's voice. Then we were aware of some purple marking, which was caused by radiation, and he started to explain what was going on, and we were all very shocked, because we had no idea.'

What had happened was that his dentist had discovered a growth that turned out to be throat cancer. Ever one for self-doctoring, Graham took things further himself when he got back from his appointment, as he soon told old friend Alan Bailey. 'The ringing up about the alcoholism,' Bailey says, recalling Graham's collapse at Christmas 1977, 'it was almost the same day of the year as the ringing up about how he'd poked something at the back of his throat and a big hole had appeared, which is what he told me. He didn't tell me the dentist did that, he told me *he* did that. I think he went back after the dentist had said something, but I think Graham must have known. So it was another Christmas . . . he'd poked a thing through his tonsil and he'd gone straight through into the back of his neck. He must have known that something was growing there . . . I had him seen immediately in Harley Street by an ENT surgeon who he knew vaguely because he was a Bart's man a few years older than us, Garfield Davies. And Garfield saw him immediately and then rang me back and said, "It's terrible, you know, it's all over the place." Garfield did a major operation on about 2 January or 3 January, took as much away as he possibly could without totally deforming Graham. That's what Graham wanted, he wanted it all in a bucket. Graham was of the old school of thought – in those days a tumour in a bucket was a tumour out, so you did a massive operation. Then Garfield sent him to the best radiotherapist of the time, and he had a little bit of radiotherapy early on to try and get rid of all the satellite things that had occurred, and then he was okay for about a month or two, except that he was completely devastated by the operation and everything: it was a major operation. Garfield was in theatre for hours trying to get everything away and leave him with a voice and everything because it was all round the larynx. It's a very difficult part of the body to operate on.'

Graham struggled on over the next few months, a mixture of chemotherapy treatment and denial keeping him going. 'There was this moment we got together and that's when we had the first shock of Graham looking really bad,' Gilliam confirms. 'And this was when it was just throat cancer then, he had had work done and he was looking like a plucked chicken, and it looked bad, but apparently it had all been pretty much dealt with. Then apparently he had had an all clear from the doctors, and everyone was like, "OK, he's over it," and then the next thing I know is I get a call that Graham's gone into the hospital. And I'm, "Oh Jesus, well, that's bad," and then I get another call saying, "They don't expect that he's coming out." I said,

"What? What do you mean he's not coming out, can't pay his bills? What?" And that was it. It happened very quickly . . . when they held him up, he was just riddled with cancer. And he'd sold his big headline story to the *Sun* newspaper about how "Python Whips Big C", but that was a month earlier, and so there's Graham once again conning people into parting with large sums of money. And it was like, "What?" It just happened very quickly. Graham was weird because he was somebody I really felt I never knew,' reflects Gilliam further. 'He was always the one I felt least at ease with because I never knew what was going on in his head. Strange man.'

Graham had thought he had beaten his throat cancer, but it had spread to his spine, making it inoperable. 'It was a nasty ten months,' Bailey says. 'In a way, in retrospect, one might have given him a bottle of gin and a thing of heroin and said, "Look, old man, your life's going to be awful for the next ten months," but Graham wanted us to do everything we possibly could. He was a dangerous sports man and he was a brave fellow and he wanted to go through it all, but I don't think we did that much good to him the last few months of his life, except eased the pain. I don't know what I'd do if it happened to me, whether I'd accept the operation or whether I'd just say, "Give me the heroin." I was the first medical person he rang. And I heard him, I could tell over the telephone that this was very bad news . . . But I think Graham sat on it for a month or two, and if you'd got in there early you might have been able to do more.'

Of course, given the climate of the time and Graham's role as a very public gay man, other things were speculated upon. 'Everybody thought he had AIDS,' Bailey states frankly. 'But I never did an AIDS test on him. I was always his doctor, but I never did an AIDS test on him and I don't think Graham was at all promiscuous by the time he gave up booze. It was a million to one chance that he had AIDS. This is not a tumour that was commonly associated with AIDS. It's associated with drink and it's associated with the pipe, but it's not one of these rare tumours that you get with HIV/AIDS victims . . . I don't think he reported it to me when he first suspected it. I think that's very likely.'

Another old friend, Bernard McKenna, saw Graham a short while before his death, but didn't realise what had been going on with him. 'I don't think he was a happy person at all. Ever. He was never relaxed in some way. But the last time I ever saw him I was walking in Belsize Park and he pulled up in a convertible Aston Martin. This was when we were having nothing professionally to do with him. And funnily enough he was going up Ornan Road where he and I had first co-written and he pulled up. And there he was in this vulgar car and Graham was dressed in something like a golfer's cap and a striped shirt and shorts with his spindly legs – he just looked like a total wanker driving this Aston Martin convertible. So he pulled up and offered me a lift and I said, "I'm only going that way, I haven't got far to go . . . I don't want a lift!" And he wanted me to get in this car to drive me, and I refused. And I remember that was the last time we ever spoke.'

By now Graham was firmly entrenched with his immediate family of Sherlock and Tomiczek in their relatively new home in Maidstone, one that Graham had wanted to name 'Dun Drinkin' '. Life had been stable between the three for the last few years, with enough money flowing, John largely sharing the master bedroom, David content to manage the day-to-day matters of the house, the entourage having been left down the pub. It was sadly convenient that the house bordered on to the local hospital, Maidstone General, the place where Graham would shortly die.

Not long before Graham eventually passed away, his mother Edith did the same thing. (His father had died in 1983, Graham noticeably bought in all the booze for the wake, although he had stopped partaking himself by then.) It was a very sad moment for the Chapmans, but by the time of his mother's death, Graham was too ill to attend the funeral, as his brother John explained: 'He was going to come to it at one time, but then he felt he wasn't able to come to it when the event actually occurred. He was upset. But when I rang him, because I was dealing, as the principal executor of her estate, with solicitors who were there to see what she had left and what proportion was his, he was commenting on that and saying, "That was kind of her," and that sort of thing. And that was it. How much it really registered on him, as a great loss or not, I don't know, because he was so ill himself at that time. He was certainly too encompassed by his own illness to do anything other than just make the normal sort of sympathetic bereavement statements that one would expect. My mother died in July, and Graham died in October [1989]. I suppose I was grateful at the time that it was that way round that it happened, rather than Graham dying first and then our mother dying afterwards, because she was protected from the knowledge of how ill he was. She knew that he'd had an operation. But her grasp on reality was beginning to go at that time.'

Just around two weeks before she died, Edith Chapman moved into sheltered accommodation in Kidworth. She remained largely unaware of the seriousness of Graham's illness. When Graham learned of her death, Graham informed everyone in his house that he wanted to be left alone for two to three hours. 'He mourned long and loud,' explains Sherlock, 'and when it was over told us that it was finished and he would now like to put all his energy into getting better.'

This, however, was not to transpire. Graham would soon be in such pain that he needed twenty-four-hour nursing; with Tomiczek away in America, he spent his last days with Sherlock.

Shortly after the death of his mother, however, Graham did something very significant – he invited David Sherlock back into his bed for what would be the last night they spent together. They held each other close, both aware of the importance of the moment and what was to follow.

'Graham's belief, or the impression that he was anxious to give everybody,' recounts his older brother, John, 'was that he was confident that that was the end of it and that he was cured, which I suppose is the way one has to approach it in that situation. Yet I was fairly certain from my own knowledge of medicine that somebody who required a radical dissection of the nodes in the neck had a seriously advanced and aggressive disease, and there was a strong chance that it wasn't the end, that there would be more of it. Then, of course, when he developed paralysis of the lower half of the body, he was confined thereafter to a wheelchair. There were secondary deposits in the spine from the tumour of the throat.'

Before his death Graham tried to make contact with some old friends, missing some in the process, including Bernard McKenna who was by then living in Portugal. 'I wasn't in and my wife, Carla, who had never met Graham or spoken to him, took the message, and Graham said, "I've just rung him to say hello," and two days later he was dead. And she said after, "He was ringing you to tell you he was dying."' His friend, McKenna, reflected on Graham's life: 'I think he did dislike himself and I think he embraced the gay movement, not as a pose, but as a piece of outrage. He didn't actually want to be heavily involved in Gay Liberation, but he wore a badge . . . it was always extravagant gestures rather than a thought-through life.'

His fellow worker, Gilliam, also always felt that at times Graham was something of a closed book. 'I don't know if Graham ever worked himself out. He was probably happier sometimes. There were moments with Graham when you did feel there was a calm descending, whether it completely descended, I don't know. I think he was still lying – it's like the last photograph of Python together – with his throat cancer – it was all basically him saying, "no problem" – it was all lying still. Now, whether he was lying to himself, I don't know. I think he probably was. Those were the moments when it was most touching because you could see he was in dire straits, but there was an optimism there that was bubbling up, him saying it was all going to be all right.'

'I like to think sometimes that we did have no secrets,' adds Sherlock, 'but in fact the reality is different. There was an awful lot, I find, that we didn't discuss. Simply because life is too complicated.'

When news spread of the severity of his illness, following a collapse at home and Graham's hospitalisation, several of his family and close friends tried to get to the Maidstone Hospital on time. Alan Bailey for one didn't make it.

'I wasn't there. I'm glad I wasn't there. I'd have been devastated. He was a patient, from that respect, and you're not often at your patient's bedside when they die; the relatives are there or the friends. We knew he was going to die, it was just a question of when he was going to die. I saw him last in the Cromwell Hospital, it was probably about three or four weeks before he died, and I said, "I don't want you to die here in hospital, I think you should go home," and I wasn't looking after him. I said that to his staff. And Graham wouldn't want to die at the Cromwell.

'But he went very suddenly bad and was taken back to the Maidstone Hospital. I knew Graham was going to die. As a friend, I didn't want to be in at the kill. I made my peace with him before he left the Cromwell. He had a very good day. I remember the ward he was in there, and I remember this stuff that he was putting down his throat to take the pain away and how he was getting the pharmacist to make it up and things like that, and that was my last memory of Graham.'

Old friends John Cleese and Michael Palin did, however, make it on time. 'All of a sudden there was the news of the collapse, and I remember driving down to the Maidstone hospital,' Cleese recollects. 'I was there most of the time, for most of his last two or three days I was in or around, not in the room when he actually died, but standing outside. Michael was there and Peter Cook and David and one or two others. It was a big surprise, because I'd had dinner with him about a year before, and he was going on and on about these free radicals and how he'd completely cut them out of his diet. He was looking a bit emaciated. One or two people said, "Does he have AIDS?" He'd cut fat out of his diet so rigidly, almost obsessively, that he was looking gaunt.'

Only a handful were present at the time of Graham's death, including his brother, John. 'There was just John Cleese, who was in the room next door, Michael Palin and David there at the time of death,' the elder Chapman recalls. 'John Cleese said it's the first time he'd ever seen anybody die. It was something, obviously, that I was familiar with from my medical career over many, many years; one knew exactly what was happening, and he was in a very, very poor way, in extremis, vomiting blood, passing blood from the bowel and unaware at that stage of what was happening. I don't know whether he ever recognised that I was there by his side. I had to rush to fly from Geneva to Heathrow and then get from Heathrow to Maidstone to the hospital. But I suppose I arrived mid-afternoon and he died early evening . . . John was obviously very moved by the whole thing, part of the response. Michael, I don't think was quite so emotional, I think he was on more of an even keel. David, I seem to remember, wanted to be involved with the proceedings after death, with the laying out and that sort of thing.'

One person who did want to be there, but arrived a fraction too late, was Graham's dear friend, Peter Cook. 'Peter was so devastated by Graham's premature death,' Sherlock says, 'and the fact that Graham had died before he got to the hospital, and Peter was definitely pretty inebriated, shall we say, by the time he got to the hospital. He was deeply shocked and had collapsed in the hospital with shock. I took him to see Graham because he was so frightened of death. He'd never seen anyone dead before, which I thought very strange for that generation.'

Graham died on 4 October 1989, one day short of the twentieth anniversary of the first episode of *Monty Python's Flying Circus*. He left behind a family of one older brother, John, and two lovers, David Sherlock and John Tomiczek (who was to die shortly after from the congenital heart problem he had always known he had).

He was commemorated in the Great Hall of St Bart's, his old medical school. John Cleese got to be the first in England to say 'fuck' at a memorial service. Eric and the other Pythons got to serenade the congregation with 'Always Look on the Bright Side of Life' (probably not an easy job given the circumstances), and old friend Alan Bailey got to eulogise him (although Bailey insisted on going on before Cleese, not wanting to be upstaged).

In his all too brief life Graham had studied medicine, tended to people, loved many – always sincerely, and had been an integral part of a moment that changed the nature of British comedy, and by default certain elements of British society. The fact that his work was, and still is, regarded on a worldwide level, is a testament to it. Alongside the work, he made his private life public, and as he would say himself, helped a number of people along the way.

But still Graham had to have the last laugh. Mere weeks before his death, he made his final public appearance, on a TV show designed to celebrate the joys of Monty Python on the eve of their twenty years of being very silly. The show was hosted by American comedian Steve Martin, a long-time fan. Given the nature of Graham's illness, he was forced to spend most of his time in a wheelchair. David Sherlock was wheeling him across the studio floor, and the guys said, 'Hi Gray, how's it going?' and he said, 'Fine, it's just this fucking cancer, that's the problem!'

Index